**DRIVER AND VEHICLE LICE**
Road Transport
148-158 Corporation S
Tel: (028) 9025 4100   Fax: (028) 9025 4086

Francis Hughes
60 Mourne Crescent
Coalisland
Co Tyrone
BT71 4NB

Your ref:

Our ref:    Badge No  AA807

Date:  23  April 2002

Dear Mr Hughes

**THE ROAD TRAFFIC (NORTHERN IRELAND) ORDER 1981 (AS AMENDED)  NOTICE OF REFUSAL OF A TAXI DRIVER'S LICENCE**

I regret to advise you that your Taxi Driver's Licence has been refused on the grounds of your convictions set out as follows:-

| NAME OF COURT & DATE OF CONVICTION | OFFENCE | PENALTY |
|---|---|---|
| Dublin Special Criminal Court 8.2.74 | Rescue forcibly a person from lawful custody<br>Belonging to proscribed organisation | Imp for 3 yrs<br><br>Imp for 9 mths (concurrent) |
| Dublin Special Criminal Court 16.8.76 | Possess ammunition with intent to endanger life or property<br>Possess firearms with intent to endanger life or property<br>Possess firearms with intent to endanger life or property | Imp for 5 yrs<br><br>Imp for 2 yrs concurrent<br><br>Imp for 10 yrs concurrent |
| Dublin Special Criminal Court 1.5.93 | Armed Robbery | Imp for 8 yrs |

The Department is of the opinion that you are not a fit and proper person to hold a Taxi Driver's Licence in all the circumstances of your case and consequently your licence has been refused.

If you are aggrieved by this decision you may, after giving notice within 3 months to the Department of your intention to do so, appeal to a Court of Summary Jurisdiction acting for the Petty Sessions District in which you reside. Further information on the appeal procedure may be obtained from your local Petty Sessions Office. You may of course wish to consult a Solicitor, Citizens Advice Bureau or any other Body as you see fit.

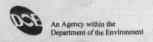

An Agency within the
Department of the Environment

MONS010.GW

Awarded for excellence

First published in 2021 by Time Warp Books

Original photographs by P. Michael O'Sullivan

**Editing**: Siobhán Prendergast, Dingle Publishing
www.dinglepublishing.com

**Layout and design**: Dennison Design, Kenmare, Co. Kerry,
www.dennisondesign.ie

**Cover artwork**: Clem Bradley, Creative Workers' Co-operative
www.creativeworkerscooperative.com

**Proofreading**: Paul Feldstein, The Feldstein Agency
www.thefeldsteinagency.co.uk

Printed by Walsh Colour Print, Castleisland, Co. Kerry

ISBN 978-1-5272-9557-5

Bookshop Distributor (Ireland)
Pádraic Ó Flatharta
SLAC
+353 (0)87 242 0319
slac.leabhar@gmail.com

**Direct Sales**: www.uplikeabird.com

THE RISE
AND FALL OF
AN IRA COMMANDER

# UP
# LIKE A
# BIRD

## BRENDAN HUGHES

### WITH DOUGLAS DALBY

Featuring Original Photographs by P. Michael O'Sullivan

Ardboe ●
Coalisland ●
Dungannon ●
Belfast ●
Monaghan ●
Carrickmacross ●
Navan ●
Dublin ●
Portlaoise ●
Stradbally ●
● Shannon

# Contents

# Contributor's Acknowledgments

This book would not have been possible without support from family, friends, and friends of friends, many of whom would prefer to remain anonymous. Special thanks to Tommy McKearney, Portlaoise Jail escapees Liam Brown, Martin McAllister and Oliver McKiernan, Jim Monaghan, Liam Quinn, and former prison warders for their invaluable first-hand input.

I would also like to thank John Bruen, Frank Hopkins, Malachy Browne, Gearóid Lynch, Justin McCarthy, Mary Mac Intyre, John Houlihan, Hugh Feeney, Patricia Mac Bride, Maureen and Eileen Shiels, Shane McCarthy, Pat Haran, Clem Bradley, Mark Maxwell, Pádraic Ó Flatharta, Stephen Boyes, Charlie and Louise Feely, Fionnan Ryan, Vicky Leahy, Ruadhhán, 'Mark', P. J., Brian Warfield, Frank Hannigan, Colm Grealy and Mick O'Dea.

Special thanks to Siobhan Harvey, the guardian of her late father P. Michael O'Sullivan's estate. Her efforts allowed me to reproduce some of his documentary photography for the first time in almost 50 years.

I dedicate my efforts to my late father, who first introduced me to the writings of James Connolly, and to my grandmother's people in Co Mayo, who inspired a life-long interest in Irish history. As a teen, it changed my life to discover my tribe around the townlands of Glengad and Pullathomas.

I would also like to acknowledge the inspiration of two dearly departed friends, Derek Dunne and Fiachra O Marcaigh. This book would have been immeasurably better with their input, but I felt their presence with every keystroke.

Most of all, I thank Brendan Hughes for entrusting his story to me. He never once lost patience with the tortuous process and we had a lot of craic along the way. He always made himself available for interviews and the many clarifications I sought. He was happy to correct whatever errors I had injected in my attempt to contextualise and illuminate his memoir.

Through this relationship, I developed an insight into the calibre of the man, his authenticity, and how he must have operated back in the day.

Lastly, several people have asked me why I chose to self-publish. Quite simply, I thought it fitting given the maverick nature of the subject, who agreed this was in the true spirit of the story. This book is tribute to the expertise of the editor, page designer, proofreader, cover artist, legal reviewers and several journalists. I trust you will enjoy the cumulative fruits of their labours.

## ON THE MUSIC SCENE...

# WOLFE TONES ARE FLYING HIGH

## Helicopter record 'takes off'

For the first time in the history of the Irish "Top Ten" record charts, an original Irish disc has jumped straight to number one in the first week of release, Mr. Oliver Barry, manager of the Wolfe Tones ballad group, claimed last night.

"The Helicopter Song," written, produced and performed by the group, has broken all sales records, selling 12,000 copies up to yesterday, he said.

Mr. Barry said that, although the record had received very little exposure on radio — it has been played on the air only three times—record dealers have been inundated for copies. Dolphin Records, he said, had ordered the pressing of a further 30,000 copies by next week, in response to the unprecedented demand.

The song theme was inspired by the recent escape of three Provisional I.R.A. men from Mountjoy Jail.

# Introduction

My involvement in this book started with a call from my good friend, Maureen Shiels.

'Dougie, can you do me a favour? Brendan Hughes wants to tell his story and he needs a hand.'

'You've lost your marbles, Maureen,' I replied. 'Or someone is speaking to you from beyond the grave.'

'No, not Brendan Hughes 'The Dark'… Brendan Hughes from Tyrone – the man behind the helicopter escape from Mountjoy.'

She had me. I confess I had never heard of this man, but the sheer audacity read like a James Bond script and would have been familiar to anyone with even a passing interest in modern Irish history.

The novelty prison break of three top IRA members in October 1973 even spawned a cheeky, celebratory song that held the top slot in the Irish charts for 12 weeks, despite a ban on the national airwaves.

I began looking through the copious contemporary newspaper coverage but discovered scant information about its planning and successful execution. Or about the people behind it. The focus was on the high-profile escapees and the embarrassment the escape itself had heaped on a self-styled 'law and order' government.

And I became intrigued about the mysterious American, Mr Leonard, whose identity had never been revealed.

After talking to Brendan Hughes for the first time, I realised that his story was about so much more than his role in this single escapade. He had packed several lifetimes into a few years.

During extensive interviews conducted in various parts of the country, including his native Co Tyrone, the stories just kept coming. He recounted his part in the birth of the Provisional IRA in East Tyrone; a series of spectacular bank robberies; a rapid rise through the ranks of an increasingly sophisticated organisation; the key roles he played in the Mountjoy escape and a subsequent mass jailbreak from the maximum-security Portlaoise Prison less than a year later; a falling out with former comrades who then tried to kill him; betrayal and long stretches in prison, ostracised.

Many books have been written about the Northern Ireland conflict, including some excellent first-hand accounts. This memoir does not pretend to be exhaustive or academic, but although events have been omitted, names and places obscured and changed, Brendan Hughes is undoubtedly a primary source, and I believe his account gives a special insight into how the IRA operated, particularly in rural areas and south of the border during the early part of the Troubles.

Many of his former comrades have scrutinised various drafts to vouch for accuracy, but the book is necessarily a trade-off, and I cannot claim journalistic rigour. Corroboration was often difficult and, of course, the fallout from The Boston College Tapes continues to discourage total frankness.

These events also took place some 50 years ago: memories fade and distort. Had his old friend Fate not intervened, he might have spent his life plying his trade as a plasterer on building sites across Ireland and the UK. Instead, he became one of the IRA's most lethal assets before becoming a prime target for the organisation he had helped create.

Had fate decreed that he be born a few years later in different circumstances, he might have become a wealthy entrepreneur. Disruption is the aspirational buzzword in modern business and without doubt, Brendan Hughes is the most disruptive person I have ever met.

And although fate deals everyone a particular hand, we still have choices to make. A character witness in his defence during one of his many court appearances described him as part of the flotsam and jetsam of the conflict, but I would argue that such a depiction does him and many like him a disservice. Anyone who took up crude weaponry against such overwhelming military odds made a very conscious decision and did not do so lightly.

His account is raw, reeks of authenticity and undermines the oft-pedalled sanctification of the IRA volunteers involved in the so-called Armed Struggle.

These were no altar boys with Armalites. These were ordinary men and women. They were young. They danced, drank and partied like there was no tomorrow. And for many of them, there wouldn't be.

As contemporary news coverage shows, they had considerable support, not only in the six counties of Northern Ireland but across the Republic too. They were not the pariahs portrayed by the authorities and the media at the time.

It is also a cautionary tale. Northern Ireland has enjoyed decades of relative calm that is taken for granted all too often. This book demonstrates just how easily events can spiral out of control, courtesy of obdurate intransigence and arrogance.

Brendan Hughes spent most of his time in jail for crimes that were for personal gain, rather than for the benefit of the IRA. With a few, rare exceptions, his former comrades shunned him and his family during these decades in prison. His previous service counted for nothing.

While he served his time, many of his former comrades would die at the hands of British forces and their loyalist paramilitary proxies. There is every prospect he would have suffered a similar fate and his story would have died with him.

That would have been a pity. His is a story worth telling.

Douglas Dalby

Ireland
July 2021

This book is dedicated to the silent people of Ireland who opened their doors to us. Our struggle depended on their steadfast support. They all paid a price; some of them the ultimate price. It is long past time their contribution was acknowledged.

*Brendan Hughes, 2021*


'I can control my destiny, but not my fate. Destiny means there are opportunities to turn right or left, but fate is a one-way street. I believe we all have the choice as to whether we fulfill our destiny, but our fate is sealed.'

*Paulo Coelho, The Alchemist*

# Prologue

I had a nose for danger, but I sensed none that spring afternoon. Sitting in a corner of that quiet pub in rural Co Meath, I barely looked up when the man strode in the door, heading past me towards the counter.

'Brendan Hughes!' he barked. 'Don't move!'

I turned to face him, weighing my options. My hand moved instinctively towards the revolver concealed under my jacket. The undercover cop was pointing a submachine gun right at me and my companion. I noticed another muzzle poking through the doorway.

He must have read my mind.

'Don't do it, Brendan!' he pleaded. 'Just don't do it!'

We put our hands in the air. He kept his gun trained on us, motioning his young partner to disarm us. The lad was so nervous I thought he might pull the trigger by mistake as he removed the pistol from my shoulder holster. We offered no resistance.

I had been free since blasting my way out of the maximum-security Portlaoise Prison 18 months beforehand, having been convicted for the daring helicopter escape of three leading IRA officers from Mountjoy Jail.

In the early 1970s, I had built a formidable reputation battling British forces along the border. I had also carried out a string of armed robberies to buy the weapons that had helped transform the Provisional IRA (the Provos) into a potent guerrilla force. I was one of the most hunted men in Ireland, but I was also in hiding from my former comrades, who now wanted me dead.

My arrest was front-page news.

A few months later, I would be sentenced to 20 years for shooting at a police officer during an armed robbery. I would spend most of the remainder of the century behind bars, banished by the organisation that I had been prepared to die for.

This is my story. Well, at least as much of it as I am able to tell. It reveals the planning and execution behind two of the most famous jailbreaks in modern Irish history. It also follows the birth of the modern IRA in East Tyrone and the formation of a secret unit to carry out special operations across the border in the Republic.

It is a story of youth, adventure, determination, ingenuity, imprisonment, betrayal, regret and death.

Photos: Maxwell Photography, Dublin

*Left: The helicopter pilot, Capt Thompson Boyes.*

*Opposite page: The Alouette helicopter used in the daring escape.*

# Irish Independent

**TODAY'S WEATHER**
Scattered outbreaks of rain or drizzle. Mostly cloudy.

(See back page)

C    Vol. 82. No. 256         THURSDAY, NOVEMBER 1, 1973         Price 4P    C

# The

TWOMEY . . . former
Provisional Chief of Staff

MALLON . . . his second-in-command

### *AND FROM THE TAOISEACH, A BITTER REACTION*

COSGRAVE . . . furious

# great escape

---

# The Cork Examiner

**Boys and Girls PUSH BIKES** now available here at £19
**FRANK JONES** Tel.: KANTURK 118

NO. 48,416         THURSDAY MORNING, NOVEMBER 1, 1973         PRICE 4p

CITY EDITION

3 PRINTS FOR PRICE OF 1 AT MacSweeny's PHOTO SHOP

Three snatched from Mountjoy in James Bond – style operation

# BIG HUNT FOR 'COPTER ESCAPEES

### Junior doctors

# Hunt for escapees stepped up

AS THE search for three Provisional I.R.A. leaders who escaped from Mountjoy Jail on Wednesday intensified yesterday, it was learned that the lift-out involved a double hijack.

## 'Copter escaper in jail

Kevin Mallon, the Provisional IRA helicopter escaper, was back in Portlaoise jail last night after being arrested near the town early yesterday morning.

# *Blushes in the Cabinet*

# THE IRISH PRESS

Vol. XLIII. No. 257      THURSDAY, NOVEMBER 1, 1973      The Truth in the News      (5p in Britain) **4p**

# COSGRAVE: 'FIND THEM'

## Provos freed by helicopter

By MICHAEL MILLS, GERRY McMORROW and ALAN MURRAY

AS ONE of the biggest Army and Garda search operations ever mounted in this country continued last night for the three Provisional IRA men who escaped from Mountjoy Jail, the Taoiseach, Mr. Cosgrave, and the Minister for Defence, Mr. Donegan, took personal charge of the operation. A special communications system was set up to keep both men in touch with developments.

Mr. Cosgrave and Mr. Donegan took control following an emergency Government meeting attended by the Army Chief of Staff, Maj. Gen. T. L. O'Carroll, the Garda Commissioner, Mr. Patrick Malone, and top officers of both Forces. The Minister for Justice, Mr. Cooney, is attending independence ceremonies in Turkey and is not due

## Gardai And Army Comb Country

### Three top I.R.A. men snatched in aerial rescue

# COPTER GRAB SENSATION AT MOUNTJOY

# Government shows incompetence–Lynch

## Helicopter escape 'poetic justice'

THE LEADER of the Opposition, Mr. Lynch, replying to the Taoiseach's statement on the Mountjoy escape, said that it would take all the resources of the Government Information Service to explain away the Government's neglect and incompetence in this particular incident as well as the neglect and incompetence of the Ministers immediately involved.

## Escape embarrasses cabinet

### Most audacious Irish jail-break ever

# I.R.A. leaders 'air-lifted' from Mountjoy

IN the most audacious and cleverly-planned jail break in the history of this country, three top Provisional I.R.A. chiefs, who were serving prison sentences in Mountjoy Jail, Dublin, were literally whisked by air to freedom on Wednesday afternoon by a hijacked helicopter which landed in the exercise yard of " D " wing of the Jail, picked up the three men who were obviously primed for its arrival, and had them over the prison walls and heading for freedom inside a minute.

# Airlifted Provos 'are now safe'

The Provisional IRA said last night that the top IRA trio who escaped from Mountjoy Jail by helicopter were now safe from the massive hunt to find them.

Seamus Twomey, Kevin Mallon and J. B. O'Hagan had been rescued by a "special unit" in an operation that was a "complete success," they said.

"The men are now safe, despite a massive hunt by Free State forces," The statement said the rescue was part of extensive operations during the past ten days.

# 'Copter Man

# PRISONERS MOVED TO PORTLAOISE

## Hi-jacked chopper whisks 3 top Provos to freedom

### By CONOR McANALLY and LIAM RYAN

WITH AN I.R.A. MAN riding 'shotgun,' a hi-jacked helicoter, from the Irish Helicopters fleet, swooped on Mountjoy Jail yesterday afternoon and within 60 seconds had carried out the country's most dramatic jailbreak.

## Army And Garda Security Ring Day And Night

PORTLAOISE will now be the main detention centre for Republican prisoners and they will be the only prisoners there. The prison will be guarded day and night by army and garda detachments.

# .T.E.

## THE IRISH

Vol. XLIII. No. 288.                    FRIDAY, NOVEMBER 2, 1973

## 'Copter pilot fears

THE HIJACKED helicopter pilot who lifted three top I.R.A. men from Dublin's Mountjoy Jail admitted yesterday that he now fears for his own life. The

### OVERHAUL OF SECURITY

# Guns guard the jails

#### By IRISH PRESS Reporters

ARMED MILITARY guards were placed on prisons containing republicans, and on the RTE studios at Montrose, Henry St., Dublin, and Athlone, as the full-scale hunt for the three escaped Mountjoy Provisionals continued last night. In the Dail, the Taoiseach, Mr. Cosgrave, announced that a full judicial inquiry would be held into the escape of the three men. Mr. Cosgrave said that the Government was taking "certain interim measures" as a matter of urgency and they had also decided

# 1

Like many other young men and women who made the decision to overthrow British rule in the North of Ireland in the early years of the Troubles – a sanitised euphemism for three decades of armed conflict – I wasn't born into a tradition of violent republicanism.

At school I didn't get taught much about 1916 or the British partition of Ireland. And afterwards, the border didn't concern me. My world was small. I was just into making a living and earning a few bob. Like many other young fellas, I was interested in fast cars, drink and women.

I first realised the IRA existed when as a teenager I heard a loud bang one day. IRA volunteers had planted a booby-trapped Irish flag on a public water pumping station near my home. A member of the Royal Ulster Constabulary (RUC), the state's police force, who tried to remove this banned symbol of Irish unity, was seriously injured.

I didn't have much of a clue about Irish history, but I knew enough to know that the IRA was on our side and the State wasn't. I wasn't political but I knew about discrimination and a feeling of being unwelcome in the society where I had happened to be born. That was in hindsight though – my own involvement only really began many years later when I had nowhere to live.

A deep experience of injustice and a thirst for action were impetus enough to embrace the Northern Ireland Civil Rights Association (NICRA), set up in 1967. Within a few years I had swapped my trade as a plasterer for a life as a guerrilla leader, regarded as one of the modern IRA's top operators.

When I took up arms, I had no shortage of immediate targets – they were walking in British uniforms along the country roads where I lived. They lay camouflaged in the fields where I had played as a boy only a few years before in Ardboe, a sparsely populated, nationalist townland on the picturesque shores of Lough Neagh.

I was born in Drummurrer, near Coalisland, in the eastern part of Co Tyrone, in 1947, but I always considered myself an Ardboe man. My mother died in childbirth when I was just two years old. The youngest of five, I went to live with my maternal grandparents and an aunt.

I never really knew my father; he wanted nothing to do with me. He took my older siblings – two boys and two girls – but he rarely visited me, even though they only lived a 20-minute bike ride away. I cycled up to his house once – but only once. It was clear that I wasn't welcome.

A few years later, my aunt got married and moved to Belfast and when my grandmother died, I was reared by my grandfather and an uncle.

I would do more than my fair share of chores around the house, but I also found time to help an elderly farmer up the road. There was no money, but he kept me in cigarettes.

I have always been comfortable in my own company. I know how to look after myself and keep a place neat and tidy. I suppose it stems from my upbringing.

I attended St Patrick's school in Mullinahoe, Ardboe, although my presence is strangely absent from school records. I hated school but I was considered bright, and I read a lot.

I couldn't wait for the library van to appear with new books. *Biggles* was my favourite back then, but he was replaced in later years by non-fiction stories of derring-do – my eyesight was eventually ruined by countless hours of reading about the exploits of explorers and people fighting Atlantic swells.

I deliberately failed the 11-plus exams at the time so that I could leave school early. In 1962, aged 15, I literally jumped the school fence to begin working as a labourer in an extension to the building. Nobody batted an eyelid – that's how it was back then – people from my background weren't expected to stay in education.

I soon became sick of the low pay on that job, so I left with a friend for England, where I worked on building sites across the Midlands. On a visit back home, I met Noreen. We married and moved to Belfast. Aged 19, I found myself with a wife and baby son just as all hell was about to break loose.

It was really my first personal experience of political violence. I bought a small house from a Protestant man – a gentleman – on Court Street, off the Crumlin Road in the north of the city. It was a mixed area where Catholics and Protestants lived in relative harmony, but things were changing fast.

The man who sold me the house was having a few drinks in a local pub when a group of Protestant loyalist paramilitaries beat him within an inch of his life for having the temerity to sell to a 'taig', a derogatory term for a Roman Catholic.

I visited him in hospital a few days later. His jaw was wired. They had also broken his ribs and one of his arms. He was black and blue all over. Although he couldn't speak, he gestured to me that we should get out as soon as possible, or we would be next.

For months beforehand, police and loyalists had been engaging in running battles two or three nights a week up and down the street. The loyalists were led by John McKeague, a notorious bigot encouraged by the inflammatory anti-Catholic rhetoric of Ian Paisley, the divisive firebrand cleric who would arguably become the most important political figure throughout the entire history of the Troubles.

We were imprisoned in our little house for hours at a time and if I happened to be out, I would make sure to stay out until things quietened down.

We decided to move back to Coalisland, where Noreen was from. Home became a cramped two-bedroom house, sharing with one of her elderly relations and his middle-aged son.

It was a case of out of the frying pan, into the fire. Housing was about to become the battlefield for civil rights, with East Tyrone the front line.

In June 1968, an elected civil rights activist, Austin Currie, and two local men, Joe Campbell and Patsy Gildernew, occupied a house in Caledon, around 20 miles south of Coalisland, in protest over its allocation to a 19-year-old single Protestant woman who worked for a local unionist politician.

At the time, more than 250 people were on the housing waiting list in the local area and Gildernew's relatives, a family that included three young children, had been forcibly evicted from the neighbouring house the previous day.

The occupation drew global attention to the wider issue of gerrymandering or election rigging, which enabled unionist minorities to wield power across Northern Ireland, even in nationalist-majority areas.

By the time the police had dragged the protesters out, the pot was already boiling over.

We took our cue from Caledon and my young family began squatting in an empty house, escaping our overcrowded surroundings and affording us a measure of privacy.

Emboldened by the power of street protests in other countries, particularly in the United States and France, and our ability to attract the world media to our status as permanent second-class citizens, we sought to expose a system built on prejudice and sectarian bias.

I may not have had the formal education of some of my peers, but I was at the sharp end of injustice, and I had begun reading The United Irishman, the monthly newspaper of the republican movement at the time.

I became active in NICRA and was among the estimated 2,000 people who marched the four miles in protest from Coalisland to Dungannon on August 24, 1968, now considered a seminal precursor to the Troubles. They could call it what they liked: I never doubted that this was war.

When we arrived in Dungannon we were met by an angry loyalist mob. The authorities banned us from marching to a planned meeting in the town's main Market Square, which only confirmed our belief that, far from being impartial, the police were a tool of a state that had been set up to ensure that we knew our station.

If my mind wasn't made up already, this was the final straw. I sought out Kevin Mallon, a local man with a reputation.

Mallon had taken part in the brief, disastrous IRA campaign along the border between 1956 and 1962, known as Operation Harvest. The State might have executed him for his alleged involvement in the killing of a police sergeant but for the skilled advocacy of Sean McBride, the famous international human rights lawyer.

He was among the activists that had helped me to break into the empty house where I was now squatting with my young family. I asked him how I might join the IRA. He insisted that he was no longer a member but suggested someone who might be able to help.

Shortly afterwards, I joined up. I didn't take any formal pledge, but I would spend the following few months learning how to strip guns and listening to lectures on guerrilla tactics from veterans of the previous campaign.

Joining wasn't a given. Many Northern nationalists continued to argue against the bullet and the bomb, advocating a campaign of non- violence. But increasing numbers of young people like me already had a bellyful of passive resistance. Our people were defenceless and under attack for demanding basic human rights.

On October 5, 1968, the authorities banned a large civil rights march in Derry. It went ahead, but the RUC attacked this peaceful protest and images of police brutality were beamed across the world.

Our demands weren't ridiculous: an end to gerrymandering, equal voting rights, and fair access to public housing. Then the British Army arrived to protect the system that kept us down. This just confirmed my belief that the only way we would ever get change was by armed resistance. I had had more than enough.

We tried politics and the State beat us off the streets.

I don't recall any fear or doubt. I hated them. I couldn't wait to get going.

**2**

In August 1969, there were riots every night in nationalist enclaves and towns across the North, including Dungannon and Coalisland. The RUC frequently resorted to using live rounds to scatter the crowds, but IRA activity in our area was minimal at that time.

What scant weaponry we had at our disposal was being funnelled into Belfast and Derry, where entire districts were coming under attack from loyalist mobs. The partisan police force, reinforced by an armed militia known as the B-Specials, stood with their hands in their pockets or even joined in.

August 12 signalled the beginning of The Battle of The Bogside in Derry, when Catholic nationalist residents erected barricades and fired stones and petrol bombs to keep marauding loyalists, RUC and B-Specials out of their narrow streets that ran beneath the city walls. Frustrated by their inability to break through, the RUC saturated the community with CS gas and fired over 1,000 plastic bullets indiscriminately into the area.

In an effort to take the pressure off Derry and fearing they would be next, the following day Belfast republicans barricaded themselves into their own areas in this deeply segregated city.

On August 13, Irish Taoiseach (Prime Minister) Jack Lynch took to the national airwaves in the Republic to issue a famously hollow threat to the British, saying that 'the Irish Government can no longer stand by and see innocent people injured and perhaps worse.' He announced that field hospitals would be set up along the 310-mile-long border that partitioned the country and called on the British government to bring in United Nations' peacekeepers.

Beleaguered nationalists were jubilant, believing that intervention was imminent. Instead, the statement fuelled loyalist paranoia and Catholic areas came under further attack. Loyalists burnt out entire streets as police looked on.

The deployment of the British army on August 14 calmed three nights of rioting but eight people had died, and thousands of nationalists had already fled to safety across the border. The intimidation continued: by the end of September, more than 1,820 families had been forced from their homes – 1,505 of them Catholic.

The IRA's entire arsenal in Co Tyrone extended to a few old rifles and handguns stored after the abortive border campaign. What would become the East Tyrone Brigade of the Provisional IRA announced its arrival using improvisation to wreak havoc. This unit would later turn large areas into virtual no-go zones for the British Army. For now though, we would have to make do with raw courage, a few near-obsolete guns, commercial explosives, clothes pegs, cardboard, wire and thumbtacks.

It had been coming for a while, but in January 1970, the IRA split into two factions. Roughly speaking, the Officials were men of words, the Provisionals men of action. A bitter, internecine feud developed on the streets of Belfast, but in rural areas like ours the distinction was largely semantic. We were all IRA volunteers with a common enemy. The finer points of republican ideology could wait.

IRA volunteers in Tyrone didn't care what the label was so long as we were taking on the British Army – now known universally as the 'Brits' – and, by extension, the Northern Ireland state.

The local IRA belatedly signalled its arrival in March 1971, when it blew up the offices of the Coalisland Pipe and Brick Company, located right in the heart of the town and opposite the RUC station, as part of a commercial bombing campaign designed to cripple the state financially.

There was all kind of speculation at the time about experts being drafted in from Dublin to do the job but the truth was closer to home. Someone who was present gave me the details.

The IRA unit acquired around five pounds of gelignite. Training and proper equipment was in short supply in those days, so improvisation was the name of the game. Delaying detonation was the main problem. The men involved didn't have a timer, so they resorted to a very primitive and dangerous method of delay. They used a simple wooden clothes peg.

For these operations, a volunteer would select the best position to plant a device, usually at a junction of two supporting walls. It would be left just a few inches away from one wall and tamped from behind to direct the blast, and the accompanying shockwave, towards that wall.

The components would be put together. First, he would place the charge, then he would fix the peg open with a piece of cardboard. Then, he would wrap a length of wire around some notches cut in the wood. When this was secure, he would introduce a battery to the detonator, keeping it well clear of the explosive charges.

The two ends of the wires would be attached to the open end of the peg by thumbtacks. After stabilising the peg, he would remove the cardboard and push the detonator gently into the charges. He would be working alone so that he would be the only casualty if things went wrong – an all too frequent occurrence.

In this case, he backed slowly out of the room and was well away when the explosives detonated 30 minutes later. This late-evening blast brought the entire town to their doors for a gawp. In later years, such explosions were so commonplace that nobody would have bothered flicking off their televisions or getting out of bed.

Anyone ever trained in explosives used to get the same piece of advice: 'You'll only ever make one mistake. The first will also be your last.'

I worked with many volunteers who were killed and maimed by so-called 'own goals'. These cost the lives of many of our people, most of them in the early years before we gained access to sophisticated, electronic detonators and more stable explosives.

**3**

Every nationalist in the North of Ireland at the time will remember where they were on the morning of August 9, 1971, particularly if they happened to be young, male and republican.

The Brits swept into working-class nationalist areas at 4 am and dragged hundreds of young men from their beds to detention camps on suspicion of involvement in paramilitary activity. Internment without trial had begun.

When I awoke to the news of Operation Demetrius, I was surprised I hadn't been scooped up in the pre-dawn raids. It would soon become apparent that I wasn't the only one they'd missed. In the cities, the IRA had got wind of what was coming and had ordered volunteers to stay away from their homes but in my case, I can only attribute my escape to weak intelligence.

Poor information meant the Brits ended up arresting innocent men while the spine of our organisation remained intact. Of the 342 men arrested that morning, 105 were released within two days.

It wasn't long before we began hearing about the violence inflicted on women and children as the army dragged their fathers, sons and brothers away to God knows where for God knows how long. We witnessed the extensive damage done to their homes with no chance of any redress, even in cases of wrongful arrest.

News started filtering through about the torture perpetrated on internees, who were being kept in filthy, damp, overcrowded concentration camps. They had the nerve to brand us terrorists, but we were the victims – they were terrorising us because we were demanding equality and dignity.

In the weeks that followed, nationalist areas erupted every night in support of the remaining internees – 'The Men Behind the Wire' – and the IRA was turning away would-be recruits by the score.

That morning, after a quick bite to eat, I left the house, half expecting to be arrested but there was no sign of any activity. I drove around looking for some friends, but everyone who hadn't been captured had gone to ground.

Out of ideas, I drove to Kevin Mallon's house at Brackaville, just outside Coalisland. I was in luck: Mallon had come home in the early hours after a good night out, completely unaware that internment had begun. I knocked and his brother gave him a call. Half-dressed and bleary-eyed, he appeared at the door.

'Have you heard the news?' I asked.

'Do I look like somebody that was listening to the news?' he growled.

'Internment was introduced this morning,' I said.

'So that's what those bastards were up to this morning when I was coming home. There were hundreds of them at Ernie Oliver's corner,' he said.

'You had better get the fuck out of here before they realise they missed you,' I advised.

Mallon told me he would be back in a minute and got himself ready.

I didn't know Kevin Mallon very well at the time, but our paths would shortly intertwine and then run in parallel for many years to come. A tall, rangy man, he was a born leader. He had the kind of presence that would fill a room.

He jumped into the car and asked me if I had access to any weapons. I told him the man in charge of them may have been rounded up. If not, he wouldn't be easy to find.

'Drive towards Ardboe,' Mallon instructed, already taking charge. We pulled up at a small cottage.

'Wait here,' he said. 'If there's a problem, blow the horn. You do have a horn in this thing?'

I appreciated the dark humour and beeped the horn so he would recognise the sound. He just glared and went into the house, returning 20 minutes later carrying a long hessian sack.

'Just a few bits and pieces from another era,' he said. 'It's a good job I kept them. Let's get the fuck out of here before he changes his mind. He doesn't seem to like you for some reason!'

'I don't give a fuck whether he likes me or not as long as he gives me weapons,' I retorted.

We made our way back to the outskirts of Coalisland and found a safe place to examine the contents of the sack. Then we got straight to work cleaning, oiling and sorting out the guns. We re-wrapped them and stored the bag in a thicket for collection that night.

As darkness fell, you could almost feel the rage.

Intent on using the anticipated riot in the town as cover, we approached the temporary dump only to discover a British Army checkpoint right beside it.

Returning to the town empty-handed, our luck changed when I ran into my quartermaster. He came back with a Thompson submachine gun – another relic but still in working order.

Four IRA volunteers with only this single weapon among them formed about 100 yards from where a line of British soldiers was confronting the rioters. Using the cover of a wall, one man crept along until he was only ten yards or so away from the enemy, level with a jeep from where a soldier was shining a search light. The volunteer stood up, opened fire and we later learned through newspaper reports that the squaddie would surely have died if a round hadn't struck a rubber bullet in his pocket. Everything went still for a few seconds before the soldiers began to return fire.

Panic ensued. The rioters scattered – and the IRA with them.

Over the coming days, weeks and months, a steady stream of people continued to try to join up. Although the Officials were still active, the Provos were in the ascendancy and I became a founding member of the newly formed East Tyrone Brigade.

Even from the early days of the conflict, we all knew the importance of local knowledge. The IRA was organised to maximise this advantage. Although the remote Army Council would set general policy, day-to-day operations were sanctioned at local level.

Some were sanctioned only after they had been mounted. A guerrilla army doesn't always have the luxury of asking permission to exploit an opportunity to attack the enemy. I would ambush Brits and police or do bank jobs on the hoof, only informing my commanding officer afterwards. In hindsight, this probably already marked me out as a maverick.

Its size and geography dictated that Co Tyrone be divided into East and West for operational reasons. Despite its nationalist majority, when the British partitioned Ireland in 1921, the county's strategic position as a buffer against fervently nationalist Donegal to the west ensured that it would become part of the newly created, pro-British statelet.

East Tyrone is characterised by sprawling boglands, bounded by the vast expanse of Lough Neagh, making it tough terrain for a guerrilla army. It could be a hard place to escape from. However, its proximity to Co Monaghan in the Republic provided a refuge and a natural base for launching operations. This was our Ho Chi Minh Trail.

The East Tyrone Brigade was a tight-knit outfit that operated with a great deal of autonomy from the urban leadership in Dublin and Belfast.

We paid no heed to the warnings about the certainty of long stretches in jail, serious injury or death. Even as we watched our comrades die, we had the invincibility of youth and the belief that we would rid Ireland of the British presence once and for all.

I never really thought about what might happen to me. When you're young, decades in captivity and death tend to be abstract concepts. Like bad accidents, they only happen to others.

At the time, none of us thought the conflict would last very long. A few years' fighting and the Brits would get mightily sick of propping up this rotten edifice and withdraw. How naïve we were.

In August 1971, the British Parachute Regiment (known as The Paras) shot dead 11 innocent nationalist civilians in what became known as the Ballymurphy Massacre. None of them were involved in the IRA and all were unarmed. It took 50 years of campaigning for the British government to eventually issue a grudging apology.

The following month, the East Tyrone Brigade killed its first British soldier. John Rudman, 21, from Co Durham in England, died in an ambush at Edendork, near Coalisland. His 19-strong convoy came under fire from a Thompson submachine gun, a rifle and shotguns.

Their casualties that day would have been much higher had a 75lb bomb intended for the follow-up operation gone off nearby, but it failed to explode. The IRA would also kill Rudman's brother, Thomas, in Belfast the following year.

A few months after the slaughter in Ballymurphy, on January 30, 1972, the Paras were again involved in mass murder, this time in Derry. The massacre of 14 unarmed civil rights campaigners in the city during a peaceful protest march convulsed Ireland, North and South, making headlines around the world. Bloody Sunday – as it became known – shook the southern Irish establishment to its core and ignited widespread latent support for a united Ireland, an aspiration enshrined in the Irish constitution at the time.

A few days later, the Dublin government was powerless to stop the British

Embassy in the city centre being burned down as an incensed crowd of at least 30,000 protesters cheered the flames and cut the fire hoses.

After a brief ceasefire in the North, the British government flew the IRA leadership to London for secret truce talks, but they came to nothing.

In terms of casualties, 1972 was the worst year of the Troubles. When it was over, 479 people were dead (including 130 British soldiers) and 4,876 injured.

During this period, I continued operating with virtually the same small group of men; looking for opportunities to take on the Brits and the police and carrying out countless robberies along the border.

We never wore masks or gloves. We never robbed a bank unless we could access the vault. We lived from day to day – for all the money we took, we never had a penny, it all went to headquarters to fund the struggle.

By this stage, I was more or less based permanently across the border in the Republic. It was far easier to operate from the South, where our cause elicited widespread sympathy, even among members of the southern police force, the Garda Síochána. But it certainly didn't afford me immunity from prosecution as a fearful Government issued orders to crack down hard on us.

In February 1972, shortly after Bloody Sunday, I was up in court in Carrickmacross, Co Monaghan, charged with having a stolen car in my possession. My co-accused, Tommy McNulty, was charged with possessing weapons. Around 100 Gardaí were deployed to maintain order when hundreds of our supporters protested outside the court, paralysing traffic. We were subsequently released.

I was arrested several times with McNulty. One such occasion happened outside our informal HQ, the family home of Feargal O'Hanlon, who had been killed with Seán South in the raid on Brookeborough police station in Co Fermanagh in 1957, an event that would spawn two of Ireland's favourite ballads, Seán South of Garryowen and The Patriot Game.

As usual, I had a pistol in my shoulder holster. McNulty ran into the house and I assured the detectives who were there to arrest us that if they let me go inside to fetch him, we would both return straight away. They agreed and I took the opportunity to dump the gun.

On the way to the station, one of the cops said to me: 'I suppose it was best to get rid of the little bits and pieces.'

They knew I was carrying.

Anyone seeking to understand how different a period this was need only look at a lavish coffee-table book called Patriot Graves: Resistance in Ireland, published in 1972. An American photojournalist, P. Michael O'Sullivan, was officially embedded with various IRA brigades operating across the North and along the border.

We were all instructed to cooperate. We needed the propaganda to keep Irish-American money rolling in, but that doesn't detract one iota from the man's bravery – he had served in the U.S. Army 82nd Airborne and was a very cool individual under fire. He had been well chosen.

The book, banned in the UK, contains graphic pictures of IRA operations – including some republished in this book, courtesy of his daughter, Siobhán. There is a series of pictures he captioned as Mallon and I. The pair made quite a contrast: one was a broad, statuesque six feet tall, the other a scrawny 5 feet 7 inches.

I had a brief stint as Officer Commanding (OC) for East Tyrone after Mallon was sentenced to one of his many prison terms. I wasn't in the position for very long. Towards the end of 1973, I was promoted to national Director of Intelligence on General Headquarters staff. GHQ was responsible for day-to-day operations and played a pivotal role in the campaign. But that job could wait.

The Army Council needed money. Buckets stuffed with dollars in Boston bars were always welcome, but the biggest source of funds was always closer to home.

IRA volunteers carried out a spate of bank and post office robberies throughout its campaign and I probably carried out more than most.

By then, I was practically on first-name terms with many of the local Gardaí. When we were detained, Mallon and I would while away the hours until our inevitable release playing cards with the officers who had arrested us. We were even allowed to send out for beer and cigarettes.

As security tightened up along the border, the Army Council ordered me to base myself further south and to raise as much money as possible. I agreed on the sole condition that I would be able to pick my own men. This ad hoc unit would report to GHQ but would operate largely autonomously, under my command.

In many ways, our unit would become a blueprint for the IRA. Instead of the same large group working together over a long period of time, units were formed into fluid cells, their composition changing from operation to operation. Information was on a strictly need-to-know basis.

I would select the personnel I required for any particular operation and when it was complete, they would return to their respective units. The individuals might be different on every job and they had no contact with anyone outside of the small group.

A unit operating like this, far from its reliable support base in Co Tyrone, was never going to exist for long, but it did some serious work. Among its exploits were two of the biggest robberies in the history of the Irish State and, of course, one of the most-celebrated jailbreaks in republican history, the helicopter escape from Mountjoy.

**4**

These days it takes about an hour to drive from Dublin to the town of Navan, Co Meath. In 1973, it would have taken considerably longer. Across the South, the roads were in notoriously poor condition and even the shortest journeys would make a mockery of a map.

Navan was an inauspicious town that happened to host a district sorting office for mail distribution across a broad swathe of countryside north of Dublin. Based on local intelligence about its lucrative contents, this would be the new unit's first major target.

I picked two of my trusted lieutenants, Seamus 'Sig' Dillon and 'Mark', to carry out the job. Another volunteer, Tony McNally, would be joining us. Sig had plenty of experience and plenty of courage. Mark was also highly experienced. I don't name him for privacy reasons.

Tony had survived numerous scrapes with the Brits over the years, including one where another volunteer, Kevin Kilpatrick, had been shot dead after they ran a checkpoint. A happy-go-lucky type, he put his luck down to cunning and quick thinking.

In our early operations together, Tony used to make bomb timers using alarm clocks. We would be driving towards a target with a device sitting on my knee. With the state of the roads, both of us could have been vaporised. We blew up place after place. We didn't stop.

I never wore gloves or a mask. I always behaved like a soldier. I was aware of the Geneva Convention and I tried to put it into practice, even if I wasn't bound by it because the Brits, officially at least, didn't recognise our legitimacy. British politicians always denied there was a war going on even though it was as plain as the nose on your face. Their army also knew different.

I believed a person should behave with some respect. There were lines. Don't get me wrong, I'd have pulled the trigger as soon as look at you, but I didn't want to do that. In many ways, I considered it a bit of a game, I suppose. I wanted to be respectable. I believed in integrity. I pictured myself sitting down at the kitchen table with my children years later and telling them 'I did that, that and that' and being proud of it.

In my mind if you're out on an armed mission and you get shot that's tough.

That held for both sides, but an execution is a different thing.

I'll give an example. I let off a cop at least once. I could easily have killed him, but I didn't. We were on a fundraising run as we called it. We had done a few robberies before we landed in a Co Tyrone market town, where we planned to take another two banks. An RUC man was sitting in his car in the main square where these banks were located. I told Sig and Tony, 'I'm going to walk across this square. If he surrenders, I won't shoot him. If he offers any resistance, I'm going to pop him. Either way, as soon as I pull my gun, you come around my back and rob the bank in front of me.'

I walked past the cop and pulled out my pistol. I told him to put both hands on the steering wheel and relieved him of his service revolver. Just then, this old woman came towards me with a machete in her hand; one of these things for cutting your way through the jungle. The cop car was between her and me and I saw the cop looking round at me as she continued her approach. I tried to fire a warning round from the Luger I was carrying but it jammed, so I used the cop's gun instead.

'If you come any closer,' I said, 'I'll shoot this cop first and then I'll shoot you.'

She turned on her heels and fled. Don't get me wrong, I would have shot both of them. I wasn't going to compromise my safety and those with me.

We were driving a Hillman Imp. After the robbery, Sig and I were lying down in the back with two Armalite rifles. I could see the cop looking at us, but I instructed Sig not to shoot him. I had already let the air out of the tyres of his patrol car, and I had his gun.

I was talking to people afterwards. When we were out of sight the cop got up, dusted himself down, walked over to a pub and ordered a large double whiskey for himself! When news of what happened reached the IRA Army Council, the only reprimand I received was for my failure to take the RUC man's notebook. Nobody berated me for not killing him.

I never received a single day's training since I went with the Provos after the split from the Officials. All my training came before this. People just assumed I knew all this stuff, but I knew nothing. But there is one thing I learned very early on. If you're going out on a job you can't expect anyone else to look out for your back, you have to look out for it yourself.

We may have been at the sharp end, but we had no shortage of support in those days. Countless people throughout Ireland provided information, places to stay, transport and other logistical support that made it possible to conduct a guerrilla war. As Mao sagely put it, 'the fish need the sea to survive.'

One such was Navan-based John O'Neill. Originally from near Coalisland, he tipped us off to the possibilities of raiding the sorting office. Over the years he would often shelter us in his own home and source other safe houses for us as well.

Nowadays, pensions and welfare payments are often deposited directly into individual bank accounts, but in those pre-electronic days cash was king. The unit spent most of early 1973 scoping the building and its activities. On the face of it, security was tight. It was surrounded by a six-feet-high wall and armed, plain-clothed police detectives accompanied cash deliveries and forward distributions to individual post offices and dole offices.

Closer scrutiny revealed obvious gaps begging to be exploited. An alleyway ran along the side of the building, leading to a reinforced office door out of sight of the road. Waste ground behind would allow a speedy getaway.

Crucially, on delivery nights, the security van pulled in like clockwork. On arrival at 10.20 pm, it would sound its horn and a young man would open the steel door, unlock the main gate, allow the van to enter and offload its contents onto trolleys, and begin wheeling them inside the building. This would take about 30 minutes.

When he was finished and had locked the gate, the armed escort accompanying the security van would wait until he had gone inside the building before leaving. Then, he would spend the rest of the night alone sitting beside the alarm button.

In the North, the unit could simply have overpowered the armed escort while the door was open, but the IRA leadership forbade confrontations of any kind with the Gardaí.

This was a smart strategy. Uniformed, rank-and-file Gardaí were unarmed and commanded widespread respect. The IRA feared antagonising a sympathetic public. As long as we were attacking the Brits or defending our homes, we could count on at least tacit support.

Initially, the unit settled on a plan to break down the office door. Then, we set about sourcing a car and a safe house. Gardaí would be combing the area looking for us and our Northern accents would do us no favours.

It was now Monday: The next delivery was due on Thursday night. I had already picked my team. We were operating far from our usual base along the Monaghan-Tyrone border. We had little idea of the roads, the terrain, or likely safe houses.

We would have to rely on others – always a necessary evil. The car and driver came courtesy of the Dublin Brigade. So far, so good.

Mark's idea for a safe house was a stroke of genius. He suggested Butlin's holiday camp in the seaside town of Mosney, about an hour's drive from Navan, across quiet country roads. Butlin's, part of a chain of family- friendly seaside resorts catering for working-class holidaymakers, was a popular haunt for nationalists looking to escape the Troubles for a week or two – the boys would blend right in.

Joe, the getaway driver, was good but he was a Dublin man with no knowledge of the country roads, so Mark spent most of Tuesday with him going on dry runs, first in daylight and then in the dark.

John O'Neill booked the Butlin's chalet and agreed to transport Sig and Mark's bags from his house, as they had been staying with him.

The IRA volunteers went through the usual pre-job ritual of emptying their pockets in case they dropped anything that might identify them. They stripped and cleaned their weapons and even the accompanying bullets, wearing gloves to hide fingerprints.

Mark parked the car they would be using to drive to Butlin's in the forecourt of a busy garage around 20 minutes from Navan. He met Joe and they drove in the getaway car back to the town. After the job, the three Tyrone boys would head for the holiday camp and Joe for Dublin. As night fell, the trio shinned the wall of the sorting office, blending into the shadows below.

**Thursday 10 pm**

They crouched in the darkness. The only light came from streetlamps on the road out front. They had a good view of the office door and the high, barred gate at the main entrance. There was little or no traffic.

**10.30 pm**

With no sign of the van, tension heightened. The minutes ticked by, but it remained eerily silent. Had they been set up? Had an informer in the Dublin Brigade spilled the beans?

**10.45 pm**

The tension broke. The van arrived, its horn sounded, and the office door opened. The young man wheeled his trolley down to the main gate, unlocked it and began bringing in the cash. The armed police detectives watched him bolt the gate and waited until he had pulled the office door shut behind him.

Whatever hopes the volunteers harboured that the armed escort might leave before the office door was locked quickly evaporated.

**11.15 pm**

The three men crept along the wall until they reached the window where the young man was sitting. They had jemmy bars with them to force the door open.

On the spur of the moment, Mark came up with an alternative.

'If we can get him away from the alarm long enough for me to break the window, I can get my arm through, and with the revolver in my hand, I can keep him away from the alarm,' he whispered.

He told Sig to light a piece of newspaper that was lying on the ground nearby and to fan the smoke under the door.

The bet was on the young man investigating the source of the acrid smoke. Fire is never a welcome addition to a place full of paper. It worked. He left his station long enough for Mark to break the window, point his pistol and warn him away from the alarm button.

The employee froze just inside the door. Sig roared from outside that he had a bomb and would detonate it if he didn't open up.

Had the young clerk kept calm and stayed down, it would have been tough to breach the door before he set off the alarm. But late at night with a gun waving inside the window and Northern accents shouting about a bomb outside, he panicked.

## 11.30 pm

Once inside, the three men moved fast. They assured the petrified clerk he would come to no harm, sitting him far from the alarm in the highly unlikely event he would change his mind.

A large pile of sacks lay in the middle of the floor. They knew what they were looking for: the ones helpfully labelled 'Final' contained the most cash and valuables. Just as the unit began to sort out the sacks, the trio heard the wail of a Garda siren. Sig crept outside to assess the situation, thinking they might already be surrounded. The others tied the young man to a set of stairs in the corner to keep him clear of the alarm after they left. The siren seemed to be fading before it suddenly became much clearer, screaming as it passed the main gate.

'I think our lift is gone,' Sig reported. 'That was Joe flying past the front door with two squad cars chasing him.'

They checked the contents of the bags to make sure they were worth the risk – no point failing to fight another day for the sake of a small return. As things stood, they could have walked away and there would have been no evidence against them, even if they were arrested nearby.

Rummaging around, they found their night's work had been more than worth it. Now all they had to do was find a way to get it out of there.

Improvisation came easy. They had often been in tighter spots. After all, that's why this unit had been formed.

Noticing a small post office van in the yard, they ordered the young man to hand over the keys. He gestured to a ring of keys on the back of the office door that would start the van and open the front gate. After loading up, they edged through the gate, locking it behind them before driving onto the now-deserted main road.

Mark donned a postman's cap while Sig and Tony sat out of sight in the back. As they drove towards the changeover car, they could still hear the sirens wailing in the distance.

'Joe used to drive a rally car,' Mark said. 'They won't catch him unless he crashes. He'll lead them away from us, towards Dublin.'

A nervous Sig wasn't so sure.

'Let's get the fuck out of town, before they start chasing us too!'

They had a smooth run to the getaway car, which then followed Mark as he drove the van to a quiet country lane, where they abandoned it. One more look to make sure they had left nothing behind, and they took off for Butlin's.

Decked out in trendy shirts, they looked like three young lads who had been in a dance hall but instead of talking about drink or women, their chat was about reviewing any possible loose ends and keeping an eye on the cash.

Adrenaline might have been expected to keep them up all night, but there was no insomnia or celebration. Completely exhausted, they all slept soundly.

The following morning, they counted their takings: £40,000 in cash. At the time, the average house price in Dublin was around £9,000. The notes were neatly tied in bundles of £5s, £10s, £20s and £50s. They placed the cash carefully in a shopping bag, covered by a couple of shirts, for transport to their superiors. Then they unloaded and stripped their weapons, wrapped them in clothing and placed them in a separate shopping bag. They placed both bags inside a suitcase and locked it.

'Both of you go and get a breakfast, I'll stay with the gear – we can't leave the chalet empty; this place is full of crooks!' Mark quipped.

After they left, he checked the place over one more time, put the suitcase in the wardrobe and left for breakfast only after the others had returned.

Sig was keen to catch the news on the radio.

'I don't know why you want to listen to the news,' Tony said. 'We are the fucking news!'

They called a Dublin contact to pick up the cash and the guns, but it would be late afternoon before two cars pulled up at the door.

'The whole place is crawling with cops after last night,' the courier explained, 'It's settled down a bit now, so we should be okay. There wasn't any point in us coming any sooner.'

The Dubs left shortly afterwards, the scout car pulling ahead of the second vehicle with its precious cargo.

It turned out that Joe wasn't to blame for leaving the boys stranded.

While he was parked on the waste ground waiting for them, a Garda patrol car pulled up beside him. Joe had no ID, tax, or insurance and was sitting in a stolen car, so he took off, dragging the Gardaí behind him. He sped out of town with two patrol cars on his tail, passing the main gate to alert the men that they were on their own. He managed to shake off the cops in the winding, country roads of north Dublin. He had also taken them away from the robbery.

Tony gave Sig and Mark a lift to the bus station. They were returning back to their native Tyrone, where they would rejoin their units. They hardly even had the price of the fare.

At the station, Tony picked up Tommy McKearney, another young volunteer from Tyrone, who happened to be going on a break. The pair headed for Dublin.

They didn't even bother to evade any of the roadblocks they encountered but came unstuck when a routine search at a checkpoint unearthed six .22 bullets, which had been mislaid by the owner of the car, who held a licensed hunting rifle. The boys had no such licence.

They were arrested and remanded in custody to Mountjoy Jail – 'the Joy' – in Dublin. The irony is that if it hadn't been for this spot of bad luck, the most daring prison escape of the 20th century would never have happened.

# 5

I passed the better part of yet another long day scanning the street from my first-floor window vantage point. The two-room Dublin flat had become my latest home and it was better than most.

It was October 1973 and winter was closing in.

I lit yet another cigarette and waited for the knock on the door. She should be here soon. I already knew she was a byword for reliability.

I first met Marion one afternoon a few weeks earlier. I had been lying down, staring at the yellowed ceiling when a soft knock came to the door. I grabbed my pistol out of habit and opened the door to find a stunning young woman standing there.

'Are you Brendan Hughes?' she asked. 'I have a message from Kevin Mallon.'

'Where are you parked?' I answered sourly. 'I don't want any strange cars outside drawing attention to this place.'

She returned my question with an icy smile.

'I only take public transport and I always make sure I'm never followed.

Plainly, this was no amateur messenger. Aside from her looks, I took to her straight away. She demanded respect and she deserved it.

'Mallon sent me about an escape plan,' she continued, matter of factly.

Kevin Mallon had been caught a few months earlier and was sentenced to a year in prison for IRA membership. He obviously didn't intend to serve out his term.

He also knew about my unit.

'Do you want some coffee?' I asked her, almost hopefully.

I wasn't surprised when she turned me down, saying she was in a hurry. The place was a mess: ashtrays were overflowing and dishes with the greasy remains of several fry-ups were stacked high between the dirty electric hotplate and the tiny sink.

'Tommy McKearney is set for release and he'll be contacting you,' she said. 'He noticed a helicopter landing in Mountjoy a few days ago to bring someone to hospital and approached Mallon with an escape plan. He wants you to do the job and to take Seamus Twomey and J.B. O'Hagan out with him.'

Twomey had been IRA chief of staff before his capture only a few weeks earlier, and O'Hagan was a veteran member of the Army Council. All three were considered prize prisoners. Their escape would be a severe embarrassment and give us a welcome morale boost.

'Tommy's due out next week and I'll be seeing you again after he makes contact,' she said.

The idea of using a helicopter for a prison escape in the North had come up before but had been dismissed for any number of reasons. For a start, the IRA didn't have a helicopter and if it had, we didn't have anyone to fly it. Even if we did manage to commandeer one, far too many things could go wrong.

'What will I tell Mallon?' she asked.

## Chapter 5

I decided to keep my doubts to myself.

'Tell him I'll do it,' I said.

I couldn't believe it when she turned to go.

'Hold on,' I said. 'You can't just barge in here and then disappear. How do I contact you, for a start? And I'll need you to contact Mallon, to work with me on this.'

'I don't work for you and I won't be working with you,' she replied curtly. 'I have plenty of work of my own to be getting on with.'

I told her I'd need clearance to take on the job – the IRA Director of Intelligence couldn't just take on projects out of sentiment or as a favour for old comrades.

'I'll also need funds,' I said.

I never let on that I would much prefer to be working on this than compiling intelligence. I knew how important my new role was, but I always preferred being in the thick of the action.

She reluctantly scribbled a phone number on a scrap of paper, instructing me to remember the details quickly before destroying it.

'If I'm not there when you call, leave a message and I'll get here as soon as I can.'

And with that, she walked out the door.

I lay back on the sofa and thought more about Marion than the message she'd carried. I was glad of her company, even for a short while. My wife and kids were in Tyrone and this war didn't look like ending anytime soon.

I've always been a great believer in fate: in its ability to screw you up and to work in your favour. If Tommy hadn't been caught with Tony, he wouldn't have been in jail to witness the helicopter evacuation and to bring the plan to Mallon. Pure chance.

It wasn't the first time I had tried to spring Mallon from Mountjoy. Mallon was always getting caught – you could never keep him out of jail!

I mounted my previous attempt on my very first visit to a prison, which was to see him. I had asked Mallon if I would be searched or whether I should even come at all – I was already on the run.

'No problem,' he assured me. 'Just walk in.'

So, I walked in with a 9mm pistol down the waistband of my trousers.

We were sitting there at a big, long table and I said, 'I have a piece here, do you want it?'

Mallon couldn't believe what he was hearing. 'I'll never get it in; I'll get caught.' he said.

Three other men accompanying me had agreed to start a fight as a diversion while I handed over the gun.

Anyway, he had refused to take it and I was forced to walk back out with it again.

# 6

My latest in a long line of addresses was in affluent Clontarf. The flat looked across Dublin Bay and Bull Island. Dublin was a very different place in those days – feeling more like a big town than a city, with distinctive villages dotted throughout.

Although suburban in character, Clontarf was convenient to the city centre and despite my soft Northern accent, I went unnoticed. Nationalists had been fleeing south in their thousands over the past few years, leaving their homes in ashes after loyalists burned them out.

Aside from the anonymity it afforded, I would take full advantage of the location for frequent strolls on Dollymount Strand. It helped me to think and, after Marion's visit, I now had plenty on my mind.

I had become very security-conscious since moving to Dublin. Being on the run wasn't new to me but I was wanted on a stolen car charge, so I had upped my game.

In Co Tyrone and along the border in Co Monaghan, I had operated with real freedom. After internment, we found support from all sections of nationalist society and doors previously closed to us were well and truly open.

I even used to venture around my hometown with a rifle slung over my shoulder. Everyone would give me a friendly nod or would simply ignore me.

We had turned East Tyrone into a virtual no-go area for the Brits and the RUC, who had to resort to air transport to and from their bases, where they were largely confined.

When I went walking in Dublin that evening, I recall watching seagulls fighting over scraps left by visitors and kids playing with a small dog. They were a welcome distraction. I knew how important this upcoming job was, not only for the prisoners but for overall morale. There had been a few setbacks of late.

In March, the IRA was about to land five tons of arms and ammunition from Libya when the Irish coastguard boarded the Claudia, a 298-ton trawler, off the Waterford coast in southeast Ireland. Other recent reversals included the formation of two new Irish army battalions to patrol the border, the seizure of 17 rifles and 29,000 rounds of ammunition on a ship in Dublin Port, and the detection and prevention of a jailbreak from Mountjoy.

And in the North, the British government had brought in sweeping new powers, including the Diplock non-jury courts – a carbon copy of the Special Criminal Court introduced the previous year in the Republic.

Irish reunification seemed to be as far away as ever amid British plans to cement unionist control of local government in Northern Ireland. We appeared to be on the back foot.

I also knew there wasn't much more I could do until I met Tommy, but he must have been confident enough to bring the idea to Mallon. Neither was a time-waster. Landing a chopper inside the jail must be a runner.

# 7

I walked the beach until after dark when hunger got the better of me. It would be the usual rashers and sausages for dinner. Afterwards, sleep eluded me until exhaustion overtook near dawn.

I have always believed that sleeping on a problem helps a person to come up with solutions. That night, it certainly gave me a start.

I knew absolutely nothing about helicopters, other than they were hard to lose once they spotted you. I had no idea where to start, but I had access to the finest volunteers in the country and that gave me plenty of confidence. I also had access to a wider circle of people sympathetic to our cause and these unsung heroes were the backbone of the struggle. They took serious risks over the years and they have seldom been acknowledged.

One such was a businessman from Coalisland, called Dermie, who used to offer us refuge when we were operating in the area. It was he who first came up with the idea of using a helicopter to mount a prison escape. Mallon and I had even discussed the possibility before his latest capture.

First thing the following morning, I rang Dermie from a public telephone to ask whether he might be available for a meeting. We arranged to meet the next evening around eight in the Co Monaghan town of Carrickmacross. He said he was due to have a meal there with some friends. I turned down his kind invitation to join them.

My mind was already in overdrive. This job would require the best volunteers and one of them, at the top of the list, happened to be available. As luck would have it, Pete Ryan was on a break in Dublin. At the time, Pete wasn't even of voting age, but was already well on his way to becoming an IRA legend. He was small and stocky, built like a tank. He feared nothing, or nobody. We had attended the same school in Ardboe. He was my friend and years later he would save my life.

Whenever he came to Dublin, Pete would stay with a friend of his who happened to be a member of a popular showband, Wee Mick and the Hoot'nanny's. The showband scene was very popular at the time, with thousands of people thronging dance halls across the country every night of the week.

The constant comings and goings around Mick's flat were great cover for an IRA man on the run. There was never a shortage of young women either, attracted to musicians and their friends.

When I arrived there, the door was unlocked. I walked into the sitting room. It looked like someone had just thrown a grenade into it. The table was covered with the remnants of last night's meals, clothes were strewn across the floor and an upturned chair blocked access to an adjacent room.

I called out for Pete but was met with silence. A young woman with red hair peeped out from behind a door.

'Who are you looking for?' she asked.

'I'm looking for a little short guy, called Pete,' I said. 'Have you seen him? I'm a friend of his and I have some money for him.'

She closed the door, and I could hear muffled voices inside. When it swung open again, there was Pete standing in his underpants.

'How many of you are in there?' I asked.

A grin spread across his face.

'For fuck sake, why didn't you say it was you?' he asked. 'What do you mean, how many are in here? What do you take me for? There's just me and her. You scared the shit out of me. I thought it was the cops. There was a lot of noise here last night and some of the neighbours got upset. There were complaints but I'll say no more about it.'

'Are you staying in Dublin for a while?' I inquired. 'I have some work that you'd like. I could do with your help, if you're up for it?'

'Your timing is very bad,' he said. 'But fuck it anyway.'

He went to get dressed and I could hear some whispered conversation. He reappeared a few minutes later.

'This had better be good,' Pete said. 'I wouldn't leave her for anyone else!'

We jumped into the car and drove aimlessly for a while. It was already one o'clock, but Pete had no interest in eating.

'Far too early,' he replied to my suggestion about getting some food. 'What the fuck sort of life do you live?' I teased.

'Look, I'm here on a break, and I'm making the most of it,' Pete replied. 'For fuck sake man, we could both be dead before the month is out. We don't drive buses you know. Our number could come up any day. Besides, all those women would miss me if I wasn't around occasionally!'

I could see he was getting impatient, which was fair enough. After all, I had dragged him away and he was supposed to be on holiday.

'Where are we going?' he asked.

'I've a job you may be interested in. That's if you don't have to go back up North right away.

'I only have a couple of weeks, but I'll give you a hand if I'm able,' he said. I told him a couple of weeks would be more than enough.

We sat in a quiet café and I ordered two sandwiches and coffees. Pete accepted them reluctantly.

'Kevin Mallon sent out word he wants me to get a helicopter and fly him out of the 'Joy,' I said.

Pete almost choked.

'A helicopter? Now where the fuck would we get one of them and who would fly it?'

I began to detail the plan that had begun to form in my mind.

'We hire the helicopter and the pilot. Then we 'persuade' him to fly it in for us. That's all I've got so far. What do you reckon?'

'So far, I think it was worth getting out of bed for,' he replied. 'When do we start?'

I asked him to come with me to meet Dermie the following evening. I would pick him up at six. It would take about two hours to get there. Even when I made the arrangement, I should have known it would take longer at that time of day. We got stuck in heavy rush-hour traffic, eventually arriving more than 15 minutes late.

'Late as usual,' Dermie joked as we sat into his car.

He knew full well it was highly unusual for me to be late. I couldn't afford to be late – my life and those of others depended on me being on time.

'So,' Dermie asked, 'it seems like you might have a problem that I can help you with?'

'He always has problems,' Pete piped up. 'He's a fucking problem himself!' I ignored the jibe. I was used to dishing it out, so I had to take it too – even from a younger man of supposed inferior rank. After all, this wasn't a conventional army.

I came straight out with it.

'Dermie, do you have any idea how to go about hiring a helicopter for a day?' I didn't go into detail, but I told him I would need to know about things like the kind of ID required and the cost.

I would also need to know whether it was possible to pay cash. I also told him any inquiry had to be very discreet.

'As luck would have it,' he replied, 'I have relations coming from the States on holiday, so I'll inquire about booking it for them. I can always cancel, but by then I should know everything you need to know. Give me a shout in a couple of days.'

The journey back to Dublin was much quicker and I enjoyed the craic with Pete. He was always great company. At this stage, I was still sceptical about the possibility of mounting an operation like this but at least we had made a start.

# 8

The two-day wait to call Dermie was torture. I loved doing jobs and I was always on the lookout for opportunities to mount an attack. But I knew this job was different. It would require patience, something I lacked back then.

That morning, I walked about a mile from the flat to call him on a payphone, relieved to be doing something to push this job on a bit. I would even have settled for some bad news to put me out of my misery. At least I could then move on to something else.

'Any news, Dermie?' I asked.

'Brendan,' he replied, 'I have all the news you want. Can we meet this evening, same time, same place?'

I knew he wouldn't be dragging me up to Monaghan for no reason. 'See you there,' I said.

'By the way,' Dermie said, 'I'm giving a man a lift and you can take him the rest of the way to Dublin, if that's alright? Big Maurice Conway.'

I was only too delighted to agree. I hadn't seen Maurice in a long time.

I was in good form when I returned to the flat and it got even better when I saw Marion standing outside.

'I've spoken to Kevin and he's expecting me to bring him some word when I go back in again on Monday,' she said.

I told her about my meeting in Carrickmacross and invited her to join Pete and I later on to meet Dermie. As usual, she batted me away.

'Not this evening,' she said. 'I have other things to do that won't keep. I'm actually very busy at the moment.'

She annoyed me in one way but, in another, her total professionalism gave me comfort. She also declined the lift I offered.

I agreed to call her on Monday evening and walked to my car to make arrangements for later on. All my cars were stolen in those days. It was easy, all you had to do was hotwire them and change the plates. You could get them made no problem.

I would always look out for plates like the model I was driving at the time, so if the Gardaí did happen to run them, they would match the make of the car.

When I arrived at Mick's flat, to my surprise, Pete was on his own for once.

'Good news,' I said. 'We have to meet Dermie again this evening. He has all the information I asked him for. And by the way, Big Maurice will be with him. We'll be giving him a lift to Dublin.'

Maurice Conway was a tall, elegant, laid-back character. After internment, he packed in his career as a schoolteacher to join the IRA, masquerading as a full-time organiser for Sinn Féin, the organisation's political wing.

As soon as Dermie mentioned his name, I had him marked for a key role in the operation. He was articulate, polite and could move easily in any company. He was also very friendly with Tommy, given their shared interest in talking politics. They would spend endless hours discussing and debating where the whole thing was going.

But Pete didn't share my enthusiasm for Maurice's company.

'Fuck me, do we have to?' he asked. 'He'll do our heads in all the way back. Could we not just put him on a bus?' he joked.

'Nope,' I replied. 'If anyone can hire a chopper, he's the man to do it. A good suit and he could pass himself off anywhere.'

Pete shot back a tell-tale grin – he sensed the logic but wasn't giving in that easily.

'That doesn't mean we have to listen to him the whole way back to Dublin,' he moaned.

I told him to be ready when I came back a few hours later to pick him up. He looked like he could do with a siesta.

'I was up all hours last night and with any luck it'll be the same tonight,' he said. 'It's like I said before, we could all be dead tomorrow.'

'If you keep this up, you'll be dead anyway,' I joked.

I drove a short distance and parked overlooking Dublin Bay to enjoy the sea breeze. I must have drifted off to sleep. A thud on the bonnet of the car jolted me bolt upright. A little kid looked at me sheepishly.

'Sorry, mister,' he said, retrieving his ball. 'No problem,' I said with a smile.

A bouncing ball wasn't something to get annoyed about. If he only knew the noise an Armalite makes when it's shooting through the roof of a car.

On one particular occasion, four of us were heading up a hill on the way to mount an operation. Mallon and I were in the back. I had a Thompson. Tony was in the front passenger seat, cradling an Armalite. We drove round a bend, straight into a British Army checkpoint.

The young guy driving us almost went to pieces, but Mallon instructed him to slow down as if preparing to stop before putting his foot to the floor.

Once he accelerated, all hell broke loose. The noise was deafening. I was sure the Brits were riddling the car with bullets. We hurtled past, Mallon and I flat against the back seat, half-anticipating that our time had surely come.

It turned out that Tony had sprayed the roof with bullets from inside the car to confuse the soldiers manning the checkpoint.

When we eventually stopped, he turned around looking at us, pissing himself laughing. I could have killed him myself.

Anyway, when I picked Pete up a short while later, he was wearing a new leather jacket from 'a secret admirer'. He wasn't giving anything else away, but the banter was enough to sustain the journey all the way to Carrickmacross. I offered to let him drive but he declined.

'On the way home, we could get Maurice to drive,' Pete suggested. 'It might keep him quiet!'

We arrived on time and Dermie picked a quiet corner in a busy restaurant.

'Okay, Brendan, here's how it works,' he said. 'I called up Irish Helicopters yesterday morning.

'I explained that my American cousin was paying me a visit and I wanted to surprise him. A pleasant gentleman told me it was very straightforward and asked me when I was planning to hire the chopper. I told him it would probably be some day next week but that I wasn't sure yet.

'Brendan, you're not going to believe this. When you arrive at their base all you do is pay them. All you need is a deposit. You tell them where you want to go, give them time to file a flight plan and get it cleared, and off you go. You don't even need ID unless you're paying by cheque. Isn't that something else? You need all sorts of ID to hire a car but when it comes to a helicopter, you need nothing.'

I turned to Maurice, 'Isn't that fucking great; you just got yourself a job!'

Maurice just looked at me and said, 'Knowing you, it won't be anything simple.'

His reply amused me no end. We had worked together before and knew each other well. I felt luck was somehow favouring me again: right man, right place.

Dermie's contribution didn't end there. After paying for the meal, he slid an envelope across the table towards me.

'I want to give you a few bob, just something to help you hire it,' he said. 'This will make things a wee bit easier for you. If there's anything else I can do, let me know. You have my number.'

I began to tear the envelope open but Dermie told me to wait until he had left.

Once in the car, I handed it to Pete, and he began counting the notes. £500.

'Which pub are we going to in Dublin?' Pete asked with a laugh. 'This would give us a few good nights.'

'Where do you drink?' I shot back. 'That should keep you going for a month.' 'Ah,' he replied, 'But I have some pleasant ladies to take care of.'

'Well, you won't be taking care of them with that money,' I assured him. 'That money has prison break written all over it. Now, put it away in case we're stopped.'

I looked in the mirror but couldn't make out Maurice's face in the dark. 'Maurice, are you awake?' I inquired.

'Awake? Of course, I'm awake,' he said. 'How could I sleep with both of you counting money and talking about prison breaks? Are you ever going to tell me what's going on?'

I gave a brief outline of the embryonic plan to break Mallon, Twomey and O'Hagan out of Mountjoy.

'And by the way,' I said. 'You'll be hiring the helicopter.'

'Didn't I know it would be nothing simple once you were involved,' he sighed.

'Maurice, this is a piece of piss,' I told him. 'All you have to do is hire the helicopter and we'll do the rest. It's right up your street. Bullshit them, pay them, job done.'

I was trying not to laugh. I knew Maurice would be delighted to have a role.

We dropped him off bang in the middle of the city centre, on O'Connell

Street. He would have no problem getting a bus or a taxi.

'I'll be in touch,' I said, as he handed me his phone number.

Maurice told me he would be around for a couple of weeks and I instructed him not to head back without telling me first.

I took Dermie's envelope from Pete and dropped him off too.

I drove back to Clontarf, parking the car a few streets away as usual. Over a late coffee, I sat by the window watching the lights flicker atop the iconic Ringsend chimney at the Poolbeg power station across Dublin Bay. I decided to end what had turned into a very good night with a phone call to Marion.

'Yes, what's up?' she asked.

'Tell our friend I have the money to do what he wants and that Dermie supplied the finance,' I said. 'I'll be waiting for Tommy to get in touch.'

# 9

Tommy and Tony were due for release on Monday. I hoped they would give me more information about the layout of the prison and what had prompted the plan. I now had access to a helicopter and the wherewithal to hire it, but I would still have to 'persuade' the pilot to alter the original flight plan and bring it down in a prison yard.

Not knowing my way around Dublin was a distinct disadvantage. I needed somewhere quiet to land the chopper on its way to the jail to give us a chance to skyjack it. I could have approached someone in the Dublin Brigade, but I wanted this kept tight – this would be a Tyrone job.

I decided I would lean a bit more on Pete. He didn't know Dublin very well either, but I didn't have any better ideas at the time. He wasn't exactly pleased to see me when I turned up at Mick's place on Saturday morning.

'Some break this is,' he moaned, when I walked in the unlocked door.

'Sure, all of life is a break with us in our line of business, Pete,' I said. 'Dry your eyes and come with me.'

It turned out the only sleep he had the previous night was in the car on the way back to the flat. Still, he washed, shaved and after 15 minutes was ready to go.

I told Pete we needed a place to land the chopper on the way to Mountjoy. This would allow us time to commandeer it and give Maurice a chance to leave. We needed five minutes on the ground, in peace. I didn't know the city well enough, so I would be depending on him.

Pete mulled things over, but nothing sprung to mind. I parked along the quays that straddle the Liffey, and we went in for coffee, hoping for some inspiration.

We sat in silence for a few minutes before Pete said, 'How about a golf course? Well, maybe it's a pitch and putt course. It's on the Blessington Road, just outside of Tallaght on the southern outskirts of the city.'

Tallaght is now the largest suburb of Dublin but before its rapid, haphazard development during the 1970s and 1980s, it was little more than a collection of sleepy villages in the foothills of the Dublin mountains.

Barely half an hour later, we were trundling along a small country lane that ran beside a golf course. It turns out I knew this part of Dublin. The owner of a nearby pub, The Embankment, was a friend of mine and I had enjoyed many a good night there.

The golf course fitted the bill, but I was concerned someone might call the Gardaí when they saw a chopper landing there, so I chose a large field adjacent to it. There was a downside to this. It bordered the main road, so we would need to work very fast. We decided we would return the day before the escape to stash our weapons.

I dropped Pete off and headed home to wait for Tony and Tommy. Pete promised to send them up to me if they turned up at his flat, which was nearer the prison than mine.

It turned out it would be Wednesday before I saw Tommy. I was obsessing about a daring helicopter escape, but Tommy had some catching up to do. I hadn't done time then, so I didn't realise the need to decompress!

Around midday on Wednesday, Tony, Tommy and Pete gathered in my flat for the first time. After some idle chat about jail, about home, and of course, women, we got down to business.

Tommy had witnessed an army helicopter land in a prison yard to airlift the IRA's former leader Sean Mac Stiofáin to hospital. It had landed in very tight space. Tommy realised immediately that the yard where republicans exercised separately was far bigger.

He approached Mallon, reasoning that if a chopper could land in a small yard, a bigger one should be no problem.

I took it from there and began sketching out my rough plan. Posing as a businessman, Maurice would pay a deposit to hire the helicopter on his friend Tommy's behalf. On the day, Tommy would instruct the pilot to land beside the golf course to pick up Maurice after a business meeting there.

Maurice and I would meet it. I would produce the weapons, arm Tommy, and I would climb aboard too. We would redirect the pilot. Maurice, the only other link to hiring the helicopter, would already be long gone.

The rest of them agreed to much of the rough plan and began looking at the getaway. That's how we always worked. We spent more time figuring out how to extricate ourselves safely because that was usually the hardest part of any operation.

For a start, we needed somewhere for the helicopter to land after the escape. We knew it couldn't be in the air for any length of time or we would lose the element of surprise. We needed somewhere quiet but readily accessible and easy to drive away from. Tony suggested the Phoenix Park, only a couple of minutes' flying time from the jail. I shot that down initially because the national Garda Headquarters was situated there.

'But it's a big place,' Tony countered. 'I was thinking about landing on the opposite side, far away from Garda HQ. There are lots of trees over there and several exits.'

## Chapter 9

We left the option open but quickly moved on.

'We'll need cars to take Tommy and the three boys away from the chopper,' I said.

'I'll get one from the Dublin Brigade,' Pete said. 'I'll tell them it's for a robbery. Tony can use this for the lads.'

I knew we were getting places fast.

'We'll also need a safe house nearby,' I said. 'But we'll leave that to Mallon, so we're not responsible if it turns out not to be safe. Wherever he picks has to be within 10 minutes of the landing site. I want everything bedded down 20 minutes out from Mountjoy Jail. We need to take full advantage of the initial confusion.'

Crucially, we also agreed the attempt would take place the following Monday, October 15, which gave us less than five days to get all this together.

I always operated that way. The minute I got a job to do it was a case of 'the sooner the better'. That way I could keep it tight, and people wouldn't have time to talk. I never believed in hanging around.

'As things stand,' I told them. 'Only the four of us, plus Maurice and Marion, know about this. Let's keep it that way. I'll let you all know when I've finalised a day and I expect you all to be available at very short notice. The only loose end I can think of for now is how Pete is going to get away from the Phoenix Park after the escapees take his car.'

'Don't worry about that,' Pete said. 'I'll get my mate to pick me up in the showband's minibus. No one will look twice at us, with all the gear in the back.'

I told them to leave in ones and twos and then had a look up and down the street to see if they were being followed or if the house was being watched. Seeing nothing, I walked to the phone box and called Maurice. We arranged to meet on Friday morning on O'Connell Street. I had plenty of other work to do in the meantime.

# 10

**Friday, October 12, 1973**

When I arrived, Maurice was already waiting. 'There's one sure thing, Maurice,' I said. 'I certainly won't miss you!'

Maurice was always immaculately dressed, and on this occasion, he sported a sharp fedora, making him look even taller and particularly elegant. He folded himself into the front seat and we joined the rush-hour traffic.

After making sure he was still up for it, I began relaying the plan as I handed over the money for the deposit for the chopper.

'Pete will pick you up tomorrow morning at 11. He'll drop you at the airport, from where you'll hail a taxi to Irish Helicopters, about a 10- minute drive. Tell the driver to wait for you while you go inside to confirm the booking.

Put down a £150 deposit and tell them a colleague will be collecting the helicopter because you have a business meeting to attend at a golf club. The flight plan should include a stop there to collect you. Time the flight to land at the jail between 2pm and 4pm, when the prisoners are in the exercise yard.'

'I'll tell the company that we're going to Mullingar for an onwards meeting,' Maurice said.

I told Maurice to take the taxi back to The Gresham, a plush hotel on O'Connell Street, and walk into the lobby, so that the driver would think he was staying there.

'I'll call you tomorrow and if everything has gone to plan just tell me that you've booked the car,' I said. 'Tommy will collect the chopper and we'll meet it at the golf course.'

I had driven around nearly full circle by the time I was ready to drop Maurice off.

'Take care of yourself,' I said. 'I'll be back in touch to make arrangements about Monday and Pete will call you later to arrange the airport run.'

Maurice got out of the car. Reaching back to shake hands, 'good luck' was all he said before striding off. Like a classic movie star, he never looked back.

It was already close to 7 pm. Half an hour later, I was standing again at Mick's unlocked door. As usual, the flat was a filthy mess but as long as I could get a hold of Pete, it was none of my business.

After the usual banter about the state of the place, I asked him to drop Maurice out to the airport the following morning.

'Just drop him there and drive off,' I said. 'He'll get a taxi to Irish Helicopters and then back to the city. Call him tonight to make the arrangements. Any problems, let me know.'

'There won't be any problems,' Pete assured me.

'Come and see me when you get back from the airport tomorrow,' I said.

I left to call Marion and we arranged to meet at the flat in Clontarf 45 minutes later. I was only back 10 minutes when I heard that familiar knock.

'You're looking very well this evening,' I ventured.

'I don't feel it,' she icily replied. 'Do you always call people out this late?'

'Only when I have some good news,' I said. 'I have scheduled the escape for Monday afternoon, and I need Mallon to organise a safe house near the

Chapelizod end of the Phoenix Park.

I don't know the area very well so I wouldn't be confident about getting one myself.

Visit him tomorrow morning and tell him you'll be back in the afternoon to collect the address.'

Marion sat quietly, taking everything in.

'Call me about five and I'll have whatever message I have,' she said.

Even at this late hour, she insisted on taking a bus. Then she was gone.

**11**

**Saturday, October 13, 1973**

I awoke early after a bad night's sleep. I knew I had to sleep whenever I got the chance because insomnia makes for bad decisions, and I couldn't afford even a single mistake. I checked my watch over and over, hoping Maurice had got the wheels in motion.

Around 12.30 pm, Pete arrived at the door.

'I dropped him off at 11 as arranged,' Pete said. 'You should have seen him. He was all dickied up like a tailor's dummy. He even had a briefcase with him. I asked him what was in it, but he told me to fuck off and mind my own business. I bet you there was a towel and a couple of sandwiches!'

He was chuckling away to himself.

'Well, you may laugh, but he'll get us a chopper if anyone can,' I said.

'I know, I know,' Pete said. 'Sure, I'm only slagging – he's the best in the world.'

'What are Tony and Tommy at?' I asked.

'They're both off visiting some relation or other,' Pete replied. 'They're due back in my place tonight. Why?'

'I want you and Tony to secure the weapons and the car,' I replied. 'I don't want everything left to the last minute.'

Pete gave me a pained expression.

'There you go again,' he said. 'You think nobody works except yourself. I'm way ahead of you. I have the car filled with petrol and have it parked offside. The weapons are ready for collection at a minute's notice. I've been busy. I knew you'd be on my case, the minute you saw me.'

I was in no mood to congratulate him on his initiative.

'You need to pick a safe place to store the weapons overnight at the golf course,' I continued. 'I think it's best to have them there tomorrow night. By the way, what did you get?'

'Two pistols, an Armalite and rounds for each,' he replied. 'Not that we'll need ammo. If we do, we're in trouble.'

'I want yourself and Tony to go out to the golf course and prepare a hide for them,' I said. 'I don't want to be hanging around with a 10-year sentence in the car if I'm stopped on the way out there.'

'I'm not sure if Tommy is back tonight, it might be tomorrow,' Pete said. 'When he gets back, I'll show him the landing spot so he's familiar with it.' He turned to go, saying he had business to take care of.

'I suppose that business involves a nightclub?' I ventured.

'You must think I do nothing else,' Pete replied. 'But you happen to be right this time. I'll see you tomorrow, all being well, and the creeks don't rise!'

'Don't worry about tomorrow,' I said. 'We'll meet here again tomorrow afternoon. I want to see all of you, including Maurice. We need to go over everything and get our timing right. I also need Tony to check the run back to the safe house. That's another thing we have to allow for when we get out of the chopper at the park. If I go with Tommy into the jail, there'll be five of us and we only have one car. I'll have to go with you and your mate in the showband bus.'

'I'm sure that won't be a problem,' Pete said. Who's going to be looking at us in a showband minibus?'

'That's fucking great,' I said. 'It'll make great press if we're caught.'

'We won't get caught,' Pete replied. 'My mate looks the part in his band gear and the back will be full of drums and things. Anyway, when did you start caring about your image?'

We had been chatting and bantering for hours. I told him I would call down to his place if I had forgotten to tell him anything.

I waited five minutes after he left before going to the coin box to call Maurice. It rang a few times before he picked up. This would be the first big moment of truth.

'How are things?' I asked. 'How's your mother?'

'Oh, she's fine, thanks for asking,' he replied. 'I've hired a car to go and see her. I put a deposit down on it to be sure.'

'Good man,' I said. 'I'll pick you up at the same place tomorrow, at one o'clock. Take care.'

I could barely contain my euphoria. All I had to do now was to get the timing right and we were away.

I picked up the receiver again, dialled Marion's number, and pushed more coins into the slot.

'My friend from Coalisland has been able to rent that vehicle and he's booked it for Monday, sometime after two,' I told her. 'Make sure to have that address for me. That's all for now, thanks.'

I walked out of the box and sat on a low wall, wondering to myself 'can it really be this easy?'

I didn't think I had overlooked anything. Timing would be the main factor. Get that right and everything else would fall into place. At that stage, I believed that was the only thing stopping us.

Once again, I wasn't allowing for my old friend Fate.

# 12

**Sunday, October 14, 1973**

Pete called to confirm everything was in order at his end. Marion had delivered the address of the safe house. I kept turning every aspect of the operation over in my head but couldn't find a flaw. Pete and Tony would have to courier the weapons to the golf course and after Tony ran the route to the safe house and was happy with it, we would be all set.

It was a bright autumn morning. The leaves were beginning to fall and last night's smog had long since lifted. People were walking along the promenade and I decided to join them.

I needed to kill time before picking Maurice up. I decided to get out of the dingy flat where the walls seemed even more yellowed than usual. I suppose I could hardly complain given my contribution. One way or another, I knew I wouldn't be here much longer anyway, but I would still miss this place.

After lunch, I set off early to collect Maurice. I always found driving relaxing, even in the city. Although I arrived early, he was there already. He ducked into the front passenger seat with a huge smile on his face.

'D-day approaches,' he said. 'Are we all fixed for action?'

'All set as far as I can tell, Maurice,' I replied. 'We'll know better after the meeting.'

We arrived back at the flat with half an hour to spare. I dropped Maurice off and gave him the key, while I went off to park the car a few streets away as usual. The rest arrived together about 15 minutes later.

'At least you're early,' I said. 'But did you need to come all at once … you're not going to Croke Park! I want to go over everything. After I'm finished, I want you to tell me if I've missed anything. Then we're out of here, we have jobs to do.'

I began a rundown of the operation.

'Tony and Pete first. After this meeting I want you to drive the route to the safe house, timing how long it takes. Later tonight, I want you to put the weapons in the hide, but you'll also have to find time to show me where it is first. We'll go there in two cars. I can drop mine nearby and the three of us can go together. And, by the way, everyone is on the dry until this operation is over. I mean it, we're all on the wagon.'

There was no need to worry about Tommy – he would be staying with me until it was time to drop him near the taxi rank on O'Connell Street early the following afternoon for his trip to Irish Helicopters.

'I don't want to go near the taxi rank myself,' I explained. 'Those drivers are nosey bastards with little else to do and they might remember my face.'

After dropping Tommy off, I planned to pick up Maurice and head for the golf course.

'We don't want to get there too early and hang around,' I said. 'People might take note.'

Maurice fished around in his pockets for the helicopter receipt to give to Tommy.

'Mr Devlin is the name I gave them,' he said.

I shook my head in disbelief.

'You know, Maurice,' I said. 'Only a Tyrone man would use that as a pseudonym.'

Tommy pocketed the receipt carefully in an inside pocket.

'What does it matter?' he said. 'It could be Mrs Devlin for all I care.'

After a lot of slagging about how good Tommy might look as a woman, I called proceedings to order again. Talking directly to Tommy and Maurice, I emphasised that until a gun was pointed in the pilot's face, no crime had been committed.

'I want you to keep in mind that until I appear with the weapons neither of you has broken any law,' I said. 'If you remember that, your confidence will show. Act like you own the chopper.'

Then, turning to Pete, I told him to be in position at 2.15 pm.

'There's no need to park near the landing spot,' I said. 'You'll hear the chopper at least a minute before it comes into view, so you can judge it from there. You're happy you know the exact place, Pete?'

'Yes, certain,' Pete replied. 'Tommy and I have been out there. There's a derelict building and we'll use it as a landmark. He'll be dropping it down nearby.'

I turned again to Tommy to ask him if he was certain of his bearings.

'100 percent,' he replied. 'I'd say the chopper will only be in the air for a matter of minutes.'

Then it was Tony's turn. I handed him the address of the safe house. He told me that he didn't know the street, but he would find it easily enough.

'I'll stay with Pete after the chopper lands in the park. Tony, you'll take the other four away. Once we get them to Tony's car, the pressure will be off. We'll hang onto the weapons and take them with us in the minibus.'

I handed Tommy the keys to the flat.

'I'll be heading now to drop Maurice along the Quays,' I said. 'Then I'll continue on towards the golf course. I'll meet Pete and Tony at a pub along the way.'

I told them this would be their last meeting here.

'I'll be moving out shortly,' I said. 'There's been far too much traffic in and out of this place.'

On the way into town, I noticed that Maurice was unusually quiet. 'Are you okay?' I asked.

'Yeah, yeah, I'm fine,' he replied. 'I'm just thinking everything over. If this works, it really will be some coup.'

'What do you mean if it works?' I said. 'We haven't put a foot wrong.'

I gave him another spare key and the address for the Clontarf flat and told him to wait for me there after the operation was over.

'Drive to The Embankment pub, and wait until the chopper takes off,' I ordered. 'Then, go back to the flat. Even if I don't get back tomorrow night, hang on for me. Unless I'm arrested, of course. If that happens, you'll hear about it on the radio.'

Maurice pocketed the key, promising to wait for a week if necessary. He got out of the car and I lost him in the Sunday evening crowds.

It should only have taken about 15 minutes to drive to the rendezvous in the pub car park in Tallaght, but the journey took at least half an hour. Pete and Tony took their chance to give me a slagging.

'Where the fuck did you go?' Pete jibed.

'I got lost a few times,' I confessed. 'As the Dubs would say, we're out in the sticks here.'

We drove together to the golf course. Tony stayed in the car while Pete and I walked towards a hedge bordering the landing spot.

'I told Tommy to come down just here,' he said.

We debated the pros and cons of the site. A passing motorist might notice us dumping the weapons or stop to see who was in the helicopter. But if we chose somewhere on the course itself, we risked arousing the curiosity of the golfers.

We decided to stick with Plan A. The weapons would be dumped in the field. Tommy would direct the helicopter to land. I would climb on board and we would fly together to Mountjoy. The chopper would only be on the ground for a matter of minutes.

Country people like us were used to finding landmarks where city folk would find none. We would hide the weapons, wrapped in green camouflage, under some briars behind a clump of yellow weeds. They would be loaded, but the safety catches would be on in the unlikely event that someone might come across them and think they were toys.

When they left me back to collect my car, I told them to meet me at the flat the next morning at 11 am.

'And remember you're on the dry,' I warned.

I was glad to see Tommy when I got back. Even a loner appreciates company the odd time.

'How did it go?' he asked.

'Grand, as far as I can tell,' I replied. 'Did you ever get that feeling that you've forgotten something? It nags and nags at you all the time but for the life of you can't figure out what it is. Maybe I'm just being overanxious?'

'I've been going over it in my head as well,' Tommy replied. 'If it's any consolation, I can't think of anything we've missed either.'

I asked Tommy to run through his role again and he went over everything without hesitating.

After we ate a Chinese takeaway, I remembered that I had promised to call Marion. Although it was late, I knew she'd be waiting for me to make contact, so I went to the phone box.

'Can you call and see our friend tomorrow morning to confirm that I'll be visiting him sometime between two and four in the afternoon,' I told her. 'I can't be more specific but tell him I have everything in hand.'

'No problem,' she said. 'Is that everything?' 'Yes Marion, that's everything,' I replied. 'Good luck then so,' she said.

When I got back to the flat, Tommy was watching TV. He couldn't sleep either. The pressure was getting to everyone.

'Come on, Tommy,' I said. 'Let's go visit the madhouse and see the two lunatics.'

When we arrived at Mick's flat, Pete and Tony were staring at the TV, but anyone could tell the lights were on but there was nobody home. 'Is there anyone else in the house?' I asked.

'Just us, unfortunately,' Pete replied.

I was in no mood for smart-ass remarks. 'Just tell me how you got on,' I said.

'We're just in the door in front of you,' Tony said. 'We stashed the gear safe and sound. All set. We also checked out the address Mallon gave us. It was easy to find and it's a nice straight run from the park – about six minutes away. It also has a garage, so we can hide the car handy enough.'

'All we need now is a wee bit of luck,' Pete said.

'That's it then so,' I said. 'See you tomorrow. Tommy and I will be off home now. We'll let you two fragile things get to bed.'

Like a pair of naughty children, the two glared at me.

'Are you serious?' Pete retorted. 'I don't go to bed this side of two in the morning. I can't help it. It's just a habit.'

'Please yourselves,' I said. 'I'll see you both tomorrow afterwards in the Park.'

Tommy and I were thinking the same thing when we got back to the flat: it was going to be a very long night.

# 13

**Monday, October 15, 1973**
**10 am**

When I pulled myself out of bed, I felt totally drained from lack of sleep. I opened the curtains to check the weather. The sky was clear, the sun was shining. So far so good.

I squinted as Tommy walked into the room, dressed to kill in a fine new suit.

'Where in the fuck did you get that from?' I asked.

'Ah, you missed that one, didn't you?' he smiled. 'I slipped it in the other day. If those other two had seen it, I'd never have heard the end of it.'

We had three hours to kill before Tommy was due to take the taxi. We couldn't risk going out in case something went wrong. It would have been just our luck to turn the wrong corner and run into the Gardaí. It was unlikely, but after getting caught over someone else's bullets, Tommy knew all about bad luck.

We stared out the window, we paced up and down, we talked nonsense, and we cursed.

**12.15 pm**

I have always believed it is much better to be 30 minutes early than five minutes late. In any case, by this stage we couldn't take any more. As we walked to collect the car, we could sense each other's relief.

I had known Tommy since the day this quiet, shy young man had turned up and asked to join the IRA. In the beginning, you couldn't get a word out of him, but after a few months in the field he was a changed man. You would have to avoid him or else you would be treated to a long political lecture. Tommy was a very clever, astute man who was also able to plan, as well as execute, an operation.

'How are you feeling now, Tommy?' I asked.

'Now we're on the move, I feel great,' he said. 'It's always the same. When I'm at base, my mind turns over everything that might go wrong, and I can get very nervous. Once I start to move, I feel invigorated. The mist clears and I feel full of confidence. Isn't it strange how some things seem insurmountable when you're waiting to go on a job but as soon as you're in the car and on your way, you wonder what the fuck you were ever worried about?'

I knew exactly what he meant. I had always felt that way and figured everyone was the same. Nobody liked facing into the unknown.

I took my time through the midday traffic. The last thing I wanted was an accident or for anyone to notice us. I dropped Tommy at a safe distance from the prying eyes at the taxi rank.

'Good luck, Tommy,' I said.

'Don't worry,' he replied. 'I'm confident now. I'll see you shortly at the golf course.'

He walked away and I drove up O'Connell Street to meet Maurice at Parnell Square. The big man was modesty itself about his role in the operation.

'All I have to do is drive your car back from the golf course to the flat and wait for you,' he said. 'Sure, what have I done?'

'Maurice, never undervalue yourself,' I told him. 'To you, it might have been nothing but you're the man who has made this all possible and you'll be remembered for it.'

He reiterated how minimal his contribution had been but thanked me for the recognition.

**1.30 pm**

We crossed the canal heading south out of Dublin towards Tallaght, giving ourselves plenty of time to reach the landing spot.

Tommy was scheduled to take off around two, and he expected to land at the golf course about five minutes later. We parked in Tallaght village, five minutes' drive away.

**1.55 pm**

As I drove towards the landing spot, a Garda car sped past, sirens blaring. An ambulance followed close behind.

I pulled into the car park of the Jobstown Inn pub and swapped into the front passenger seat. Alarm bells were already ringing in the back of my mind. Maurice inched the car back onto the main road but when we turned the next bend, my heart sank – there had been a serious crash.

Emergency vehicles were blocking the very junction at the laneway leading to where we needed to be. They would see the helicopter landing only a few yards away from them. A medic was trying to pull someone out of one of the cars. There were cops everywhere.

The Gardaí waved us on.

'What are we going to do?' Maurice asked. 'The chopper is due any minute.'

I realised that without the weapons there was no chance of taking the helicopter. Even if we could pick up the guns, the place was crawling with Gardaí and we would be intercepted long before reaching the prison.

'Drive on as far as The Embankment,' I ordered.

In the distance, we could hear the helicopter approaching. 'Do you have the number for Irish Helicopters?' I asked.

After a frantic search of his wallet, Maurice produced a business card. His hands were shaking with tension and nerves.

'I'm going to tell them you've been involved in a traffic accident and that you'll have to call off the flight,' I said. 'When the pilot hears you've been in an accident, he'll think the commotion below him was about you. Then it all depends on Tommy. If he keeps his head, we might just get another shot.'

By now, the chopper was already on its descent. I dashed into the pub to find a phone. Fortunately, it was working.

'Hello, you have reached Irish Helicopters. How may I help you today?' a young lady answered.

'My name is Malachy Devlin,' I replied. 'My brother has hired a helicopter to fly him to Mullingar. Are you familiar with the booking?' 'Yes,' she replied. 'They've just taken off.'

'I'm sorry I didn't catch them,' I said. 'My brother has just been involved in a car crash and is badly injured. He won't be able to take the flight. I don't know how badly, but he's been taken to hospital. I'm on my way to see him.

I stopped to call because I hoped that I might have caught you before the helicopter took off.'

The woman told me to hold the line while she radioed the pilot to let him know. As I stood there, Maurice came in to tell me that the chopper had taken off again.

The phone crackled back to life.

'Hello, just to let you know they are on their way back here again. There is no harm done. I am really sorry to hear about Mr Devlin. We would be happy to reschedule, or you can let me know what your brother wants to do when he's on the mend. Thank you for calling.'

**2.30 pm**

We walked outside, utterly deflated. After all the planning, we had come unstuck by a simple car crash. I thought about the men in Mountjoy anticipating our arrival and the bitter disappointment and recriminations that would surely follow.

I resolved to call Marion immediately, in the hope of getting a message into Mallon to put him out of his misery. I knew she probably couldn't get into the jail again at that hour, but I called her anyway.

'Marion, I have bad news for you,' I said. 'There was a car crash near to where the helicopter was due to come down. I had to abort the mission. Call out to my flat at about half-eight. I'm still hoping for another crack at it.'

'Alright,' she said. 'I'll see you later. Is everyone okay?'

'Other than feeling like shite, we're all fine,' I said. 'See you tonight.'

We scratched about in the car park for another few minutes, not quite ready to move.

'Well, fuck that Maurice,' I said. 'Wasn't that a stroke of bad luck. How could you allow for something like that? I only hope Tommy kept his cool. We may be able to salvage something out of this mess.'

I could see the disappointment etched on his face.

'Cheer up, Maurice,' I said. 'We did our best, but fate pissed on our efforts.'

I drove past the accident scene, seeing no point in avoiding it because there wasn't a checkpoint. Only two Gardaí remained, directing traffic. Half an hour before or after and we would have been up and away.

# 14

We didn't say much on the way back to the flat. Maurice and I were first to arrive. I threw myself down on the sofa and closed my eyes. Bad luck played its part, but with hindsight I should have chosen a more isolated spot. I wasn't beating myself up too badly though – it's always easy to be wise after the event.

Around five o'clock, a soft knock came to the door. Tommy lurched in, red in the face and out of breath.

'Fuck me, that was one ordeal,' he blurted. 'When I saw all those flashing lights, I thought all our numbers were up. The pilot had a better view than me and told me it was a traffic accident. I suppose he's used to figuring things out from the air.'

I didn't waste any time grilling him about how he had handled the situation.

Tommy related everything from the time he arrived at the office, telling the staff he was there on behalf of Mr Devlin.

'They already had the chopper warming up. I didn't realise that a helicopter has to tick over for 30 minutes before it can take off. Anyway, they checked my receipt and told me to climb on board. I told the pilot where to go and he knew where it was. He got clearance to take off and up we went. I was saying to myself, this is the business. I was wondering to myself, what had I been worried about, this was a piece of piss.'

I interrupted only to ask him whether he had been able to converse with the pilot.

'Yes, we had headphones,' Tommy said, before continuing his story. 'We flew out over the city and I was really enjoying it, until I saw all those flashing lights right at the landing spot. I nearly had a heart attack. Tommy, I said to myself, you're heading back to the 'Joy but not in the way you intended!

'Then I remembered what you told me about not having done anything wrong and I got a grip. I was afraid my face might have given me away, but the pilot was concentrating on landing the chopper. When we touched down and found nobody there, he asked me for further instructions. I told him to give it a few minutes in case the accident had delayed Mr Devlin.

'I knew by then that you wouldn't be coming anywhere near the place. From where we were, we could still see the flashing lights at the accident and cops everywhere.

After a few minutes, two people approached the helicopter, and they didn't look too happy.

"What in the hell do you think you're doing," one of them roared above the noise of the engine. "You're not allowed to land just anywhere."

'The pilot asked me if I had obtained permission and I told him that as far as I was concerned, Mr Devlin had filled out all the necessary paperwork. The pilot said he couldn't sit there any longer or he would be in serious trouble with his boss. So, after apologising to the two men, he took off again.

'I joked to the pilot: "Maybe they thought we were going to steal their golf balls!"

'He turned around with a smirk on his face. "Yeah," he said. "It's a serious business when somebody tries to steal your balls!"

'This helped to ease the tension, and before long the radio message came from base explaining that Mr Devlin had been involved in a traffic accident and would be unable to take the flight. I pretended to be worried, and we engaged in some small talk for the few minutes it took to return to base.'

'Do you think they bought it?' I asked.

'I'd say so,' Tommy said. 'I went into the office and asked whether we owed them any money. I wanted to leave everything as clean as possible so we might go at it again. Just as the receptionist was telling me that Mr Devlin was due a refund, the phone rang. It was the cops. Someone had complained about a helicopter landing without permission at a golf course and they would be out to interview someone about it.

'I said Mr Devlin would be in touch about the refund and I assured them he would also be more than happy to answer any questions about the permission. I realised immediately that this would scupper a re-run.'

'Fuck it,' I said. 'They won't find us, but it closes the door on Mr Devlin returning to Irish Helicopters. When the cops see there's no paper trail, it'll make them suspicious. At the very least, they'll leave word that Mr Devlin should contact them. They might also check the hospital admissions and the road accident report too. We'll have to write off the money. I think it's curtains for Mr Devlin.'

I congratulated Tommy on his handling of the situation, feeling sure that we might get another crack at it because of him.

That's the advantage of working with reliable people. People who can think on their feet, who can improvise when the situation demands it. Someone else might have panicked, but Tommy had left something for us to work with.

The hours ticked by. There was still no sign of Tony or Pete. I kept checking the street, wondering what had happened to them.

Around seven o'clock, a knock on the door made us all jump. Maurice opened it cautiously while I covered him with a revolver. Our missing comrades probably didn't get the welcome they were expecting.

'Where the fuck were you?' I demanded.

Tony went on the defensive immediately.

'We were never far away, but you hardly thought we were just going to waltz in. We had to be sure you hadn't all been arrested. As far as we knew, the cops could have been staking this place out waiting for some stupid asshole to walk into their trap. It was only when we saw you at the window that we decided everything was okay. Now, you tell us … what in the fuck went wrong?'

I spent the next hour explaining the vicissitudes of fate and was nearing the end of the story when Marion arrived.

'I take it the whole thing is a total fuck up?' she said cheerily, not the least fazed by what appeared to be a fatal blow.

'No way,' I said. 'We start putting Humpty Dumpty back together again tomorrow. We had a bit of bad luck, but it's not game over. Thanks to Tommy here, we still have options. He kept the door open and we're going through it.'

I spent the next hour or more detailing events to Marion, so she could relate them to Mallon. I knew he wouldn't exactly be thrilled. When you're sitting in a cell, you tend to expect miracles. It's an entirely different story when you're outside, operating in the real world. I knew Mallon would come round when he calmed down.

I called a halt to the huddles that had formed around the room.

'I think that's enough for one day,' I said. 'Marion, you have the distasteful task of informing Mallon how it all went wrong, but you can tell him I'll be putting it all together again, starting first thing. You can also tell him I promised to do this job and I've never let him down.

We'll just have to consider today as a dry run. The lessons learned will ensure we don't repeat any of the few mistakes we made next time out.'

Marion said she would relay the message and return the following night with his reaction.

She declined a lift with Pete and Tony, which kind of made me feel better that it wasn't personal!

'You must be joking,' she laughed. 'I wouldn't get in the car with you two mad bastards. God knows where we'd all end up. At least if I take the bus, I won't get arrested.'

I liked the way she had lifted the gloom and lightened the mood. She also shared the dark humour that could make life bearable.

'Thanks a lot,' Pete retorted. 'It's nice to know you're appreciated!' I ordered them all to leave in small groups.

'Ladies first,' Marion said, opening the door. 'I'll be here around four tomorrow, Brendan, if that suits?' 'I'll be here,' I said.

Tommy was staying. The others staggered their exits.

'I'll be in touch over the next few days,' I told them.

Maurice said he would be returning North on Wednesday and I thanked him again for his role in the operation. It didn't matter – Mr Devlin was burnt.

I didn't have to warn him to keep his mouth shut. Maurice Conway wasn't that kind of a talker.

I had promised Mallon I wouldn't fail again, but I knew we would have to deal with even more variables next time out.

I had to assume the Gardaí knew that something suspicious had taken place and would be keeping a close watch on Irish Helicopters.

Our accents would most certainly link the strange events to the IRA. They wouldn't know why the IRA might want a helicopter but that didn't help me. The next attempt would have to be completely different.

The first time out the entire operation had hinged on being able to hire a helicopter. The mistake had been to land it in the Dublin area. Next time out, it would have to land somewhere far more out of the way.

Personnel-wise, Tommy couldn't go near Irish Helicopters again. Maurice would be gone, but I still had Tony and Pete.

I stayed up into the wee small hours, drinking coffee and cursing our bad luck but I also tried to put it behind me. I knew this job would be more than worth the trouble if we managed to pull it off.

The following morning, I would get Pete to arrange for the Dublin Brigade to remove the weapons from the golf course. Then I would wait for word from Marion. Maybe I would be sacked entirely from the operation, for all I knew.

The one thing I did know was that I couldn't let this go.

# 15

My first thought the next morning was that yesterday had all been a bad dream. It's not easy to accept failure, especially when you're not used to it. But my mind was already racing with a new alternative and the more I thought about this plan, the more I liked it. This put me in better form.

Around 10 o'clock, Tommy stuck his head around my bedroom door. I could see he was still taking it hard too.

'I'm heading away to see my family for a couple of days, if that's alright with you?' he asked.

'No problem,' I said. 'I won't need you again until Thursday. As long as you're back by then?'

Tommy just grinned at me. There was no way in hell he wouldn't be seeing this through.

I enjoyed having the place to myself until Marion came around as scheduled around four.

I suppose they weren't in the best of form inside?' I ventured.

'You could say that,' she replied. 'I explained what had happened. He couldn't believe a simple car accident blew it all to bits. I told him it was still on, but I could see he had his doubts.'

'What did he say?' I asked.

'He said that if it was anyone else, he would have no faith at all but because it's you, then it might just be worth another go.'

It wasn't as if Mallon had much choice, I thought, but I didn't voice this to Marion.

'Can you visit Mallon again tomorrow?' I asked. 'Tell him I already have another plan, but I'll need some support with the logistics. I want you to tell him I need £1,000 and a Yank. Or someone with a strong American accent.'

'I can see him getting the money, but a Yank is a different matter,' she said, puzzled.

'Don't worry about it,' I assured her. 'Kevin will contact GHQ, and someone will be found – him or her, it doesn't matter. It may take a few days, but that Yank is out there somewhere. Just let me know about the money as soon as you can. I know the Yank will probably take a bit longer to organise.'

'Okay,' she said. 'I'll be back tomorrow.'

She had only left when Pete and Tony arrived.

'Well, have we still got the job, or are we sacked?' Pete asked.

'Sacked?' I mocked. 'Why would we be sacked? Who else would they get as mad as us?'

Then I began outlining Plan B, emphasising that this was last-chance saloon. The boys bought into it but voiced their doubts over the central requirement.

'A Yank?' Pete asked. 'Where in the hell are you going to find a Yank?'

'I just need an accent,' I explained. 'A good strong American accent will do. Don't worry, we'll get him or her somewhere.'

I ordered them to come back to the flat at the same time the following day.

'And tell the Dublin men that we'll need a car in about ten days' time,' I said. 'What did you do with the other one, by the way?'

'I gave it back to them,' Pete said. 'They had a job for it and seeing as how I wasn't using it myself, I let them take it.'

Tony said he had thought about a possible alternative source for a car next time out.

'Do you remember Joe from the Navan job – the guy who got chased all over the place?' he said. 'He can get us one and do the driving too if necessary.'

I agreed it might be better to use someone we had worked with before.

After they had gone, I realised how tired I was and decided to get an early night. I needed sleep. Whatever about a second chance, I knew there wouldn't be a third.

# 16

**Thursday, October 18, 1973**

I opened the window a crack to breathe sea air and disperse some of the fug lingering in the flat. I enjoyed Tommy's company but welcomed the solitude. After checking the street as usual, I sauntered out the door and across the road to the rickety wooden bridge leading to Bull Island and Dollymount Strand.

I mulled the new plan over and over as I strode along the beach.

The more I went over things, the more it came down to the character of the Yank. The entire operation would hinge on finding someone who could play the part.

From a distance, I heard someone calling out my name. I looked around to see Tony scampering towards me. For Tony to walk, never mind run, there had to be a very good reason. He would drive even when walking was quicker; in his world, walking was for fools.

'What the fuck are you doing out here?' I asked, as he gasped for breath. I was talking to the top of his head; he was bent over, hands on his knees. 'You should get more exercise,' I said.

## Chapter 16

'Exercise doesn't agree with me,' he panted. 'Look at the state of me after this!'

'Is there anything wrong?' I asked. 'Is everything alright with Pete?'

'Never mind Pete,' Tony replied. 'He's sleeping and I had terrible trouble sneaking out without him.'

'I can't believe you said that with a straight face,' I said. 'It couldn't have been that difficult. You two don't exactly have a reputation as early risers. If nothing else, you had the element of surprise on your side!'

'I wanted to get you alone to ask you a big favour,' he said. 'I want the job of taking the chopper into the 'Joy. I don't suppose you've given that job away already?'

'I was keeping that job for myself,' I replied. 'Why should I give it to you instead?'

'Well, for a start, I know the layout of the prison and you don't,' he replied. 'You don't want to land in the wrong yard now do you?'

'Yeah, you have a point there,' I agreed.

When I told him I'd think about it, he couldn't hide his disappointment. As job interviews went, he had certainly done his homework.

'Come on man, you don't have to think about it,' he said. 'I know you.'

I turned and began walking again. The truth is, I had already earmarked Tony for the job for the very reason he had given me, but it would have been far too easy to tell him that straight out.

'Brendan,' he persisted. 'We've been operating together for years; you know I can do it.'

'I'm not questioning your ability to do the job,' I replied. 'But I may have something else in mind for you, that's all.'

Like a dog with a bone, Tony wasn't about to give up that easily. He kept hounding me the entire length of the beach.

He was wrecking my head and I knew from bitter experience I couldn't get rid of him.

'Look, you're giving me a hard time,' I said. 'I came out here this morning to get away from all this shite. And now here you are breaking my balls over a job.'

'I know,' he said. 'But all you have to say is yes and I'll fuck off and leave you in peace.'

The grin stretching across his face signalled victory.

'Alright, so,' I laughed. 'You've got the job but if you get stuck in there, I won't be sending another one in to take you out again!'

'You're the business, I won't let you down,' he said.

'Can I finish my walk now?' I asked.

'Look, I'm really sorry I disturbed you, but it was the only way I would get the job... and I really want this job.'

I just shook my head. I had enjoyed the craic, so I invited him to walk with me.

'It'll do you the world of good,' I said.

But for Tony, it was a case of Mission Accomplished.

'Do I fuck want to walk with you,' he said. 'You want to see what I left in my bed, to come here to see you! I'll talk to you later. The weapons have been dumped and everything's tidy.'

And with that, he turned away. He was about to walk off when something obviously struck him. He took a few steps back towards me.

'Shake on it,' he said.

I shook his hand, smiling at his enthusiasm as he punched the air. He knew a handshake meant everything to a country man. He also realised that if this went right, he would go down in history as the man who had flown the helicopter into Mountjoy Jail.

I carried on walking after he left. The entire day stretched out ahead of me. I knew even then it was a rare luxury I should savour.

**17**

**Monday, October 22, 1973**

The thump on the door woke me with a start. Bleary-eyed, I fumbled for my pistol in the early morning dark and sat bolt upright, expecting the Gardaí to fill the room.

'Hughes,' a voice shouted. 'Hughes, get the fuck out of that bed.' Recognising Tony's voice, I stumbled towards the door.

'What the fuck are you doing here at this hour and where's your fucking key,' I asked. 'You scared the shite out of me banging the door like that.'

Tony turned to Pete as they walked into the flat.

'I told you we would wake up the grumpy bollix in a panic,' he said. 'We forgot the key. I don't carry it with me all the time. If I'm arrested and they find it on me, they'll know I have another place and I don't need that kind of grief.'

I looked at my watch. 7.30 am. 'What the fuck are you two at?'

'We're getting an early start,' Pete said cheerily. 'We couldn't relax thinking about this operation. I can't wait to see their faces on TV when we pull this thing off. It'll be all the sweeter if we do it this time.'

I told them to sit down while I got dressed and asked them to make me a cup of coffee.

'I can't believe you two. Up at half seven in the morning and on a Monday too,' I said.

After a gulp of coffee, I felt a bit more human and began laying out the day ahead.

'Your only job today is to recruit one reliable person from the Dublin Brigade to get us a stolen car and a driver to take you away from the helicopter,' I said.

'Here's how we're going to do this. Let's assume the job is next week, on Halloween. I want this guy to have a clean car in place at 2 pm. His instructions are simple. He finds a car and parks it somewhere safe. Then he changes the number plates, using ones from a similar model so it doesn't stick out. Tell him to hold onto the original plates. I want him to put them back on the car after the job, before he abandons it, to confuse the cops. I want confirmation that the car is ready early next week.

'Tell him he has to pick up four passengers after a robbery. They'll be armed and will leave their weapons in the car after they're gone. He needs to drive these four volunteers to a pre-arranged spot to another clean car for them to complete the getaway. He also has to arrange a safe house for them to lay up.'

Tony objected to the plan immediately.

'You can't seriously be considering relying on the Dublin Brigade to do all this – they'll make a pig's ear of it,' he said.

'I realise that,' I said. 'Give me some credit for sense. This is just another layer of security to make them believe this is what we're at. Meanwhile, I want you two to get me three clean cars. These can't be stolen – their owners will have to drive them. We'll be using these three cars for the job.'

'After the Dub picks you up from the helicopter, order him to the new drop-off point, where the three cars will be waiting. This will break the link between you and him.

'Now, listen very, very carefully to this next part. After the Dub has dropped you off at the three clean cars, it is absolutely vital that he hides the stolen car. He can't dump it before nightfall under any circumstances. After he secures it and puts it under cover, he has to remove the weapons and any other material you may have left behind. I don't want you taking a mask with you or having anything else on you just in case. Then he has to wipe it down, inside and out before he puts the original plates back on.

'No abandoned car near the helicopter will give the cops a bigger area to search. When they do eventually find the car, it will have its original plates and no fingerprints or other clues. This will throw them completely and give us even more time to escape the dragnet.'

Pete nodded his approval.

'I don't see any problem with any of that,' he said. 'It all sounds straightforward – wee buns.'

'To both of you, maybe,' I said. 'But these people need to have everything explained in detail. You have to leave them in absolutely no doubt about the importance of carrying out every single thing you tell them. I don't want to have to listen to bullshit excuses later. Impress on them that if anything goes wrong and it's found to be their fault, someone will pay a heavy price. Bluff them into thinking this is a very big robbery. Remember, it'll be your asses out the window if you land in that chopper and find it's been a no-show.'

Tony said it might take a couple of days to pull together but promised it would be done. I could sense their excitement.

The enormity of this job had really sunk in after the failed first run.

I got up to wash the cups.

'You've got very domesticated in your old age,' Pete needled.

'Unlike you pair, I try to keep the place a wee bit tidy,' I replied. 'I'm expecting Marion after a while and I don't want her to think that I'm like you pair of dirty bollixes. The last day she was here, I couldn't even offer her a cup of tea.'

'Sure, you don't drink tea anyway!' Tony shot back.

I showed the pair of them the door and warned them to choose the Dublin volunteer well; he had a vital role to play. Tony said he already had someone in mind.

'I've worked with this man before and he's okay,' he said. 'He's 100 percent from a security point of view.'

Pete looked at him sceptically.

'I don't know how you can say that' he said. 'You just can't rely on them. Great intentions but no experience.'

'One last thing,' I said. 'Have a think about a place to land the chopper after leaving the prison. I don't want to use the Phoenix Park – I've been giving it a lot of thought and it's much too obvious. When the alarm goes off and they realise three men are in a helicopter, straight away they'll think about possible landing spots nearby. They'll know we won't be in the air for long. A park is the most obvious, so we can't use one.'

Pete piped up immediately. 'I know. We can use Baldoyle Racecourse.'

'A racecourse?' I murmured. 'I don't know about that. We'll never get Mallon away from it, he'll be off backing horses!'

'There's no danger of that,' Pete said, laughing. 'It used to be a racecourse, but it's lying empty now and it's wide open. It has road access and it's not a place you would think of right off.'

'Sounds good,' I said. 'It's definitely worth a visit. Take another look and if you still think it might do the trick, let me know and I'll have a look too. Where is it, by the way?'

'It's on the northside, up the coast a bit,' Pete replied. 'It's only about four miles from the jail. You'd be there in minutes. It's also in a part of Dublin where there's great support, so safe houses shouldn't be a problem.'

'One more thing,' Tony said. 'Where do our three drivers go after they've dropped everyone off?'

'They go home,' I replied.

'They'll all be at the same place for the pickup, but they'll be driving the three men to separate safe houses in different areas. That way, if the cops do stumble across a house, they'll only recapture one of them. Also, everyone should be hiding safely within 10 minutes of the helicopter landing, five if possible. It'll be up to Mallon again to find the safe houses. He's in jail with a heap of Dubs. He'll provide the addresses and we'll send a car to each of them. Simple.

'Marion will have the addresses before the weekend. You two will pair each driver off with a single address and take them on individual dry runs beforehand. We have to make sure there are no roadworks, traffic or obstacles on the routes around the expected pick-up time after the escape.

'I really don't know why I'm even wasting my breath talking to you. You've both done this kind of route work loads of times. Just because it's a helicopter, doesn't change the basic rules. It's just another getaway, just another job. Get back to me this evening or tomorrow evening at the latest.

Now go. You have the whole day ahead of you for a change.'

# 18

After they had gone, I stared out of the window for a long time, pondering the numerous loose ends. The chances of a road accident scuppering us had been slim, but I was determined to learn from this unlikely mistake.

I needed somewhere to hijack that chopper without any interference, and I was weighing up a couple of options. A destination north of the city had its own risks. For many people in Dublin, even the mention of the word 'North' conjured images of the border, and the Troubles. These were the last things I wanted anyone thinking about. We needed to tell Irish Helicopters that we'd be flying south.

That narrowed my options, but Seán Treacy in Co Laois sprung to mind. If anyone was my man, he was.

Like Mallon, Seán had joined the IRA at a young age and had taken part in the Border Campaign. More recently, he had fought in Derry, evading capture by British forces after several firefights.

I went over what I had so far. The part after taking off from the prison was more or less sorted. The confusion created by the use of a helicopter would play into my hands and I aimed to take full advantage.

I was also hoping that the laziness (and the arrogance) of the Minister for Defence, Paddy Donegan, would also work in my favour. He was known for using army helicopters like a virtual private taxi service. Perhaps the warders might think a surprise ministerial visit was in the offing when they heard the rotor blades approaching?

I wasn't even thinking about the yard itself and how they would get on board the chopper – that would be up to the people inside to sort out.

I was now turning my thoughts to what might happen afterwards and how the first alarm calls would confuse the cops. I was trying to visualise how they would react at first. As always, I tried putting myself in their shoes.

They would get a call saying prisoners had escaped from Mountjoy. Their very first question would be: How? This would be followed by: Did you see what they were driving after they got out?

I was guessing that when someone mentioned the word 'helicopter' it would throw them completely. There's no way they could see this coming. They would be completely blindsided and powerless until they found the chopper. Only then would the search kick in.

I estimated we had at least 15–20 minutes before they got their act together. That would be all I needed. They would have an empty helicopter and nothing else to go on. No burned-out cars, no sightings of armed men, nothing.

I also surmised that radio traffic would jam every channel used by the prison staff, Gardaí and the army. In those days radios were still fairly primitive, allowing only one voice at the time over any channel. One person would have to stop talking before the other could get on the air.

My mind was racing at a million miles a minute at this stage, when a knock on the door startled me. Even though I had been gazing out the window, I had been lost in my own thoughts.

I relaxed when I heard Tommy's soft voice.

We decided to take advantage of the late autumn sunshine for an afternoon stroll on the beach. After our usual counter-surveillance scan, we skipped across the road and over the clackety wooden bridge towards the sea.

We weren't long on the spit of sand when a Garda patrol drove slowly past, stopping a few yards in front of us.

'Do you have ID?' I muttered to Tommy. 'Nothing,' he murmured.

'Just keep walking past them and talk away,' I said. 'I doubt it's anything to do with us.'

We strolled on, keeping a careful eye on the two Gardaí sitting in the car. Eventually they drove off.

'I'll bet they won't be as calm in a couple of days,' I laughed.

We sat down in a sheltered hollow in the dunes, looking out over Dublin Bay. I knew by what Tommy was saying that my new plan had made quite an impression.

'It's not very often that I'm in the right place at the right time,' he said. 'Happily for me, this looks like one of those times. What do you want me to do this time around?'

'For now, Tommy,' I said, 'I need you to poke holes in the plan. I need to eliminate any errors. This has to be bullet-proof. Tony is in charge of the getaway from the chopper. Himself and Pete are off right now putting it together.'

It was then that Tommy dropped a bombshell.

'I'm afraid you won't have Pete after tomorrow,' he said. 'I brought word for him to report back to his unit in Tyrone.'

'Well fuck that, I really could have used him,' I said, wondering who to contact to countermand the order.

I was in no position to complain though. I knew it was the price of secrecy. Very few people knew about this unit's existence, let alone the operation we were planning. I weighed things up and decided that keeping things tight was more valuable to me than losing one of my top men.

'I suppose we'll have to manage without him,' I said. 'Does he know yet?'

'Yes, I met him just before I knocked on your door,' Tommy replied. 'Normally he would be happy to be going back to work but not this time. He cursed and swore for five minutes solid while Tony was laughing his head off at him.'

I was bitterly disappointed. Even at such a young age, Pete Ryan was very cool in tight situations. He was brave and his humour was good for morale. Tommy shared the disappointment but lightened the conversation, which reinforced my belief that I was lucky enough to have other reliable men at my disposal.

'It's a pity it wasn't him going in on the chopper,' Tommy said. 'I would have loved to commandeer his job!'

We lost track of time and it was only the gathering dusk that caused me to check. It was nearly six o'clock.

'Fuck,' I said. 'We have to go. Marion will be looking for me. I sent her to see Mallon to get some things for the job. If I've missed her, she's going to be really pissed off.'

As soon as I opened the door, I spotted the piece of paper on the floor.

'Missed you,' it said. 'Back tomorrow afternoon. BE HERE.'

Tommy was reading the note over my shoulder. I could see him smiling.

'If I were you, I'd be here tomorrow,' he chuckled. 'She seems like a cranky person.'

'She's just efficient and reliable, that's all,' I replied, defensively. 'I don't blame her for being annoyed. I should've been here.'

# 19

**Tuesday, October 23, 1973**

The day dawned wet and miserable. I watched people pacing the beach, their heads bowed low against the wind. As I sipped a morning coffee, a bleary-eyed Tommy came in. He had no watch on him, so had no idea of the time.

'It's half past nine,' I replied to his inquiry. 'I'm waiting on those other pair to arrive.'

It was only then I realised Pete would probably be gone already.

'I expect he's gone, alright,' Tommy said, when I voiced my thoughts. 'I was ordered to tell him it was very important and very urgent. That's why he was so upset. He had no way out of it.'

As we sat at the window, the conversation turned to politics. It wasn't a topic that particularly interested me.

'Where do you think it's all going?' Tommy asked.

'I've really no idea, Tommy: I just live one day at a time,' I replied. 'If I start getting into the politics of everything that I do, I'll get lost. I'm not a political person as such. I prefer to be just a volunteer. I know I should take a greater interest and maybe I will, but I'll get this job out of the way first.'

I hoped this would be enough to shut down the conversation. Before Tommy could regroup, the key turned in the door and Tony walked in. I was delighted with the reprieve.

'I thought I'd lost you too,' I said.

'Yeah, it's a pity Pete had to leave,' Tony said. 'I had to give him a lift to Carrickmacross to meet someone. I doubt we'll be seeing him for a while.'

'How did you get on yesterday?' I asked.

'Not too bad,' Tony replied. 'We're not quite there yet but we're getting there. I got hold of Joe, the Dub. He's confident he'll have everything in place by Wednesday, or Thursday at the latest. I have to meet him again tomorrow evening to finalise things.'

'The three cars and drivers, what about them?' I asked.

'I've only got two so far, both our people. They know the area. They don't know what it's about, but they don't ask a lot of questions either. I've told them where to be and as soon as they know where they're going, I'll drive the three routes with them to make sure they're all clear.'

'When do you think you'll get the third car?' I asked. 'I'd like to have that end of the job squared off as soon as possible.'

Before Tony could answer, Tommy jumped in.

'I know someone who'll suit us,' he said. 'He'd be delighted to help. I have his phone number and I'll contact him later on today. He'll be at work now, but I'll get him after six. He knows the city like the back of his hand. He's very careful and totally reliable.'

'Did you manage to take a look at the racecourse?' I asked Tony.

'Yeah, yeah I did – and it's ideal,' he said. 'When we were there yesterday around half-three it was deserted apart from an old guy walking his dog. I'd also say that people around there were used to choppers arriving there belonging to horse owners and trainers.'

'I never thought of that – that's a bonus,' I said.

On any job, I would attempt to satisfy any questions that might arise in the mind of a casual observer by factoring in a likely innocent explanation for what was going on. If that didn't work, it would at least create an element of doubt rather than alarm.

'Tony,' I said. 'When you next meet Joe, make sure he is absolutely clear on when he is to dump the car. Remember, he has to clean it out thoroughly and rub it down inside and out. He'll have all evening to do this. Make sure and tell him to have everything he needs available in the garage beforehand. I told you before, I don't want to be listening to excuses later on.'

'I'll be meeting Joe shortly and will emphasise the orders – yet again!' Tony said.

I still wasn't happy, so I asked Tommy to go along to make doubly sure that the message got across.

After they left, I made my umpteenth coffee and lit another cigarette.

You could set your watch to Marion. At four o'clock, I heard her knock at the door.

'Where were you yesterday?' she asked, sounding none too happy.

'I've been very busy,' I replied, trying not to sound too apologetic. 'How did it go with Mallon? Do we have money? And what about the Yank?'

'We have funding and GHQ is looking for your Yank,' she said. 'The bad news is that it could take a day or two, but the good news is that they have someone in mind. They'll be in touch when they have him.'

She handed me an envelope and I began counting it. £1,000.

'They wouldn't give me any more; in fact, they thought this was a lot of money,' she said.

'Miserable fuckers,' I said. 'You'd think I was drinking it. How am I expected to pull off a job this size on pennies? Mind you, thinking about it, there should be plenty here depending on how much the hotel in London costs.'

'You've lost me,' she said.

I admit I had dropped this in to get her interest and possibly to impress her.

'Okay, here's my plan, so you can fill Mallon in,' I said. 'I'll need his help with a few things.'

'Such as?' she grinned. 'Being inside kind of cramps your style a bit.'

'There's no need to be a smartass,' I said, enjoying the craic. 'I need him to get me three, separate addresses in Dublin for himself, Twomey and J.B. to go to, that's all. Same drill as before times three.'

'I'm going in there tomorrow and I'll ask him so,' she agreed.

'Tell him the chopper will be landing to drop them off at a racecourse out at Baldoyle,' I continued. 'You can also tell him it's closed so he won't be backing any horses! Tell him the safe houses all have to be within a 10-minute drive of the racecourse. I want everyone stood down and hidden within 20 minutes of that helicopter taking to the air. And one last thing. Tell him we're aiming for Halloween night – broomsticks, witches and all that. That's only eight days away now. I need pressure put on GHQ to get me that Yank.'

'I don't know what influence they have on GHQ,' she said.

'Marion, we are talking about Kevin Mallon, Seamus Twomey and J.B. O'Hagan,' I said. 'If they don't have pull then nobody has, you know that. If they want this thing done, tell them to get the finger out and get me a Yank who can talk. That shouldn't be much trouble. I've never met any Yank who couldn't bullshit his way anywhere!'

I could see Marion was taking everything in. God, she was attractive, but this was no time to think about chancing a relationship.

Anyway, she gave no inclination of being interested in anything but business. As small talk goes, this was as good as it ever got between us.

'Let's go over it one more time before you go,' I said. 'I need a Yank by Friday at the latest. In the meantime, try to get me three addresses by Thursday, but certainly no later than Saturday. I have some work to do around them and I need a bit of time.'

I told her that when I was a kid, we used to go out on Halloween night and play jokes on people. We did things like removing people's gates and leaving them a good distance away.

'This Halloween I'll be removing something a lot more serious – three prisoners from Mountjoy and the entire country would be laughing with us,' I said.

She gave me one of those looks – a mixture of bemusement and indulgence – and assured me she would return with news on Thursday evening. 'If you need me before that, give me a call,' she said.

I was never much of a drinker, particularly when I was planning an operation, but tonight I would allow myself a beer with a bite to eat. I knew that time would not be my own very shortly.

Tomorrow, I would go to see Seán Treacy. He lived in a townland called The Heath, a short distance from Portlaoise Prison, a place we would both come to know all too well.

I hung around for a while waiting for Tommy and Tony, but they never showed up. I ended up heading out on my own for a couple of quiet ones.

# 2O

**Wednesday, October 24, 1973**

I needed to make sure everyone else was feeling the pace, so I wanted some company on my trip to see Seán. We only had a week left to make this happen.

The minutes ticked by as I waited for the two boys to appear. I had been expecting them back the previous night, so relief tempered my annoyance when I heard them laughing outside.

'I thought you would both have been here last night,' I growled.

'We went around to wee Mick's place and the craic was too good to leave,' Tony said. 'Anyway, we made good progress yesterday, so we were in great form. We spoke to Paul, Tommy's man. I have to say I was impressed; he's sound. Joe was supposed to be out last night getting a car. They have loads of old number plates to make up fake plates. All I need now are those addresses, then I can tell our men where to go. Have you any idea when we'll be getting them?'

'Saturday, at the latest,' I replied. 'Hopefully before.' I want you to spend next Tuesday taking the three drivers on their separate routes. I want to be completely sure there are no surprises, or delays on any of them.'

'Here,' Tony said, pointing to Tommy, 'Do you know what he asked me last night when we were having a beer? 'He wanted to know would I swap places with him and let him go in the helicopter instead?'

'I expect you swapped,' I said, knowing full well what Tony's answer would have been.

'Did I fuck,' Tony said. 'I told him he'd have to fight me for it!'

He laughed, punching Tommy on the arm.

'Enough of the messing,' I said. 'I have to see Seán Treacy today. Tommy, I want you to come with me. Also, boys. There is one more thing you might not want to hear. Everyone is on the wagon from Sunday. Both of you will be staying here from then on. No more drink, or women. You'll be sleeping, eating and drinking this job until it's over. Okay?'

They both agreed. It was more of an order than a question.

I told Tommy to get himself ready. It was already half-eleven and it would take about two hours to drive the 40 miles or so to The Heath. This was pre-motorway and the journey out of Dublin would pass through several small villages and towns with the inevitable delays along the way.

I wanted to scope out a potential landing site for taking over the helicopter during daylight, an increasingly precious commodity as the days grew shorter. I declined Tony's offer to accompany us.

'Three men in a car is only inviting trouble,' I said. 'Cops are inclined to stop people when there are three or more in the car. If you've nothing better to be doing, go and give Joe a hard time. Sit on him until he has his job done.'

'Alright, so,' Tony agreed. 'I'll do that. Don't worry though, he'll come through alright.'

I was driving a Hillman Avenger. These cars were plentiful at the time and even its bright red colour wouldn't have attracted any notice. It had Dublin plates and I reckoned it was clean enough. I hoped the driving licence with the false name on it would get me past any checkpoints. At the time, Irish driving licences didn't have photographs and there was no way of checking identity.

The uneventful journey through Naas, Newbridge, Kildare and Monasterevin passed largely in silence. My lack of interest in politics seemed to have done the trick. After a couple of hours, we turned into Treacy's pub, a landmark in The Heath.

Back then the bar was little more than a small, thatched cottage with windows that kept it dark on even the brightest of days. When your eyes had grown accustomed to the light, you would be able to make out the counter. Seán's mother usually stood behind it like a sentry. A slight lady who always wore a black apron, she never said much, even if she knew you well. A large, menacing Alsatian would be sitting at her feet. The customers were all locals. Just like the dog they viewed everyone with suspicion. When a stranger walked in, the hum of conversation would cease, resuming only after they had taken time to weigh you up. They would engage you in a friendly way but only to find out who you were and what business you had there. It wasn't an area that attracted many strangers.

Like all good publicans, Seán had a great sense of humour. I have always been inclined towards people who enjoyed a joke. He was also one of the most reliable people I knew. Along with Ned Bailey, he ran the IRA in the area. When they gave their word, it was as good as money in the bank. It was said that Seán took part in blowing up Nelson's column in Dublin in 1966. Whatever the truth in the story, he was now a senior member of the IRA GHQ staff. He led a logistical support unit that organised the movement and storage of arms. It sorted safe houses, provided transport and kept its ears to the ground for information.

We parked the car out of sight at the back of the pub but entered through the front door. Seán's mother was at her post but there was no sign of the dog.

'Is Seán around?' I asked, deferentially.

'I'll go and see,' she said. 'Who's looking for him?' 'Tell him it's Brendan – he knows me well,' I said.

She disappeared into the gloom of an open door behind the bar. After a few minutes, she came back and told me that Seán would be out shortly.

'Will you have a drink?' she asked.

'Not just now, thanks,' I replied. 'Where's the dog today?'

I could tell she was weighing up whether to tell me or not. She wasn't one for giving any information, however innocuous.

'The poor thing isn't at all well,' she relented. 'He ate something down the field and hasn't been right since.'

She settled back in a chair and looked away. I knew the conversation was over and I didn't press her further.

Seán appeared a short time later, drying his hands as he came to greet us.

'Great to see you lads,' he said. 'That fucker of a dog isn't well, it shat all over the place.'

I could see Tommy looking at Seán's outstretched hand. 'It's okay, I just washed them,' he laughed.

'What can I do for you, lads?' he asked, as if IRA business cost him no more thought than pulling a pint.

'We need your help as usual,' I said, inviting him to go for a walk to discuss things in complete privacy.

When we reached a field about 100 yards down the road, he pressed me for specifics, and I was only too happy to oblige.

'Seán, we're going to do a job the likes of which the IRA has never done before,' I said. 'We're arranging a jailbreak with a difference.'

We're going to fly three prisoners out of Mountjoy by helicopter. We need to land it somewhere beforehand, somewhere around here. Have you any ideas?'

'A helicopter,' Seán repeated. 'That's different, alright. Can I ask you where you're going to get one of those? It seems a bit far-fetched to me, but

I suppose you wouldn't be here unless you were serious. And why would you need to land here?'

'I'll come to the rest of it in a minute but first things first,' I said. 'We're going to hire it and we need to land it here so we can get control of it. We've a small problem though; we've tried already and failed so that's made things a wee bit trickier.

'The chopper will only be on the ground for five minutes max. The guy who hires it for us will leave with you, his job done. He only needs to get it here. I'll want a safe house for him. Another volunteer will take his seat and give the pilot a new flight plan.'

'A safe house won't be a problem,' Seán said. 'But finding somewhere to land the helicopter is a different story. It's not exactly something you can hide or do quietly. I'll call Ned Bailey – if anyone can sort this, he can.'

Ned was another republican of the old stock. He was a crafty old devil and feared nothing. I had stayed many times in his home. His wife, Beth, was just as committed and they took many risks together.

Seán told us to wait in the bar, saying he would be back in about half an hour.

We thought that nursing a couple of pints would help us blend in a bit, but it didn't work. We had barely taken our seats at a corner table when two locals walked in and looked us up and down. After an hour or so, our patience was wearing thin.

Seán eventually returned with Ned and another man I recognised immediately. His name was Jim Hyland, nicknamed 'The German'.

The three of them pulled up seats beside us and I could see the other few heads in the bar sinking lower into their pints.

'Sorry about the delay, lads but we have the very place,' Seán said, excitedly. 'Jim and I have already had a look at it, that's what kept me.'

He stood up again and disappeared behind the bar, muttering something about having to attend to the dog. When he returned after a few minutes,

Tommy noticed that he was drying his hands again. Instead of sitting down, he headed to the door.

'Are you coming, or are you staying here?' he asked.

We jumped up and followed.

'Ned told me where to go,' Seán said. 'You can tell me if it works, or not. We'll speak to the locals; they won't give us any trouble.'

'You won't be telling them what we're doing though?' I asked.

'Of course not,' Seán said. 'I'll be telling them I'm organising some publicity for the pub that includes aerial photographs. We'll have a chat with them after the job's done. Don't be worried. Most people around here are sound.'

We tagged Seán along some backroads for about six miles before stopping beside a large field near a place called Stradbally, a quiet village now famous for its annual Electric Picnic music festival. I noticed two hills in the distance. They stood out against the flat landscape of the Irish Midlands. I also noted farmhands working on the last of the harvest and indicated their presence to Seán.

'What if they're still here when we arrive?' I asked.

'Don't worry about them,' he assured me. 'They're all customers of mine. I'll be telling them about the publicity shots – all those photographs I'm going to get taken from the air. By the time the chopper touches down, they won't pay it any heed. Afterwards, they'll be all talk about the escape but not a single one of them will mention what took place here. Don't worry, Ned and I will keep on top of it. Anyway, by that time, it'll all be done and dusted.'

This remote spot was ideal in so many ways. The scenery was picture-perfect, with multi-coloured fields stretching for miles around. It would fit nicely with the story that our Yank, Paul Leonard, would be spinning about picking up a photographer.

Seán couldn't have chosen a better spot. We would only be on the ground for a few minutes, just long enough to change our men and give the pilot new instructions. No fuss. No big show. All very tidy. Well, as tidy and discreet as you could be when hijacking a helicopter!

This place had presence. It wasn't like landing in any old field, or a place surrounded by bogland. We knew the landscape would impress the pilot and would fit in nicely with the picture Mr Leonard would have been painting for him.

I congratulated them on being so quick on the uptake and then asked Seán if he could requisition a rifle and two handguns.

'I can get those, no problem,' he said. 'I'm holding a bit of stuff that's in transit north. I'll just borrow them if that's okay with you?' 'I'll clear it with GHQ; that won't be any trouble,' I replied.

'Will you clear it for sure?' he asked. 'It all belongs to Belfast. You know what they're like when someone takes their stuff. They can be very awkward to deal with.'

'Don't worry, Seán,' I assured him. 'I have clearance from GHQ for anything I need.'

As the light faded, we wound up the meeting, anxious to blend into the rush-hour traffic returning to Dublin.

'One last thing,' I said to Seán as I went to drive away. 'The man you'll be taking away to the safe house may need some clothes bought. I don't know yet but if needs be can you take care of it?'

'Certainly,' he replied. 'That won't be a problem. What's he like, this Yank?'

'I don't know. I haven't met him yet.'

Seán looked troubled.

'You haven't met him yet, and you want me to put him in a safe house?' he asked.

'Don't worry,' I said. 'He'll be well checked out long before you have to put him in a car, or a safe house. Seán, we're planning to move next Wednesday, the 31st, Halloween. We'll need the safe house lined up and the weapons stashed nearby here the night before. If the Belfast crowd come to collect their stuff before that, remove what we need. If they ask, tell them you got an order from GHQ. Contact me if anyone gives you any problem.

'I'll be back here in the meantime to show the Yank where to land. You don't need to be around. I know my way. I'll call you if I need to meet you. I'll just say that I'll see you tomorrow or something like that. I don't have to tell you not to discuss this with anyone who doesn't need to know. Don't talk on the phone either – someone is always bound to be listening.'

I knew even as the words tumbled out of my mouth that these men knew all this anyway; they had been at this game a lot longer than I had and they were still going strong.

I turned the car towards the main Dublin road. Tommy had hardly spoken a word since we arrived.

'You were very quiet,' I said. 'Well, what do you reckon?'

'It looks the business, alright,' he said. 'I can't see any problems, except for the workers.'

'I'm not worried about them,' I replied. 'By the time Seán and Ned have finished filling their heads about photos, they won't pass any remarks. To them, one chopper looks like the next. Afterwards it won't matter. Nobody will say anything out of place. They're very tight around here.'

We blended into the busy traffic along the way. There was little conversation. I knew Tommy was turning the plans over in his head, looking for holes. We were very alike when it came to strategy. Other volunteers might be willing to take a chance, we always tried to minimise the risks.

Things were falling into place but the key to the entire operation was still missing – where was the Yank?

When we returned to the flat, Tony was waiting. I filled him in quickly on the day's progress and then asked whether Marion had been.

'No,' he replied, 'I haven't seen a sinner since you left.'

It was already dusk, and the streetlights began to flicker. A light drizzle mingled with the smoke from tens of thousands of chimneys, generating a sulphurous smog.

'What are you two for doing?' Tony asked. 'I'm going to make something to eat,' I replied.

Tony feigned surprise and I knew he was winding up.

'You're going to cook?' he said. 'Well, count me out. I don't want to be poisoned before this job is over!'

'You just want an excuse to be off to wee Mick's,' I retorted. 'You're not fooling me!'

'Come on, Tommy,' he said, 'Leave this grouchy fucker here, he's an oddball. He likes his own company, unless there's a woman involved of course!'

Tommy protested that he would have nowhere to stay if he left. 'Don't worry,' Tony assured him. 'I have somewhere for you.' He told me they would be back the next morning.

'Hold on, just a minute,' I said. 'What about Joe? Has he got the car?'

'The Dubs were out looking last night but came up blank,' Tony said. 'They'll be out again tonight. Don't worry, they'll get one.'

'But I do worry, Tony,' I replied. 'That's my job. Christ, it's only a stolen car we want, not a fucking tank. What kind of outfit are they? They really are fucking useless; I've never seen the likes of them.'

'Relax, they'll come up with the goods,' Tony assured me. 'I told you he was okay, and I know he won't let us down.'

I wasn't convinced. I had enough to worry about without sweating the easy stuff.

'I want both of you to pay him a visit tomorrow,' I said. 'Tommy, you pretend to be from GHQ. If he has no car by then, I want you to light a fire under him. Okay?'

'No problem,' Tommy replied. 'I'll make an impression on him.'

As they turned to go, I ordered them to be back by 10 the following morning at the latest.

'No excuses,' I said. 'We're getting too close to lift off. We have to tighten things up. We can't afford a single slip.'

'We'll be back first thing,' Tommy said.

I knew there would be no problem. That was always his nature, from the first time I met him.

I lit a cigarette and sat by the window. I needed to go over everything again before making something to eat. This had been a good day.

Having the Yank in place would be the next massive step. Of course, I still had to determine his or her quality after they turned up. A thought struck me: I should have asked for two Yanks instead of just the one. It would have given me a choice. But it was too late now, I was stuck with whoever showed.

It turned out I needn't have worried. Luck would be on my side this time. The Yank who eventually arrived would exceed all my expectations.

# 21

**Thursday, October 25, 1973**

I slept like a dead man. After eating, I went straight to bed, exhausted. The tension and stress were beginning to take a toll, but in the morning, I woke up mentally and physically refreshed.

It was only around nine and I wasn't expecting the two boys for another hour. Marion should be here in the late afternoon but that would depend on whether GHQ had found the Yank or whether she had any addresses for me.

I boiled a couple of eggs, making a mental note to do some shopping. The bread was stale and I had used the last of the butter. At least I had plenty of coffee.

I had just finished and cleared up when the door opened and the pair of them walked in. 10 am on the nose. I eyed them up but neither of them looked the worse for wear. Tommy asked for a coffee. I told him where to find it and to clean up afterwards.

'Any word on Pete?' I asked.

'No,' Tommy replied. 'It'll be a few weeks until we see him again, but we'll probably hear about him first, knowing him!'

I was in no mood for banter.

'And what about you two?' I asked. 'Any developments?' Tony knew me far too well to let me shove him around.

'I don't suppose you have the addresses yet?' he shot back, looking over his shoulder as he put the kettle on.

'Not unless there's a carrier pigeon on the window ledge,' I said, knowing I had just been outflanked.

'How would I have the addresses when I only asked Mallon for them yesterday?' I countered.

'I can see this is going to be one of those days,' Tony said. 'Grumpy bastard!'

'I told you Marion should be here with them later,' I continued, ignoring him. 'Are you losing your memory or something?'

He just looked at me with a big smile and said, 'Just winding you up, you need to relax a bit.'

I protested that I was in great form but would be happier still if they visited Joe and put a fire under his arse. Tony assured me for the umpteenth time that Joe would come across and Tommy said he would make doubly sure.

'When I see him, I'll be emphasising the position he'll be in if he lets us down,' he said. 'I know how to talk to him.'

I could afford to smile. Tommy was impressive when he built up a head of steam.

'When do you want us back here?' Tony asked. 'I'm going to check out Baldoyle again to see if there's anything going on around the time we intend to land. I'm also going to drive and time the route to the three cars. After that, the only thing we have to work out timewise, is how long each of the three cars will take to get to the separate safe houses. I won't be able to do that until I get the addresses.'

'That's the business, Tony,' I said. 'I'll see you both back here around five.

You can update me then. The more times we go over things, the less chance we have of coming across any nasty surprises.'

It was only half-eleven and having nothing much on, I decided on a walk. I knew I would miss this place, but little did I know just how often my mind would fly here to escape the walls of my cell.

On my way back a couple of hours later, I went into the usual café for a coffee and some decent food. I opted for fish and chips and I had just tucked in when a patrol car pulled up outside and two Gardaí sauntered in. I observed them discretely with every mouthful. They were on a break and paid me no heed. I finished, paid and even nodded to them as I left.

Once outside, I kept checking behind me until the café was out of sight. As I neared the flat, I glanced back again to make sure there was no sign of them. When I closed the door, I checked the window, breathing a sigh of relief when I saw the street empty. I flopped down, closed my eyes and must have drifted off because I was startled by the signature knock on the door.

I opened the door a crack and peeped out. And there was Marion with that broad smile on her face.

'It's only me,' she said, 'I'm a wee bit early, but I had nothing to do so I came out to see you.'

'I didn't know you were that fond of me,' I said, flirtatiously.

'I'm not,' she said, still smiling but leaving me in no doubt that I had been shut down. 'I'm here on business.'

'That's fine, I'm all business myself,' I said, trying to row back a bit.

'You were sleeping,' she said, accusingly. 'You can't be very busy if you have time to sleep during the day.'

'You don't know the half of it,' I countered. 'I only do that to fool people into thinking I'm doing nothing.'

'Bollocks,' she replied.

She kept smiling but I could see she had already switched gear.

'I have the addresses you asked for,' she said. 'All of them are only five minutes from the racecourse.'

She handed me an envelope and I found four addresses inside.

Trust Mallon to give me an extra one. This would give me a choice and confuse whoever had given them to him.

I put them away safely in my pocket. Tony and Tommy would be the only other people to see them.

Her business concluded, Marion turned to leave, but I asked her to hang on for a few minutes.

'You know we're aiming for the 31st,' I said. 'Well, that morning I'll need you to visit Mallon and tell him we're in business. I might be able to let you know sooner but I don't even know for sure if we'll be ready to go by then. Any word on our Yank?'

'The last I heard they had found someone and were in the process of getting him to Dublin,' she said. 'Don't worry, as soon as he arrives, I'll bring him to you – I have no use for him myself! If he's not okay, you can blame Twomey – as far as I know he's the one that got him.'

'I don't care who got him,' I said. 'If things go wrong, I'll end up carrying the can.'

'Don't worry, I'll stand up for you,' she soothed.

I knew she was deadly serious. Providing I didn't fuck things up, she would be on my side if things went wrong again.

'Getting back to Halloween,' I said. 'If I haven't confirmed everything beforehand, stay by the phone from early morning. I'll give you the final word as soon as I can, but I should be able to let you know much sooner than that.'

'You can depend on me,' she said. 'I fully expect everything will work out fine this time.'

She gave another of those smiles. I also noted it was the first time she had given the plan the thumbs up.

As she was letting herself out, she told me not to fret. She was a difficult woman to figure out.

You never knew what she was going to say next, but you could depend 100 percent on her honesty and reliability.

It had already gone half-five and I was expecting a progress report from the two boys. Watching the evening news when they arrived, I turned it off to concentrate on what they had to say.

What Tony imparted raised my blood pressure.

'Joe is still struggling with getting a car, but he says he has one arranged tonight for sure,' he said. 'Tommy had a stern word. I think he knows how vulnerable he'll be if he fails.'

'Yes,' Tommy chimed in. 'I think I convinced him of the merits of doing his job. But to tell you the truth, I have more faith in him now, since I met and spoke to him.'

Tommy was smiling, but it was a cold smile. I knew Joe would have got the message but I was still anxious about the lack of progress.

'We drove the route to the changeover,' Tony continued. 'It takes between three and four minutes; and another five to where Joe intends to keep the car until he dumps it later on. All I need now are the addresses.'

I reached into my pocket and pulled out the envelope.

'Here are your addresses,' I said. 'Maybe you'll stop bitching now.' Tony took a moment to study them.

'I'm not entirely sure of two of them, but the other two are close enough to the racecourse. I'll time all four of them on a run tomorrow afternoon around three o'clock. When I've picked three, I'll take each driver to them separately.'

'Don't let the drivers know anything more than the one address,' I instructed. 'And make sure they know not to discuss where they're going among themselves. After you've briefed them and they've driven their routes, appoint one of them to be in charge. Then, all you have to do is inform him where to be. He can tell the other two. I don't want them to be speaking or even looking at one another while they're waiting on you to arrive.

'Remember, all the weapons are to be left in Joe's car for him to dump. I don't want armed men running all over the pick-up point. No running. No shouting. Just walk calmly from the one car to the three others. Be as normal as possible. That way nobody will take any notice.

'I'll be sending word into Mallon to brief the other two men on how to behave but you'll be reinforcing this during the flight, Tony. By the time you reach the pick-up point, back at the prison they'll still be trying to figure out who's gone and what they're going to do about it. Special branch detectives will be all over the place, trying to get on top of the situation. We're in the clear until they locate the abandoned helicopter.

'Don't forget you're in charge. Take no nonsense from anyone, even if they are senior officers. They'll appreciate it afterwards.

'One last thing. We don't want the helicopter taking off and following you from the air. Before you leave, make the pilot stop the engine. This will ensure it can't be operational again for half an hour or so.'

'Let's go and eat before you head off for the night,' I said. 'Where are you staying tonight, Tommy?'

'I'll stay here – I need a good night's sleep,' Tommy replied. 'This bastard never goes to bed!'

'Don't mind him,' Tony said, echoing Pete. 'He's just not up to it. We could all be dead tomorrow, given the life we live.'

'I'll be dead shortly if I live with you, you mad bastard,' Tommy retorted.

From the window, Tommy watched Tony walk down the street. He was shaking his head in puzzled amusement.

'There is no end to that man,' he said. 'Always on the move, how he keeps it up I don't know.'

'Fuck me,' I said. 'I forgot to tell him to be back by 10 tomorrow morning.'

'Don't worry,' Tommy replied. 'He forgot to take the addresses, so he has to come back. Tomorrow's Friday – he'll know that he has to run the routes on a workday, so I expect we'll be seeing him. We discussed this on our way over here and we've arranged to finish our end of the business tomorrow. We have the addresses now, so relax. He'll be here.'

We scrubbed ourselves up, put on clean clothes, and ventured to The Yacht, a popular bar and restaurant within walking distance along the coast. We even enjoyed a couple of pints with our dinner.

We were in good form but the gloom of the flat soon brought us back to earth. It was a poor substitute for our real homes.

As I lay on my bed that night, tossing and turning, there was consolation that others were also likely to be having the same bother sleeping. At least I was in control – the prisoners were completely in the dark. The previous let-down would also have shaken their confidence. I had no such negative feelings. I was starting to really warm to this job. From experience I knew that once I got it past a certain point, it would take on a life of its own. And all I had to do was guide it in the right direction.

**22**

**Friday, October 26, 1973**

I turned on the news as usual, but the weather forecast was really the only thing I was interested in. A stormy day next Wednesday might scupper a flight, especially one hired for taking photographs. The flat wasn't quite cold enough yet for me to see my breath, but the chill wind coming in from the Irish Sea told me winter wasn't far away.

For what it was worth back in those days, the long-term forecast looked good. High pressure out in the Atlantic was expected to hang around for another week.

We needed all the breaks we could get.

Tommy ducked his head out of the bedroom just as I was sitting down to my first coffee and cigarette.

'You know where to find the stale bread, if you want it,' I muttered.

'No thanks,' Tommy grunted. 'Don't you ever buy groceries, or do you eat out all the time?'

'No, it's only just now,' I said. 'I'm too preoccupied. The shop is only two doors away, if you want to go and buy something.'

Tommy thought about it for a moment, telling me he was worried his accent might make him stand out.

'People are forever taking stock of me,' he said. 'Tell me, do I look strange?' I burst out laughing. Looks-wise, he was the most ordinary of people. 'What's so fucking funny?' Tommy asked.

'Tommy, you're a very intelligent man, but that was a silly question,' I replied. 'You couldn't look suspicious if you tried. You even hired a helicopter, and nobody batted an eyelid. Would paranoia have anything to do with it?'

'I give up on you,' he said, as I continued laughing. 'Normally you make sense but you're making no sense at all.'

The more he said, the funnier I thought it was, so he eventually let it go. Tony walked in just as Tommy was making another two coffees.

'Good morning,' he intoned, as if he was a doctor doing his rounds. 'And how are we all today?'

'Fine,' I replied, still smiling 'I'm surprised to see you so early. Normally, you're on the wrong side of the right time!'

'At least you're in better form today,' he said, hamming up the bedside manner. 'As for me, I'm working now, and the closer I get to the end, the more attention I pay to time-keeping. You should know that. What's for breakfast?'

'Stale bread,' Tommy said sourly. 'He never shops. But don't eat it all because we got nothing yet ourselves.'

'Fuck off,' Tony said. 'I'm not eating your stale bread. I'd rather starve.'

'Suit yourself,' I said. 'Who do you think I am, your mother? There's a shop two doors away if you feel like going.'

'Coffee's fine for now,' Tony said. 'You do have coffee, and milk?'

'Help yourself,' I said. 'I will,' he replied. 'Otherwise, I'll get nothing!'

'Now you're getting the idea,' I said. 'I told you before, your Ma is in Coalisland, not here.'

'Are you two getting it up for me?' he asked, indignantly. 'What did I ever do on you?'

'Would you ever get a coffee and sit down?' Tommy replied. 'You're making the place look untidy, standing there.'

Tony looked around, shaking his head.

'You have some brass neck, the pair of you,' he said. 'Have a look around. How could anyone make this place untidier than it already is?'

I put an end to the craic, much as I was enjoying it.

'That's enough nonsense for now,' I said. 'We need to get down to business. We've only got five days left and we have loads of things to tidy up. Joe and the three addresses spring to mind immediately.'

'I'm on top of that,' Tony replied. 'By tonight we'll have everything in place. I'll be able to give you all the times of the runs. I'll arrange to meet the drivers separately tomorrow and tell them where to go.'

'And I'll deal with Joe,' Tommy interjected. I glanced at my watch.

'It's gone 11, shouldn't both of you be off?' I said.

'We're already on our way,' Tony said. 'What are you up to today?' 'The same as yesterday, waiting on my Yank,' I replied.

'Good luck with that,' Tony said. 'If he doesn't show, I'll hire it myself, if you're stuck!'

'You might have to do that yet,' I replied, even though I knew this would never work. We had gotten away with a Northern accent once, but that chance had gone.

'Fuck off now, the both of you,' I said. 'You're putting me in bad form with your negative bullshit. Everything is going to turn out okay. Just be back here at five. If I'm not here for some reason, wait for me. If I'm missing it'll be to do with business.'

I had to concede Tony was right when he said the place had become a bit of a kip. For shame's sake, I knew I would have to tidy up a bit before Marion returned, hopefully with the Yank in tow.

I had barely finished doing a half-decent job when she knocked at the door. Standing beside her was a tall, thin man.

'I hear you're looking for a Yank,' he said, smiling. 'I am he!'

Marion all but pushed him in the door and turned to leave but I put my arm across her to stop her, while inviting the Yank to go inside and make himself at home.

'What's the story?' I whispered. 'Where did you get him, and who is he?'

'All I know is that his first name is Liam,' she replied. 'That's all I know about him. I was told by GHQ that he has been cleared to work with you. You wanted him, now you have him. Good luck. For what it's worth, in my opinion he's okay. You can call me once you're ready. I'll bring whatever word there is to Mallon.'

And with that, she brushed away my arm and left.

I hadn't realised just how difficult it would be to work intimately with a stranger. I had operated with Pete, Tony, Mark, Sig and Tommy for years. I knew how they would behave in a tight situation. Now I was relying on someone I didn't know from Adam – someone who wasn't even Irish in my mind. For the first time, I began to doubt the plan I had drawn up.

I introduced myself and the Yank did likewise. First name terms only.

'I'm Liam,' he said. 'I'm Irish but I've lived in America for more than 15 years, since I was very young. I have the accent to prove it.'

'Do you know why you're here?' I asked.

'No, I just heard you wanted a person with an American accent,' he replied.

I wasn't altogether happy at this 'take it or leave it' attitude. What was GHQ playing at?

'I asked for someone with a steady nerve who could bullshit and pass themselves off as someone else,' I told him, with a slight air of menace. 'Have I the right person?'

'There's nothing wrong with my nerve, don't worry about that,' he replied. 'And I can bullshit all day long if you want. If I knew exactly who I'm supposed to be, and what I have to do, I would have a better idea of what you're looking for. I'm not a conman, by any means, but I can talk my way around most situations.'

I was used to weighing people up. I guessed he was around my age, somewhere in his mid-20s. He had a dark complexion, which I learned later came courtesy of his Mexican mother. He struck me as confident, unassuming and determined. He appeared gentle, but if you looked carefully, you would see he was made of stern stuff. I came to a quick conclusion that he was more than capable.

It turned out that my judgment was sound. I was talking to Liam Quinn, who had already proven himself a highly rated IRA volunteer. Liam had travelled from San Francisco to join the IRA two years before and had been in action around Derry, a city where daily engagements with the Brits were almost guaranteed.

'Nobody has told me why I'm here,' Liam continued. 'I'm up to 90 wondering what's going on. I can only assume it's something special if you're going to all this trouble.'

He declined my offer of coffee, saying that he was keen to get down to business.

'It's hard to know where to start,' I began. 'It's a long story, but here goes…'

I ran through the events of the past few weeks, the failed attempt to spring the three senior IRA men and the hastily concocted Plan B. All the time I was talking, I watched his face, and his body language. He never interrupted me once. All the while, he sat back in the chair, completely relaxed. He didn't seem the least fazed.

When I had finished, he said he knew absolutely nothing about helicopters and certainly couldn't fly one. It was the first time I had seen him looking puzzled.

'So,' he asked. 'Where do I come in?'

'It's a lot simpler than you think,' I explained. 'You might be familiar with this craze that Americans have for tracing their Irish roots?'

'Yeah,' he said, with a slight irritation in his voice. 'I've heard of it, but it doesn't interest me at all.'

'No, maybe not,' I continued. 'But you could get very interested in it if you had to?'

'I suppose this is where the bullshit comes in,' he said.

'Kind of,' I replied. 'It's as much about who you'll have to bullshit that's important, but I'll get to that.'

He accepted a coffee when I offered for a second time.

'If you insist,' he said. 'I suppose it's that instant crap you all drink here. I hate it, but I'll take one anyway. It's just one step better than nothing.'

I was really beginning to warm to this guy. He had a sharp humour that I wasn't expecting. He would fit in nicely.

I put the mug of coffee in front of him – black, no sugar as instructed – and continued the briefing.

'Your job will be to hire the chopper,' I said. 'What do you think?'

He sat forward in the chair, took a drink from his coffee, swallowed and grimaced.

'God almighty, that's awful stuff,' he said, before nodding as an indication that he was up for the job.

I couldn't help but laugh at his preoccupation with my coffee.

'I'll give you all the information you need,' I said. 'I'll also be providing new clothes that I hope will say things about you. I want people to think you're one of those rich Yanks with money to burn. This entire operation hinges on your performance. You're the key to those prison gates. It'll all come down to how you sell yourself. Do you think you can handle that? If not, I'd rather know now.'

Liam made unwavering eye contact.

'I've been hanging around for a long time waiting for something as big as this to come along,' he said. 'Just tell me in detail exactly what I have to do.'

'Okay,' I said. 'Here's how we'll do it. You will become Mr Leonard. I'm going to give you enough money to go out and buy some fancy clothes. A suit, three shirts, shoes, and luggage. When you choose, make sure that everything looks expensive. This is about image. When I'm happy that you fit the bill, you'll be flying to London where you'll book into the plushest hotel we can afford.

'And this is where the real bullshit comes in. When you're at the hotel reception, I want you to appear to be a mouthy American, full of your own importance. I want you to tell the desk staff that the purpose of your trip is to trace your ancestors. These ancestors were English people who were sent to Ireland in the last century to put manners on the uncouth natives.

'Now, listen carefully to the next part. After you've booked in, collected your room key and are about to go up to your fancy room, you turn around, as if inspiration has just struck. You ask the receptionist: By the way, do you happen to know if they have helicopters in Ireland because I would love to organise some aerial photographs of my ancestral lands? Tell them that you're stuck for time. Also, tell them you'd feel safer in the air given the stories you've heard about shocking violence engulfing the place.

'If a chopper is available, instruct them to book it for next Wednesday, the 31st, to give you a couple of days to fly to Dublin. And don't forget to leave a very generous tip!'

When I was finished, Liam grasped the plan immediately. I wanted the hotel to make the booking with Irish Helicopters. Unlike someone with a Northern accent, a wealthy American booking from an expensive London hotel would attract no suspicion whatsoever.

'You betcha I can do it,' he said, accentuating his American twang.

Liam wanted to rest so I showed him into the room where Tommy had been staying. I was relieved to find it reasonably tidy and he put his small holdall on the bed.

'I'm expecting some people with a report,' I said. 'The walls are thin so we might disturb you but just try to ignore us.'

A while later, Tony and Tommy arrived back in great form. 'I take it you had a successful day,' I said.

'Not bad at all,' Tony said. 'I'll fill you in but tell us how you got on first.'

'I got my Yank,' I said. 'He's down in your bed, Tommy. He has nowhere to stay. Are you okay to kip with Tony tonight?'

'Only if I have no choice!' he replied.

'Now, dare I ask, do we have a car?' I asked.

'Yes,' Tommy said. 'Joe came through with one at last. He's fitted it with false plates and parked it up in a hotel. We looked it over and it's good. Four doors for easy access, big, fast and powerful too. Just the job.'

'What about the addresses?' I asked.

'I picked the three I wanted,' Tony said. 'We drove to each of them from the racecourse, and the longest is six minutes away.'

'That's driving normally?' I asked. 'No speeding and no special effects?'

'Exactly the way you wanted it,' Tony replied. 'Like two grannies.'

The pair smiled, relieved to be reporting progress after days of frustration.

'Now, all we have to do is tell the three drivers where to go,' Tony said. 'Show them their routes and make sure they get familiar with them. We'll do that tomorrow. By the way, I had another look at the racecourse at about the same time we intend to be there next Wednesday. It was quiet, there was absolutely nobody around.'

'That's great news,' I said. 'Now we're going places. Tomorrow, I'll get our man kitted out with new clothes and if we have time, I'll show him the landing site in Stradbally.'

Tony said he and Tommy would go straight to work again the next morning, rather than reporting in. They would be back the following evening.

I told them to have their overnight gear with them.

'Don't forget,' I said. 'From tomorrow night we all stay together until this job is done. Pick a couch to sleep on; I'm clean out of beds.'

Both of them just laughed.

'Don't worry about us,' Tommy said. 'You know we're well used to sleeping on floors, sofas and uncomfortable chairs. You name it, we've slept on it!'

I was happy that I now had every part of this jigsaw.

It had been a great day. I felt I was holding success in the palm of my hand and the odd time I also allowed myself to think about what that would mean. It wasn't just a successful escape; this would be THE escape – the one everyone would be talking about for days and years to come. I knew this one was special, but I couldn't allow myself to dwell too much on that – after pride comes the fall!

No, this had to be just another operation.

The star of my show was resting on the bed probably still unaware of the extent of mayhem he was about to unleash. Mr Leonard was on his way into the history books. He just didn't know it yet.

# 23

**Saturday, October 27, 1973**

Liam was ready to go into town. I told him to take a bus but to return by taxi, instructing him to walk the last half mile or so. 'Remember,' I said, 'The clothes you buy must scream respectability and wealth. Classy, not vulgar.'

My confidence in him grew with every conversation.

'You never asked me what you have to do after you're in the chopper,' I remarked.

'No, I didn't,' he said. 'But I expect you're going to tell me.'

'Okay,' I said. 'Here's how I see it going. There's a place called Stradbally about 40 miles from Dublin, as the crow, or helicopter, flies. I've arranged for you to land there. That's where we'll be giving the pilot his new flight path.

'You'll be telling the pilot you need to land to pick up a local photographer and his equipment for aerial shots of the beautiful, golden fields below. After it touches down, you'll open the door and walk away. You'll be taken to a safe house, where you'll be well taken care of. If you need clothes or anything else, they'll sort you out. Any questions?'

Liam shook his head, asking only how he would get back into the flat after his shopping spree. I assured him I would be here.

'I've got nothing more important to do today. If you happen to be back early enough, we'll drive out to the landing site.'

After he headed off, I tidied up, wondering what to do with myself for the rest of the day. I decided to brief Marion on progress so she could tell Mallon everything was going to plan. The walk to the phone box would give me a chance to grab a decent coffee and an early sandwich.

We arranged to meet in the flat at one o'clock. I knew it would be one of the last meetings there. A lot of people had been in and out of the place over the last couple of weeks. Neighbours might take no notice now but after next Wednesday, they might put two and two together. I couldn't take that chance.

I knew of a flat in Rathmines, a southside Dublin area full of rental accommodation, where I would blend right in. GHQ told me it was available, and I resolved to ask for the keys.

Cold and early as it was, there were families out walking and playing on the strand. The sea air was like a tonic. It all seemed like a million miles away from the plot I was hatching.

I wished life would soon get back to normal, but I could hardly remember what normal was any longer.

I was starving by now and I decided to chance the café, one last time. As I finished my meal and drained the last of my coffee, I was getting up to leave when the same two cops came in again. I nearly got stuck in the door as I tried to pass them. Again, I made a mental note not to go there again. Even though they had never spoken to me or caught my accent, they'd seen me once too often.

I kept a wary eye behind me as I made my way the short distance to my flat. I saw nothing unusual. If only they knew.

I had barely turned the key and sat down to enjoy my first cigarette, when Marion arrived at the door. She came in, smiling as usual.

'Can't you stop smoking those things, you're going to kill yourself!' she lectured.

I studied her through the haze, trying to work out whether she was serious or joking.

'Can I do nothing right?' I protested. 'I only smoke three or four a day.' She wasn't buying this lie.

'They stink, and you stink as well,' she said. 'You would do well to stop. Anyway, what do you want me for?'

'This is it,' I said. 'The message Mallon is waiting on. You can tell him this when you see him on Wednesday but I'm going to tell you now because I have all the bits together.'

'It's a few days away yet,' she cautioned. 'Shouldn't you wait a wee bit longer, just to be sure?'

'No,' I said emphatically. 'I'm on top of this now, and it won't change. If you haven't heard from me by ten on Wednesday morning, tell him what I'm going to tell you now.

'We'll try to arrive by three o'clock that afternoon, but it may run slightly over. Tony will be in the helicopter. He'll have three weapons with him: an Armalite and two handguns. Tell Mallon no more than three prisoners will be able to board, or it won't be able to take off. He'll have to control things down in the yard.

'The chopper will fly to Baldoyle Racecourse, where we'll have a car waiting. This car will take them to a car park at a nearby pub where three other cars will take them to separate addresses. Now – and this is very important – I want no display of weapons at any stage. No weapons at the helicopter. No weapons at the racecourse or at the pub car park. I want a quiet, controlled, changeover; it'll give us more time.

'Tell him all three weapons must be left behind in the first car. The Dubs have orders to store that car until nightfall and change the plates back to the originals before cleaning it thoroughly inside and out. No fingerprints. Then when they leave it somewhere, the cops will be unsure if it was the getaway car. The Dublin Brigade will have taken care of the weapons too, of course.

If everyone follows these orders to the letter, the cops won't be able to narrow the search to a particular place. I want everyone off the streets and bedded down 20 minutes after leaving Mountjoy Jail. The cops will be like headless chickens until they find the helicopter, and this could take them a while. What do you reckon?'

'It's the bee's knees, if it all goes to plan,' she said.

'It will all go to plan,' I protested. 'Show a little faith.'

'You do sound very confident, alright,' she said. 'I'll tell Mallon exactly what you just told me.'

'By the way, Twomey chose our Yank well. He's a class act.'

'Good luck to you all,' she said. 'I don't pray, otherwise I would pray for you because I think you need it more than most.'

I wasn't a man for prayers either, but I appreciated the sentiment.

'I nearly forgot to tell you,' I said. 'I've decided to move out of here. There's been far too much traffic in and out. We'll be gone on Sunday, Monday at the latest. I'll be in touch with my new details.'

My mood dipped every time she left, but now I didn't have time to dwell on it.

About 10 minutes later, a knock came at the door. I was expecting Liam back, but I wasn't taking the chance. I opened it a crack, with a gun in my other hand. I needn't have worried. There he was, weighed down with carrier bags reeking of opulence.

'I absolutely hate shopping,' he said, dumping the bags on the sofa and flopping down on an armchair. 'I knew this would be the worst part of the job!'

Looking at his retail plunder, I could only laugh.

'I take it you had enough money?' I asked, hopefully.

'Piles,' he said, grinning. 'I'm going to look like a movie star.'

I checked my watch and decided it was too late to drive to Stradbally. We would have to go tomorrow.

'Okay so,' I said. 'Put on the suit and the rest of the gear. I want to see how you look.'

'Come on man, give me a break,' he replied. 'I've been on my feet all day running from shop to shop trying this on, trying that on. My head is up my ass. Alright, alright. If you make me a cup of that awful coffee, I'll do it.'

I told him to relax for another minute and went to boil the kettle. I also mentioned that we would be moving out to a clean flat.

'What do you mean, a clean one?' he asked. 'Why not just clean this one up?' When I saw he wasn't joking, I burst out laughing.

'Jesus, no,' I said. 'I mean, clean from a security point of view. We'll be moving across the city to Rathmines. The new flat hasn't been used before. We'll leave tomorrow. It'll be a busy day. We'll pack up here and drive to the landing site, so that you'll recognise it no problem. The others will move our gear in the meantime and wipe this place down. We won't be coming back.'

It was only then that I began cursing myself for a massive oversight.

'Shit. I just remembered about your ticket,' I said. 'I should have told you to book a flight to London while you were in town. I'm sorry but you're going to have to go back and do it now before the travel agencies close. Look on the bright side, at least you don't have to put on those new clothes for me!'

'I don't know which is worse, trying on clothes, or going back into town,' he replied, with a wry smile.

'Do you still have enough for the flight?' I asked.

'Yeah, yeah, plenty,' he assured me. 'Just give me the details.'

'Book your flight for early Monday morning, returning early Tuesday afternoon, to give yourself plenty of time to take a taxi to Irish Helicopters before they close – it's only a 10-minute drive but there will likely be a queue at the airport taxi rank, so you have to factor that in.

'When you get to their office, tell the driver to wait for you, go in and confirm the booking made from London on your behalf. After you've tied up any necessary paperwork, take the taxi to the Royal Dublin Hotel on O'Connell Street, book in, and call me from a public phone nearby. Don't use your room phone or even a public phone at the hotel reception. The Rathmines flat has a phone in the hallway. That's one of the reasons I've chosen it. I'll give you the number and I'll be waiting for you to call. Then, I'll come and pick you up.'

'I'd better get going or they'll all be closed,' Liam said. 'Take a taxi straight there and back this time,' I ordered.

I gathered up the bags and laid them carefully on his bed. Then I began planning my exit. The cops would leave no stone unturned once they got their teeth into investigating this escape. Moving was no big deal. IRA men travelled light. Some spare clothes and shoes, maybe a radio, that was it. No photos, no letters, no forwarding address.

By now Liam had been gone for over an hour. I expected him back shortly. I paced the flat. I felt the tension building and I couldn't relax. I was really pissed off with myself for forgetting to instruct him to book his flights, but it made me even more determined not to overlook anything else. I began going over the plan again in minute detail.

After a while, Liam reappeared, clutching an envelope. 'Done and dusted,' he said. 'Tickets to Hell!'

'You look a bit more relaxed this time around,' I said.

'I had a pint of the black stuff to give me energy,' he replied.

'That's allowed,' I said. 'After you've tried on the clothes you can relax. It won't take a minute, then you're done for the day.'

He went down to his room, and I could hear a lot of paper rustling, and the odd curse. Then he appeared, pirouetted, and bowed low in front of me like an actor on stage. I was amazed at the transformation. It's as if he had read my mind. He had bought all the right stuff. He had created my stereotypical, brash Yank.

Just then, Tony stepped in and did an abrupt U-turn, bumping into Tommy standing in the doorway behind him.

'Where the fuck are you going?' I asked him. 'Shit, I thought it was a cop!' he said.

'When did you last see a cop dressed like that, you eejit,' I said. 'You've been watching too much television. A fucking cop? This is the Yank.'

'I wish you'd stop calling me that,' Liam said. 'I'm Irish. I'm only pretending to be a Yank.'

'Christ, you're doing a pretty good job of it,' Tommy said.

'Enough of this nonsense,' I said, as if chiding a group of small children. 'Where do we stand with the safe houses?'

'I took each driver separately,' Tony said. 'I showed them where to go, timing each route again. Six minutes was the maximum. I heard your voice as I warned them: no speeding, no screeching tyres. I told them Tommy's mate, Paul, would be in charge. I'll notify him early on the day and he'll instruct the others. They'll drive their separate routes one last time again to give them the final all clear. Then they'll be at the rendezvous no later than 2.45. I think that covers everything.'

Tony was rightly confident, but I knew he was also looking for a bit of pat on the back, which I was happy to deliver.

'It's 100 percent,' I confirmed. 'Very efficient indeed.

Remember that I want both of you to stay here tomorrow night, but I'd prefer if you collected the key for Rathmines. At least you'd have a bed there and it might be better to launch this job from a clean location. Tomorrow, when Liam and I are at Stradbally, I want you to clean out this flat and move all our gear. One last thing – I want you to go into town and pick up a map of the Stradbally area, but don't open it – I don't want any prints on it. Liam will need it to show the pilot where to land.'

Tommy cast a cold eye at the cramped, two-seater sofa he was expected to sleep on.

'I'm for collecting the key, Tony,' he said.

'You may as well,' I said. 'Because you won't be going back to wee Mick's and there won't be any drink or late nights until we've done our work.'

The pair turned to leave, nodding a cursory greeting in Liam's direction.

'Liam and I are off to Stradbally in the morning,' I said. 'When we get back to the city, we'll go straight to Rathmines. Before you leave here, wipe the place down. Whatever about us, I don't want Liam's fingerprints left here, just in case. The fewer clues we leave the better.'

'Yes, we'll do that no problem,' Tony said. 'We have all day.'

I told Liam to leave his new ID and plane tickets on the table, ordering Tommy to guard them with his life.

'Once you've finished here tomorrow, take all Liam's paperwork and his bags with you to Rathmines,' I said.

'Is that all, are you sure you don't want the kitchen sink as well?' Tony jibed. 'Just don't forget anything and make sure to buy the map,' I replied. Liam had been watching the barbed exchanges with amusement.

'Do you guys go on like this all the time?' he asked. The three of us just smiled at him.

'We know one another too well – it's really a sign of respect,' I explained.

Tony was having none of it. Gesturing towards me, he said, 'He's hard to listen to at times: he can be a grumpy bastard.'

**24**

**Sunday, October 28, 1973**

My last day in the flat dawned cold and cloudy, but I awoke refreshed. Things were moving fast and that's just how I liked it.

We took a cursory look under the beds and around the furniture, making sure there was nothing lying around. Liam had already put his bags and paperwork on the table for Rathmines. Everything seemed fine. One last look around before I closed the door. I would miss this place and the beach, but you couldn't afford to get sentimental in my line of work.

When we stopped off for breakfast, I called Seán to let him know we were on our way and, although it was pointless, that there was no need for him to be there. He instructed me to come straight to the pub and we would go back to the landing site together. It was nearly noon by the time we arrived. We found Seán clearing autumn leaves out front.

Looking Liam up and down with a grin, he asked, 'Is this the Yank?' Before I could introduce him properly, Liam jumped in.

'I'm sick of you guys calling me a Yank,' he said. 'I'm fucking Irish. Okay?'

'Jesus, he is easily upset,' Seán chuckled. 'Sure, we love Yanks around here… As long as they come to drink in my pub!'

Putting a friendly arm around Liam's shoulders, Seán continued, 'Don't mind us, we're only getting it up for you. Come on around the back. We'll leave your car here and use a local one.'

I was wary of going anywhere near the building. 'Where's the dog?' I asked.

'Ah, he's coming on just fine,' Seán replied. 'Thanks for asking.'

'Seán, I'm not inquiring after his fucking health,' I said. 'I just want to know where he is!'

Seán just laughed.

'You're as safe as houses,' he said. 'He's locked in the shed. He wouldn't touch you anyway.'

I just looked hard at him but said nothing.

Seán introduced Liam to Jim Hyland, who would be driving, saying he would catch us before we went back to Dublin.

'Ned is out there waiting on us,' Jim said.

'You know what he's like, Brendan. He worries a lot. He's a fussy old bollix, but what can you say? Nothing goes wrong when he has anything to do with it.'

Seán, Jim and Ned went back a long way together. When Ned heard what we were up to, he insisted on seeing us personally to assure us of our safety and security on the day of the job. When we arrived, he was standing near the gate to the field.

'Brendan, great to see you again,' he said. 'And who's this man?'

Before I could introduce him, Liam spoke up, 'I'm Liam, and I'm Irish.' Ned looked at me, puzzled.

'Just a joke we're having,' I said. 'He doesn't like being called a Yank. Even though that's why he's here.'

'Leave the young fella alone,' Ned said, kindly.

## Chapter 24

'Pass no remarks on these two, they're always getting it up for people.'

Turning back to me, he asked, 'What do you think of this place? It has quite a history, going back to the 9th century.'

'What's it called?' I asked.

'In Irish it was called Dun Masc, which in English became Masc's Fort. It's now known as the Rock of Dunamase. You are walking in the footsteps of Diarmuid MacMurrough, King of Leinster. Even Strongbow fought over it. Our old friend Cromwell rendered the castle unusable by battering it to pieces with cannon fire.'

I was slow to admit that Irish history wasn't my strong point.

'Well,' I replied, 'We're certainly in some notable as well as disreputable company here. I wonder will we be in the footnotes of history ourselves after this?'

This raised a laugh before I again voiced my concern about the men who still hadn't finished their late harvest work in the nearby fields.

'Jim has all that boxed off,' Ned assured me. 'We know everyone around here and I guarantee you there won't be a problem with any of them.'

I told Liam I would be giving him a map to show the pilot where to land.

'Once you come within sight of this place, put the map away in your pocket, and don't lose it, whatever you do,' I instructed. 'From then on, use visual directions.'

Liam just stared at the rocky outcrop, topped by the castle ruins. 'I couldn't very well miss this place,' he said.

'No,' Jim agreed. 'We were thinking along those lines when we chose it. It's the kind of place Americans photograph all the time.'

'I can see you guys aren't too fond of Americans,' Liam remarked.

'Nothing could be further from the truth,' Ned told him. 'We don't mind them at all. All we're saying is that they take a lot of pictures of places like this. Sure, isn't that a good thing?'

I was delighted with the location. It ticked all kinds of boxes. It had presence. Anyone could see why someone would want to photograph it. A pilot wouldn't think twice about being asked to land here.

'Liam,' I said. 'Have you seen enough?'

'Yeah, I guess I've seen all I want to see,' Liam replied. 'I doubt if anyone could miss it.'

I thanked Ned and Jim again for their help, telling them their contribution had been crucial.

'After this goes up, best keep your heads down,' I warned. The Special Branch will know for sure that you had a hand in it, and I don't want to give those bastards an excuse to pick you up.'

'I just want to see their faces and laugh at them,' Ned said. 'That's all part of it: Sicken the fuckers.'

I could only smile.

'You're as mad as the rest of us,' I told him. Ned made a point of shaking Liam's hand.

'Good luck young fella,' he said. 'I'll see you again after the job's over. Maybe you'll let me buy you a pint… Just to celebrate.'

# 25

As usual, there was little conversation on the way back to Dublin. The men of The Heath had a way of casting a spell on everyone they met.

After a few wrong turns, I eventually found our new base. There was a small, wrought-iron gate, sealing off a narrow path leading up to the front door of a Georgian red-brick. I had no key, so I knocked on the main door, hoping for the best.

Tommy opened it. The dark hallway gave little clue as to what kind of place it was, although I knew several tenants would be sharing this old roof.

'Come on in,' he said. 'We're through that door there, indicating a brown door on the right, at the very end of the musty corridor.'

'What's it like?' I asked.

'Just another flat; two bedrooms, four beds, and a living room-cum-kitchen-cum-dining room,' Tommy shrugged.

'Does it come with lights?' I asked, sarcastically, after stumbling on a loose floorboard.

A bare bulb flickered.

'Sorry about that,' Tommy said. 'Turns off after one minute. I timed it.'

'Old habits,' I thought to myself.

The light didn't improve the place. It badly needed a lick of paint. Tommy saw the doubt on my face.

'This place really is okay,' he assured me. 'Don't judge it by the hallway; it's not too bad.'

My humour didn't improve after I walked through the door. Threadbare, faded carpet with a strange, oriental design covered the floor. The rickety table in the corner looked like it was propped up under one leg to stop it falling over. In the other corner there was a shower, half-hidden by a mouldy curtain. I was already regretting having to move.

Our things were stacked in a neat pile on one of the beds. I told the lads we had to clean the place before we could even contemplate eating.

'Fuck knows who was here before us,' I said.

I was going to send Tony off for some groceries, but I had second thoughts. He would only come back with sweet crap like biscuits and cakes. We needed real food like bacon, sausages, eggs, bread, milk and so on. I sent Tommy instead. Tony looked at me in disgust. Now, he would have to work.

'You have a poor opinion of me,' he complained.

'Only regarding shopping,' I told him. 'You eat shit; drink too much; smoke too much; and take absolutely no exercise. Look at you, you couldn't walk half a mile, without having to rest.'

I turned to start cleaning up, and I knew he was making faces at me behind my back. I could only imagine the names he was calling me, but I also knew it was the kind of banter that kept an operation going. It was expected, given and taken on all sides.

Liam just stood there wondering what the hell he should be doing. I told him he was now part of this unit and he would have to do his share. After we ate, we got right down to it. I needed their input to make sure there were no gaps. So, we went over everything yet again.

## Chapter 25

'By the way, did anyone check the phone in the hallway to see if it's working?' I asked.

Tommy said he had tried it earlier and it was fine.

'Liam, what time is your flight tomorrow, again?' I asked.

'10.30,' he replied.

'I'll leave you on O'Connell Street but well away from the taxi rank,' I said. 'I don't want to be seen. You need to be at the airport early because I want you to change what's left of what I gave you for English banknotes. They're worth the same but I don't want you to have any links with Ireland. Also, make sure to memorise the number of the phone in the hallway here. I need you to call me after you've booked into your hotel. Don't use your room phone or even a phone in the hotel itself. Go to a payphone a few streets away. By the time you call me, you'll know if the helicopter booking has gone through okay.

We'll leave here at half-seven tomorrow morning. I don't want you rushing around the airport. I don't want you to draw any attention to yourself until you reach your London hotel. Then, of course, I want you to draw plenty of it! After you return to Dublin and have settled into your hotel here, take a walk down and call me from a coin box. I'll meet you at the same spot where I'll be dropping you off tomorrow morning.'

'No problem,' Liam said. 'I've been going over this again and again.'

It struck me how calm he appeared. I still hadn't realised how seasoned an operator he was. Turning to Tony, I asked if Joe was ready to go.

'All set,' he said. 'He's been checking the car every evening to make sure. I've also been in touch with Paul. He'll be standing by from Wednesday morning and has already arranged to notify the other two drivers. They all know that part of the city well. Any problems and they'll be able to improvise, taking alternative routes. These are mature, steady men. Trust me, they'll do the job.'

I gave Tony £150 in small-denomination notes.

'If the three men inside run into unexpected difficulties for whatever reason after you land at the racecourse, at least they'll have money to take a taxi to somewhere safe,' I said. 'Give them £50 each when they're in the helicopter, so they'll have money in their pockets.'

To reassure the others of Liam's ability more than anything else, I returned to his part of the operation.

'Now, Liam, you know the line of chat to give to the receptionist in the London hotel?' I asked. 'I don't have to go over that again, do I?'

'Listen here,' Liam drawled, 'You guys ain't got nothing to worry about. I'll bring back your bird, consider it done!'

Heads nodded in approval. He could have been in Hollywood.

'Okay, so,' I said. 'Once you've confirmed the hire, take the taxi to the Royal Dublin Hotel. When you get inside, drop the charade. Revert to being a nobody. The more non-descript you are, the better. After you get settled in, go down the street and call me. Give me 10 or 15 minutes and I'll be there to pick you up. 'Now, we'll go over again what happens on Wednesday. We need to be above Mountjoy Jail between three and half-three. We'll allow 35 minutes to fly to Stradbally. Another 15 minutes on the ground and another 35 minutes to the prison. You need to be leaving Dublin airport in the helicopter no later than half one. If we're early we can kill some more time on the ground but if we're late, we're screwed. Have you got all that?'

'Brendan,' Liam intoned in a tired voice. 'You've already told me everything umpteen times. I have it all in my head already, but I take it I can always improvise if things go wrong?'

'Yes, of course you can,' I said. 'But only as a last resort. You're a vital cog in this wheel but everything has its place and timing will be crucial. We only have a two-hour window to land in the jail. People get nervous when things don't go to schedule. Nervous people make mistakes.'

It was already 11 o'clock and I called a halt.

'We all need to get some rest now,' I said. 'It's going to be a tense few days. But you know the story boys. It's just like any other job we've ever done. Once we start the car and head off, the nerves will settle, and it'll all be grand.'

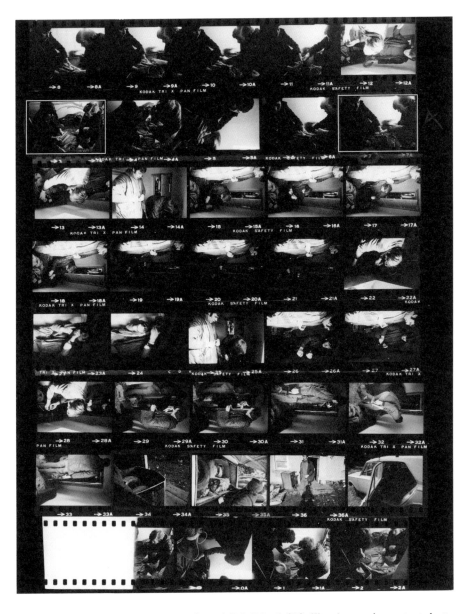

*One of P. Michael O'Sullivan's negative contact sheets.*
*Chosen images are highlighted.*

147

43/4

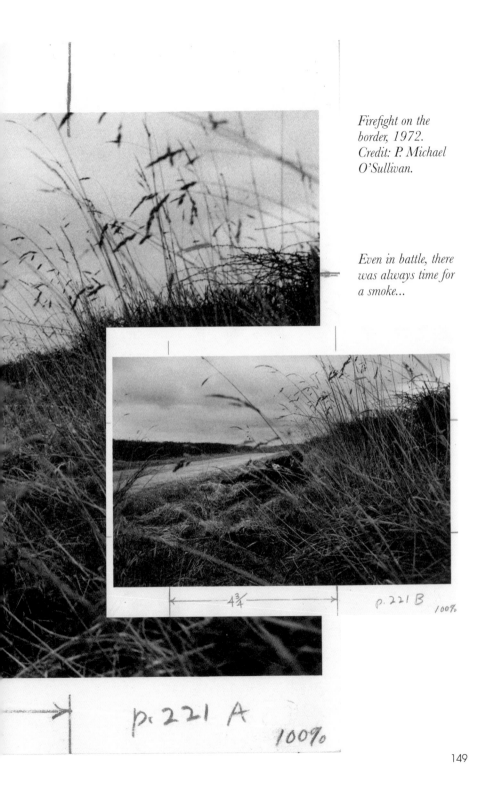

*Firefight on the border, 1972. Credit: P. Michael O'Sullivan.*

*Even in battle, there was always time for a smoke...*

p.221 B
100%

4¾

p.221 A
100%

149

4¾

*P. Michael O'Sullivan was an outstanding photographer who was granted unprecedented access to IRA operations.*

KODAK TRI X - PAN FILM          KODAK SAFETY FILM

➤13A    ➤14    ➤14A    ➤15    ➤15A    ➤16    ➤16A    ➤17

p.221C 100%

p 2/26    66½    8½"
66

KODAK TRI X PAN FILM

➤7A    ➤8    ➤8A    ➤9    ➤9A    ➤10    ➤10A    ➤11

*Like all guerrilla organisations, IRA members used their knowledge of the local terrain to give themselves an edge against superior forces.*

152%

The IRA became increasingly proficient in explosives. As the conflict progressed, the technological prowess at their disposal improved from these early years of command wires.

*IRA* volunteers
prepare to mount an
operation.

april.

*Brendan Hughes relaxes during one of his many periods of detention in Monaghan Garda station.*

9⅞                                    → 231

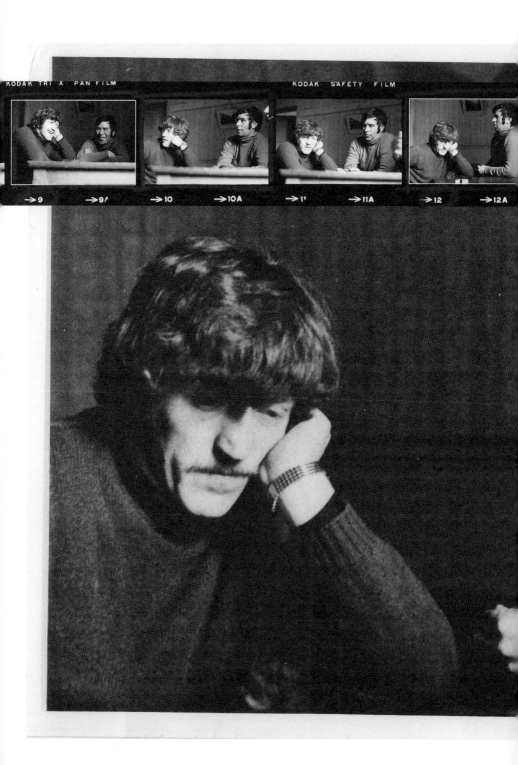

→9  →9/  →10  →10A  →1'  →11A  →12  →12A

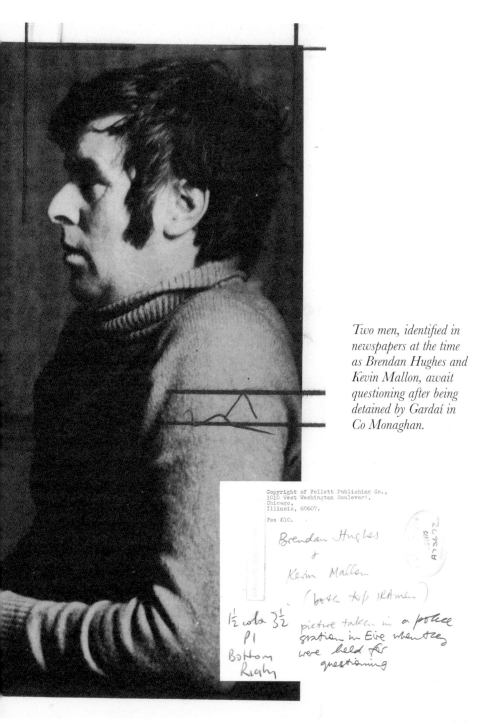

*Two men, identified in newspapers at the time as Brendan Hughes and Kevin Mallon, await questioning after being detained by Gardaí in Co Monaghan.*

161

# 26

**Monday, October 29, 1973**

The morning dawned wet and cold. I needed a clear day on Wednesday but with November fast approaching, I knew the odds against us were tightening and playing things by ear never appealed to me.

Liam was first into the bathroom. Washed and shaved, he sat waiting for some smart remarks about his new wardrobe, but none came. Nobody was in a joking mood this morning and, anyway, we didn't want to sap his confidence. We all showed him the absolute respect he deserved.

I told him to take only the basics with him in case he left anything personal in either hotel by mistake. I gave him what was left of the money, reminding him again to change it to Bank of England notes at the airport. He picked up his smart suitcase, which contained only a couple of spare shirts and toiletries. After giving himself one last look in the mirror, he led the way out to the car.

I had parked nearer than usual to where I was staying, judging that the bigger danger came from the notice a well-dressed Yank might attract in dowdy bedsit-land.

'How are you feeling?' I asked, as we headed towards the city centre.

'I have an entire flutter of butterflies doing loops in my stomach,' he admitted.

'My mouth is dry – but other than that, I'm just fine. Don't worry, I won't let you down.'

I eyed him in the mirror. He didn't look nervous at all. He was his usual calm self.

I pulled over to the kerb at Parnell Square. Liam made to open the door but before he did so he put out his hand to shake mine. I wished him good luck and told him I'd be waiting for his call later that evening.

'If everything goes to plan, I'll only say that I'll be seeing you tomorrow,' he said.

With that, he closed the door and melted into the morning office crowd. I watched him for a moment, then I started the car and drove back to the flat.

I was more than a little nervous myself. I knew the next few hours were crucial.

I drove past the flat 20 minutes later. Everything seemed quiet but I parked around the corner this time. I walked the few hundred yards to the front door and along the dank hallway. When I entered the room, Tony and Tommy had just finished eating.

'How's Liam?' Tommy asked. 'Steady as a rock,' I replied.

'It's going to be a long day,' I said. 'What are you two up to?'

'We're going to run one final check on Joe and our three drivers,' Tommy said. 'Maybe we'll have another look at the racecourse. It'll be our last visit until we land there on Wednesday.'

'The car, Tommy, check the fucking car again,' I said. 'I don't want to sound like a broken record but I'm really nervous about it after all the messing about. The last time Joe got a car, he ended up being chased all over north County Dublin.'

Tony only laughed: 'They never caught him though, did they?!'

UP LIKE A BIRD

After they left, I sat down to have a worry to myself. I missed the flat at Clontarf, its views and salty air. The nearest water to this place was a stagnant canal. As I lit yet another cigarette, I could see Marion calling me a smelly bastard but knew this wasn't the time to consider giving up.

I kept turning the job over and over in my mind. Hard as I tried, I couldn't find any holes. That didn't stop me worrying every detail to bits. There were so many moving parts, and everything had to go right, or nothing would. I seemed to be checking my watch every few minutes. It was still only one o'clock.

I decided to find somewhere to eat, just to give myself something to do. I remember thinking to myself, 'Things are very bad, Brendan, when you go out to eat just to pass the time.' Maybe I should have gone with the other two? No, I was much better off keeping my head down.

I returned to the flat around three. I did my usual check around the street, before approaching the gate. Everything seemed to be okay, so I went in. The boys weren't back yet but that didn't surprise me. They didn't like lying around a flat any more than I did. But I was stuck now. I couldn't chance going out again in case I missed Liam's call.

They came back about seven o'clock, chatting and joking as if they had no cares in the wide world. Just as I was asking them how they'd got on, the phone rang. I rushed out to answer it, just ahead of a young man from another flat, who was none too pleased when I grabbed the receiver.

'Hello,' I said.

'Is that you Brendan?' came an American twang. 'Yes.'

'Good,' the voice replied. 'I'll be seeing you tomorrow evening.'

'I'll see you then, so,' I replied, my heart thumping as I returned the handset to its cradle.

'It's all yours,' I told the young fella I had wrestled the phone from, apologising for any offence. He scowled at me, without saying anything. I shrugged my shoulders and left him there.

I pulled the door of the flat after me, adopting a poker face. I relaxed into a chair. They stared at me.

'Well, are you going to tell us or what?' Tony asked. 'Did he get the helicopter?' I couldn't hold back any longer.

'He got it, alright. I don't know any more details, but he fucking got it.' Tommy and Tony linked arms and did a mock jig in celebration.

'We fucking did it, we fucking did it,' Tommy roared.

After punching the air a few times, we sat down to let it sink in.

I asked the pair of them if they had any change for the phone. They rummaged around in their pockets and produced a few coins. I took what I needed and rang Marion.

'It's me,' I said. 'I'm just ringing to confirm that you can deliver a positive message tomorrow. Tell him we'll be there on Wednesday between three and four.'

'No problem,' she said, and hung up. A true professional to the last.

I clawed my way down the unlit hall towards the chink of light at the open door and found Tommy and Tony where I left them, slouched on the faded sofa.

'Well, boys,' I said. 'Tell me, how was your day? Are we all set at your end?' 'We're all set, ready to move,' Tony said.

'Okay,' I replied. 'I don't want to talk any more about it right now. I'm going to lie down and have a rest. Don't forget though, both of you are confined to barracks.'

I lay there for hours listening to the low murmur of their voices drifting in from the other room, punctuated by the usual reassuring stream of laughter and curses. Somehow, I managed to nod off eventually in yet another strange bed. I awoke several times that night but forced myself back to sleep again.

# 27

**Tuesday, October 30, 1973**

The flat was quiet. The boys had probably been up chatting half the night. I boiled a couple of eggs, made some toast and washed it all down with what Liam called 'that awful instant coffee'.

I hoped he was able to enjoy some better stuff in whatever fancy hotel the travel agent had booked him into. I expected he would be on his way to the airport shortly for his return flight, due around noon.

I wondered how in the hell I was going to kill time. The proverbial calm before the storm. Talking of which, I checked outside to see whether the weather had improved. It hadn't.

Life on the run was full of boring days but I never got used to them. Up North it had been different. There was always the chance of a bank job or the prospect of taking a pop at some Brits to keep you ticking over.

I decided to take a run across to my old beachfront haunt in Clontarf. Not to the flat, of course, just to Dollymount Strand. It would only take me 20 minutes to reach it. I planned to be back by 12. A walk would be no harm and maybe I had already guessed it might be my last one there for a very long time.

I left a note on the table for the two boys, telling them where I had gone. I doubted they would surface for another couple of hours anyway. I told them to wait in the flat until I returned. If the phone rang, they were to answer it, just in case.

I parked near the sea in Clontarf around half-ten. The bracing wind did me the world of good. I felt the tension draining away but the walk ended all too soon and I drove back to the flat. When I opened the door, the boys had just finished eating. I knew the strain was starting to tell on them too. The air was blue from cigarette smoke.

'Any calls?' I inquired.

'No,' Tony grumbled. 'How in the fuck would we get any calls? The only one who knows the number and knows we're here is Liam, and he's on a flight.'

'Not anymore,' I countered. 'He landed 20 minutes ago. He'll be finding out shortly if he's getting a helicopter or getting arrested.'

We lay around the flat, irritable, getting in one another's way and talking rubbish. Time dragged.

At six o'clock the phone eventually rang. I jumped up and ran down the hallway, taking my chances in the darkness.

'Hello, is that you Brendan?' Liam said. 'I'll see you in 15 minutes.' I tore back inside.

'Boys,' I said. 'See you later. I'm off on a date with a Yank!'

I drove through the fading light towards Parnell Square. The streetlights were just about cutting through the grimy drizzle. Newspapers were blowing along the pavements. It was a typical, miserable, late October evening.

I saw him straight away, studying a movie billboard. When I blew the horn, he turned, saluted and smiled. I couldn't wait to hear how he got on. As we drove, he began filling me in.

'Well, did they confirm your booking?' I asked.

'They sure did,' he said. 'They couldn't do enough for me. Even gave me a cup of terrible coffee, just like yours!'

'Never mind the fucking coffee, tell me the full story,' I said.

I decided to drive out of the city in the opposite direction to the flat to give him plenty of time to drop every tiny detail.

'The helicopter is booked,' he said. 'My pilot is a Captain Boyes. I got into the hotel in London around half-two. I booked in and paid immediately with English notes, as ordered. I walked away from the desk before doing a Colombo on them. When I was a few steps away, I turned around and said, "Oh, by the way, can I ask you something?"'

'The receptionist was only too happy to oblige, especially after I had produced a handsome tip. Then I gave her the spiel about being an English-American who wanted to trace my ancestors to the 19th century estate they had once owned in Ireland. I told her I planned to travel to Dublin the following day to continue my search, but time was tight. I asked her whether there might be a company in that backward country that would hire a helicopter for a day to fly me and a photographer out to take some aerial shots, and, if such a thing were possible, could she book it for Wednesday on my behalf.

'She looked me up and down, wondered why a nice American like me would want to go to such a goddamned awful, and dangerous, country, informing me that she wouldn't go to Ireland if you paid her. I insisted that I had to find out everything I could about my ancestors, and this was my best chance while I was on this side of The Pond. She said she would make a few calls, inquiring whether I would be dining at the hotel. I told her I would and she asked me to come back to the desk after dinner. About an hour later, I returned, and she handed me a piece of paper with all the details of the booking she had made on my behalf. She remarked that she would rather use a car herself, telling me that flying was a very expensive way to travel.

'I tipped her again, thanking her profusely. Money was no object to this rich Yank!'

Then Liam handed me a piece of paper with the booking details.

I pulled the car over to read it. It had everything: contact name and phone number, even the price. It was hard to believe. I pulled off again.

'So, what arrangements have you made with them?' I asked.

'I have to be there at 11.30 to fill in some paperwork. Take-off is scheduled for 12.30. They say it's a 30-minute flight to our destination, ETA one o'clock. That should give you loads of time to get to the jail.'

Thinking furiously as I was driving, I realised the timing was off. If Liam took off at 12.30 and landed around one, it would be far too early. He would have to push back the time.

'Liam,' I said. 'First thing in the morning, call Irish Helicopters and reschedule the flight. Tell them you can't take off until 1.45. I don't want to be over Mountjoy until three o'clock, at the earliest. We don't have a huge window. The prisoners can only access the exercise yard between two and four. Allowing for the fact that they might get out late, I want to be there at three.'

'Yes, I understand,' he said, not the least put out. 'It won't be a problem. I'll call as soon as I get up.'

When I dropped him off at the hotel, I ordered him to go straight to his room.

'The less people see of you, the better,' I said. 'Don't go to the bar. In the morning, eat in a café. Call a taxi from the hotel but leave quietly so that nobody notices what time you get out of there. Don't carry anything with you. Leave your cases in the room and cut the labels off the clothes, so they won't know where you bought them. And before I forget, I want to tell you that you've done exceptionally well.

'I won't be seeing you again until you get out of that helicopter in Stradbally. From now on, I'll be working on the assumption that you'll get the helicopter okay and you'll arrive on time. We'll be waiting there for you.'

I wished him the best of luck and we shook hands one last time before we parted.

Back in Rathmines, I went through my usual routine before opening the door of the flat to find my friends waiting for me, anxious for news. I didn't speak for a minute, ratcheting up the tension as their eyes followed me around the room.

'For fuck sake, tell us,' Tony pleaded desperately. 'Are we in business, or not?'

'Tomorrow,' I said. 'I'm going to put a helicopter under your little fat arse. And you are going to take it into Mountjoy Jail to collect that bollix Mallon! Tomorrow we go down in history. Yes, we have a helicopter!'

They sat staring at me through a nicotine fug. For a minute they were speechless.

This was one of those moments all volunteers live for. Excitement, thrills and an overdose of adrenaline. We were all on a high, seeing all our efforts about to pay off. I imagined how Liam must be feeling and Mallon and the others. We were all drunk with excitement.

We sat into the small hours, talking and going over our respective roles. We had a good feeling. I had a good feeling.

We were ready.

# 28

**Wednesday, October 31, 1973**

After a fitful night, tossing and turning, I got up in the half-dark and made straight for the window. The weather looked like it might just favour us.

I'd only just poured a mug of coffee when I heard the others stirring. We ended last night on a high. We smoked endless cigarettes, dizzy with nerves. This morning we were silent.

Time dragged. Eventually, we couldn't wait any longer for the traffic to clear. Piling into the car, we headed out of Dublin towards The Heath. When we arrived at Treacy's bar around half-eleven, Seán and Jim were waiting for us.

'All set?' Seán asked.

'Looks like it,' I said. 'I'm expecting the chopper to be here between two and three. We should all be at the field by a quarter-to-two just in case. How's everything at this end?'

'Brendan,' Seán said, 'We always have things in order, you know that! Ned has us fucking tortured.

He is checking is this right? Is that right? We're all a bag of fucking nerves!'

Just then Ned came out of the bar. He repeated Seán's question, but I was in no mood to go over the entire rigmarole. Instead, I skipped through my mental checklist.

'Seán, have you got the weapons ready?' I asked.

'Yes, they're in place,' he said. 'I cleaned and oiled them. They're dumped yards from where you need them. I also have a house arranged for Liam. I'll take him there myself. He'll be well taken care of.'

I turned to Ned.

'I don't want you near that helicopter under any circumstances,' I told him. 'Have you any idea the pressure you'll all come under after this job goes down? You need to make sure you've nothing lying around your house or anywhere on your land. They'll be searching everywhere. This is going to drive them nuts.'

Ned wore a knowing, country smile.

'I'm way ahead of you,' he said. 'Jim and I have been making everything safe. It's all hidden. As soon as you leave here, I'm off home. By the time the chopper is on its way, half the country will have seen us going about our usual business. And we'll make sure they know what time they seen us too!'

**1.30 pm**

Chatting and having the craic provided a welcome distraction but Seán was keeping a good eye on his watch and told us it was time to go. We had 15 minutes to get to the field.

The journey took 10 minutes. When we arrived, Seán and Tony went to break out the weapons concealed under some hay bales in the next field. They returned with them a few minutes later. Tony unwrapped their plastic coverings and began checking their breeches, one by one, to make sure they were safe. The last thing we wanted was an accidental discharge.

I looked around the field; the farm workers were still off in the distance. Seán read my mind.

'Relax,' he said. 'They all drink in my pub. I know every last one of them. They'll all be at the bar tonight and this won't even get a mention. There will be plenty of pints raised to the escape but what happened here will be forgotten. Don't worry, these are good people.'

They were obviously well on top of the situation, so I relaxed and went on with my own preparations.

We had parked in the middle of this large field, making sure that Seán's car obscured the pilot's view of my number plates. I doubted very much he would remember the vehicle registration anyway but there was no point in taking needless chances.

I told Tony to keep all of the weapons out of sight during the approach to the jail.

'Until the screws see the weapons, it'll keep them guessing,' I said. 'Put them on show only when you have to control the situation. The later you take them out, the less time they'll have to react. Those screws won't have a fucking idea what's going on until you're on the ground. Did you get all that?'

'Loud and clear,' he replied.

I barely had time to finish my last instructions when we heard the unmistakable sound of a helicopter in the distance. We all looked up at the little dot growing bigger as it came towards us.

'Here we go,' I said, half to myself. 'Remember, behave normally until it touches down. After that, we'll play it by ear. Whatever you do, don't let the pilot turn off the engine.

Tony, you're in charge of the weapons. Just show them to the pilot. Don't threaten him. We need him to be calm.'

By this time, the dot had taken on the distinctive shape of a helicopter. The French-made Alouette II circled overhead just once before coming in to land.

We all faced away from the downdraft. As it settled on the ground, and the engine pitch changed, I walked up to the pilot's door. Opening it, I leaned in tight towards him and shouted politely above the roar of the rotors:

'Good afternoon. I am a member of the Provisional IRA and I want you to fly somewhere for me. Please don't make this any harder than necessary.

We are armed, but we don't want to use our weapons. Do you understand what I'm telling you?'

The whine from the engine and the spinning blades was deafening. The pilot said nothing at first and then looked around for his passenger. Mr Leonard had already left. In his place sat a grim-faced Tony with a gun in his hand and two others resting across his knees.

The pilot turned towards me again. I tried to force a smile of sorts in an effort to put him at ease. 'Where do you want to go?' he asked.

'I want you to fly to Mountjoy Jail,' I roared above the whine. 'I need you to pick up three passengers. Two of us will go with you.'

He never flinched. As he stared at me, I recall thinking, 'This man is made of stern stuff and could cause me a problem.'

Then he just smiled.

'So, you want me to escape with three prisoners? What if we're shot at?'

'The weapons are only for show,' I said. ''There will be no shots fired by us unless absolutely necessary. This would be a very last resort. If we don't fire, they won't fire.'

'This helicopter can only carry a maximum of five people,' he shouted in a calm voice. 'If you send two men with me, I can only take two more.'

By this time Tommy had climbed in the back. I gestured to him to get out. 'Now,' I said. 'There's only one going in. You can lift three out.'

'Theoretically, yes,' he said, in a refined, clipped accent. 'I have to warn you though that if the area I land in is too small and if, as I expect, it is surrounded by a high wall, then there is a distinct possibility we won't be able to take off again. We may not be able to generate enough lift to get off the ground.'

'Can we do anything to avoid that situation?' I asked.

'I could hover just above the ground,' he said. 'It may work, or it may not. I'll certainly give it a go.'

He was now smiling openly. He seemed completely relaxed and in total command of himself. Fate had favoured me. Thompson Boyes was a veteran pilot who had spent a couple of years transporting police around Uganda before being forced to flee when the tyrannical Idi Amin seized power in 1971. By strange coincidence, he was born not a million miles from me, but his background could hardly have been more different. I would have loved to have had a pint with him later, but it never came to pass. He may have been of unionist stock but was very much his own man. Then aged 47, he was also a very experienced pilot, renowned for calmness under pressure.

I looked at my watch, it was time to go. In hindsight, what happened next would become life-changing, but not in a good way.

Tony demanded the map of Dublin we carried on operations. We had used it time and again to find our way around the city over the previous few months. I told him just to look out the fucking window and he'd know where to go but he insisted. In the heat of the moment, I was stupid enough to hand it over.

'Whatever you leave behind you in the helicopter, do not leave that map,' I shouted very slowly and carefully. 'Our prints are all over it.'

'I'll look after it with my life,' he promised. Closing the door of the chopper, I went through a final mental check. I remember saying to Capt Boyes that he would be getting free beer on the back of this for a long time. I smiled at him, but he only nodded. He was a tough man to read. He also had an unwanted mission to complete and an armed man sitting beside him.

While all of this was going on, Seán had left with Liam before I had the chance to thank him again and say a final goodbye. The helicopter took off and, nose down, it started to gain altitude. Tommy and I were alone in the field. We watched it until it faded into a small speck and then we got into our car and headed back towards Dublin.

We had arranged to lie low at a safe house in Newbridge, a nondescript town halfway to the capital. As we drove, both of us were praying for front-page news.

# 29

In the main exercise yard at Mountjoy jail, republican prisoners were playing a pre-arranged football match. Mallon, Twomey and O'Hagan were there to cheer on this youthful exuberance. They were also keeping an ear open and scanning the skies across the walls. Nothing.

Twomey was quietly cursing to Mallon.

'They're late,' he kept repeating. 'Another no show.' Mallon told him to relax.

'I have full confidence,' he said. 'Brendan has never let me down.'

The prisoners knew this North v South match would go ahead whatever the weather, but none of them knew why.

Veteran IRA man, Joe Cahill, who was caught on board the Claudia, led a group of prisoners back inside the republican D Wing when the expected arrival time had passed. This left the inmates in the yard short of numbers to subdue the warders.

A few minutes later, they heard the thrum in the distance. Mallon got to his feet and extracted a pair of white handkerchiefs from his pocket. The noise came closer and closer. When the helicopter was around 100 feet overhead, it circled once and then began its descent. Some prisoners continued their game, others looked up.

Mallon began to wave the handkerchiefs as a semaphore to guide the pilot down. The screws appeared paralysed as the chopper made its descent. One prisoner from Derry had just walked into the yard, curious about the descending chopper. He spotted Tony with a rifle and ran back inside in panic.

'Get back, get back,' he screamed to those inside. 'The SAS are landing in the yard.'

When reality dawned on the warders that it wasn't the Minister for Justice paying them a visit, it was already too late. A group of prisoners, who had been made aware of the escape, began pinning their captors back.

By this time, Mallon, Twomey and O'Hagan were running, half-crouched, towards the door of the chopper. Once inside, Tony handed Mallon a pistol. Tony ordered them to sit down and stay still. They were upsetting the trim of the five-seater as the pilot struggled to keep control.

'Get the fuck out of here,' Mallon screamed at him.

The engine squealed in protest, and then, like a cork from a bottle, it shot into the air, clearing a rooftop with only a few feet to spare.

The men looked down on the total bedlam they had left in their wake.

An inquiry recorded that one screw was shouting, 'Close the gates, close the gates.'

They were open to allow a delivery lorry through. Another admonished him: 'Shut up you fool!'

O'Hagan later recalled a screw running towards them, intending to hurl a concrete block at the helicopter.

'He didn't get far,' he said. 'The escape team in the yard blocked him off.

I held onto the inside door handle. It wasn't properly closed, and I was afraid Seamus might fall out. We were rising now. We couldn't hear the cheers below for the noise of the helicopter, but you could see the men jumping up and down and striking the air with their fists.'

The screws had no idea who had even escaped. There weren't any protocols for this situation and trying to herd dozens of prisoners back to their cells for an identity check was no easy task.

For the next few days, the jail echoed to songs like 'Fly me to the Moon' and 'Up, Up and Away' as the prisoners celebrated. They broke out whiskey and vodka to toast the escapees.

One of the inmates, Belfast man Liam Brown, nicknamed 'Farmer', had jumped on a screw and held him down as the helicopter shot skyward. Later, this prison officer went around telling his colleagues it had taken four men to restrain him. Farmer knew the truth and never let him forget it.

At a subsequent trial, he was acquitted for his role in the escape but four others, Gerry O'Hare, Michael Fox, Donal McCarthy and Michael Nolan each received one-year sentences.

Meanwhile, above in the chopper, the smiles and hand signals said it all. The deafening roar of the engine made conversation practically impossible.

Tony distributed the cash to all three men. He had already instructed the pilot where to land and indicated the exact spot when the racecourse came into view. Capt Boyes circled once and glided to earth.

'That bastard Joe isn't here – we have no car,' Tony roared, spitting with rage when he didn't see anyone there to meet them.

Mallon had assumed command by now and told him to take it easy. 'Don't worry,' he said, motioning to his gun. 'We'll soon get a car.'

The three men ducked low again as they left the chopper. Tony ordered the pilot to turn off the engine and he complied, happy that his ordeal was over. Tony held out his hand and Capt Boyes shook it. He mouthed a polite 'thank you' to the pilot and joined the others, who were already trying to break into a van parked on the racecourse perimeter.

Squealing tyres signalled the arrival of a Dublin taxi. A sheepish-looking

Joe was leaning out the window. 'Did anybody order a cab?' he quipped.

'Where the fuck have you been?' Tony cursed, in no mood for humour.

'You're not going to believe this,' Joe replied, speaking a million miles a minute. 'Some piece of shit stole our car. I'm telling you, nothing is safe these days! I went to check on it this morning and there it was – gone! We had to go into town and hijack this taxi. I have the driver tied up in a shed at the back of my house. I'm sorry, it's the best I could do.'

Tony just shook his head but they were still in business. Only ten minutes had elapsed since the helicopter had cleared the walls of the 'Joy.

Joe drove the short distance to the changeover. The three walked quickly to the waiting cars, leaving the guns behind. Tony ordered Joe to hide the getaway vehicle as instructed.

'And don't forget to keep it until after dark,' he said, before joining Mallon in the third car.

'Nice and easy now, we have lots of time,' Tony told the driver.

Six minutes later they were slipping into the safe house Mallon had organised. Less than 20 minutes had passed since they had been scooped from the exercise yard.

'One sugar or two?' their delighted hostess asked them when they arrived.

In a later interview, J.B. O'Hagan said the success didn't really sink in until those first, precious minutes in the safe house.

'It was only later, when we were sitting back with a cup of tea in our hands, that we fully appreciated the achievement,' he recalled. It was a real spectacular. However, all credit is due to those on the outside who planned and carried out the escape. They were the real heroes.'

In Newbridge, Tommy and I listened intently to the radio. When it came, the newsflash was brief and to the point.

'Three prisoners have been airlifted out of Mountjoy Jail by helicopter,' it said. 'A nationwide hunt is now underway to find the missing prisoners and the helicopter.'

'Good luck with that,' I thought to myself. I was ecstatic with joy and relief.

For once, the articulate Tommy was almost lost for words. He kept repeating, 'We done it, we done it!'

On a separate scanner, we monitored the chat on the Garda frequency, giggling like naughty school kids. Instructions were being issued to set up roadblocks.

'Who and what are we looking for?' one said.

'Three prisoners escaping in a helicopter,' another replied.

This would invariably produce an avalanche of curses and the obvious question of how exactly a roadblock was expected to stop a helicopter?!

Later that evening, Tommy and I made our way towards Dublin. No-one was even looking at cars going into the city.

The celebration dinner at the flat wasn't exactly the fatted calf. Two boiled eggs and burnt toast washed down with some of my apparently awful coffee. We weren't hungry anyway – we were still pinching ourselves.

Around half-eight, I'd had enough. I had an idea where Mallon and Tony might be heading, so Tommy and I went to join them. Mallon and I were friendly with two sisters from Co Tyrone who were working in Dublin. The relationship was never more than platonic, but we loved their company. The craic was good, and they always had news from home.

Tommy and I arrived at their place around nine. They welcomed us in, offering each of us a bottle of beer.

'I don't suppose you had anything to do with that today?' one of them asked, mischievously.

I denied everything with a tell-tale grin. Before she could press me further, a knock came at the door. One of the girls peeked out the window and screamed with delight.

'It's Kevin and Tony,' she spluttered, before opening the door and throwing her arms around Mallon.

'Jesus, you're a sight for sore eyes,' she screamed. 'You boys are all over the news. Every cop in the Free State is out looking for you. And here you are in my flat. It's like Christmas.'

Mallon turned to me.

'Well done, as usual,' he smiled. 'But you were fucking late!'

'Well, at least I delivered,' I replied. 'I'm getting as good as the milkman for delivering!'

'Yeah, I'll remember that,' he laughed. I peeled off to have a word with Tony. 'Well,' I said, 'Where's the map?'

I knew by his face he had fucked up.

'Brendan, I lost it in the confusion when the car wasn't there at the racecourse,' he said. 'I'm sorry, what more can I say?'

I didn't want to ruin the celebrations breaking out all over the room, so I almost whispered to him, 'You know what this means? It means jail, Tony. Our fingerprints are all over it.'

It was a bitter blow and took some of the shine off the job for me. I was always very careful to cover my tracks, to leave no clues, and especially, no fingerprints. And now, here I was, completely exposed, on the biggest operation I had ever carried out.

It would be wrong to say it was no fault of mine. I had to bear some of the blame for allowing him to take it in the first place. I would pay a very dear price for this very bad mistake.

There was no point in dwelling on it. The harm was done, so I said no more. The party was already getting into full swing. Tommy asked me what was wrong, and I said, 'Nothing.' He knew by my face not to repeat the question.

I couldn't have known at the time that there would be another major fuck up. After Joe had left the changeover, he drove the taxi to the garage where he intended storing it. He switched off the engine, closed the door and left. Later that night he returned with another volunteer to dump it. The pair failed to wipe it down or even to remove the weapons. Maybe the nerves got to him.

As they were leaving the garage, the commandeered taxi stalled, and they couldn't get it going again. It was dark and the weapons were hidden under the seats. The pair pushed it out of the driveway.

A man happened to be walking past. Dermot Teeling was selling An Phoblacht, a republican newspaper that Sinn Féin members distributed in pubs around the country at the time. The pair recognised Dermot and asked him to help them push the car. This would be enough to get him three years in jail. His fingerprints were later found on the boot and the Gardaí already had them on file.

Our old friend fate had just stepped into his life with drastic consequences.

They got the taxi going but the area was crawling with cops and the two lads probably just panicked. There were checkpoints everywhere. They ended up abandoning it several miles away, leaving the guns inside.

Forensics were primitive enough at the time, but the Gardaí had a field day when they found that taxi containing three weapons and its forensics treasure. We had been extremely lucky to have been as successful as we were.

The cops and the Government were at sixes and sevens. Paddy Cooney, the Justice Minister, had been abroad when the shit hit the fan. His head would have rolled anywhere else, but somehow, he kept his job.

Raids were taking place all over the country. The usual suspects were taken in for questioning. The authorities were chasing shadows. They ranted and raved on television and radio. Politicians north of the border scorned and ridiculed the southern Government. I'm sure, privately, these right-wing authorities were swearing revenge for the embarrassment we had heaped upon them.

To rub salt into their wounds, a band called The Wolfe Tones released a catchy song celebrating the genius of the escape. The Government promptly banned it from the airwaves, but it reached number one in Ireland and topped the charts for 12 weeks. Over the next few months, we would be passing shops and open windows belting out the chorus of The Helicopter Song:

'Up like a bird and high over the city,
Three men are missing, I heard the warder cry,
Sure, it must have been a bird that flew into the prison,
Or one of those new Ministers said the warder from Mountjoy.' – Brian
Warfield

# 30

I kept an even-lower profile than usual for the next few days. I intended returning to my position as GHQ Director of Intelligence but as it turned out, I wouldn't be in the job much longer – 13 days to be exact. I had been on the run for more than two years, but it took the cops less than two weeks to arrest me over the helicopter escape.

Somehow, they also knew exactly where to put their hands on me. I have had plenty of time to think about this over the years. I can only conclude that I had been handed up. It is the only way they could have captured me so quickly.

I was leaving the Rathmines flat on a cold November evening. Earlier, I had called a woman volunteer, whose job was to drive me around and give me cover as her husband in the event of us being pulled over. She wasn't known to the authorities and she actually owned the car she was driving. I was walking towards this car when a man approached me flashing a badge.

'Special Branch,' he said. 'What's your name?'

'John Patrick Murtagh,' I bluffed.

I had a fair idea this wasn't a random check.

'I am arresting you on suspicion of being a member of an illegal organisation,' he continued. 'Put your hands on the roof of the car.'

I didn't resist and he frisked me. I was unarmed. I usually carried a gun with me in the countryside, in case I had to commandeer a car in an emergency, but in the city, I rarely felt the need.

He handcuffed me, bundled me into the back of an unmarked garda car and sat beside me as another officer drove the few hundred yards to Rathmines Garda Station. They put me into a small interview room, leaving me alone to stew for a while. Every so often the door would open and an eye would appear at the crack. After staring at me for a moment, it would disappear again. They had arrested the woman too and threatened to charge her too unless I confessed to being a member of the IRA.

'I'm telling you boys, don't let her out, whatever you do,' I told one of my interrogators. 'She is one mad bitch. Hold on to her at all costs!'

After that they didn't try that one again and they promptly released her. They probably knew they had nothing on her and I wouldn't be giving her up.

Around 11 that night, they moved me by armed convoy to the Bridewell, Dublin's main Garda station, situated near to the Special Criminal Court where I would be tried. I was taken inside, and a cop signed for me, like some parcel. Then they put me in a cell on the first floor. They didn't disturb me again for the rest of the night.

Early next morning, they woke me and asked did I want to wash. I followed a Garda to a small sink with soap and a towel. It wasn't much of a wash, but it was all that was on offer.

When I got back to the cell, I found a pot of tea, a beaker of milk, a hardboiled egg, and two thick slices of stale pan bread with a pat of butter. It reminded me of the flat in Clontarf – minus the coffee!

It didn't take long for the serious stuff to start. I was taken downstairs for interview, as they call it. The designated Interview Room was just a cell by another name. The furniture consisted of a small rectangular table, tight against a wall, and three chairs. A Special Branch detective was sitting on one of them. He invited me to sit and another Garda in civvies joined us. They introduced themselves, giving their names and ranks. I don't remember either.

'What is your name?' one intoned, formally. 'John Patrick Murtagh,' I replied.

'Come on, now,' one of them said, 'We know you're Brendan Hughes. Why don't you stop all this nonsense, and just tell us the truth?'

Once I realised they knew exactly who I was, I thought the best course of action was to shut up. I told them I would be observing my right to remain silent. For the next few hours, they nagged and questioned me. They would change personnel every 30 or 40 minutes. Two in, two out.

In an effort to engage, the training manual probably advises empathy. The old 'good cop, bad cop' routine. At one stage one of them said to me: 'Look, Brendan, I'm sure you're tired of all these questions. Why don't we take a little break? Tell me, do you play football? Let's talk about football for a while.'

I fixed him with a stare, saying: 'I don't play football. I don't watch football. And I know fuck all about football. But let me tell you something else for nothing. If I did know anything about football, you are the last people I would discuss it with.'

I fell silent again, so he changed tack.

'Look at the state of you, sitting there facing all these years in prison. Mallon and Twomey are out there drinking and enjoying themselves. They're probably walking about in carpet that depth,' he said, indicating about a foot deep in luxury.

I ignored all of this, and so it carried on, hour after hour. I did get the odd cup of tea, and a dinner of sorts.

It always seemed to me that when you get arrested, the smart thing to do is let them get on with it. Making explanations and excuses is like struggling after you've stepped into quicksand. The more you talk, the more you struggle, the deeper you go. So, it's best just to shut the fuck up.

Back in the cell, I had hardly laid back on the dirty bed and closed my eyes when I heard the lock in the door. A big smiling face appeared. It was the duty sergeant or some such like, the man in charge of me. He looked around to make sure nobody was looking and said, 'Brendan, I know the grub here is really bad. I'd like to give you a couple of sandwiches. My wife gave them to me for my lunch. Do you want them?'

This act of uninvited kindness took me by surprise, but I was all the more grateful for it. They were delicious. No matter how dire things may be, there are kind, generous people about. I didn't get his name but, if ever he reads this, I would like to thank him for the food, but more for being a decent human being. In those hectic days, decent people in positions of power were getting harder to come by.

I eventually fell asleep and they left me alone until morning. The following day was a replay.

At some stage, I was taken to stand in an ID parade. The person who walked along the line in front of us failed to pick out anyone.

During one of the interrogations, a disreputable little man obviously decided I was having things too easy. The prick, who was to my right, leaned forward, clenched his fist and put it in my face.

'I'm sick of you,' he said. 'If you don't start talking, I'll give you this.'

And he pushed his fist into my face.

I turned to face him. I rubbed my chin and said to him, 'Come on, you miserable little shit. Give it your best shot. I know your kind. You're just a bully. All bullies are cowards. Come on, what the fuck are you waiting for?'

I continued to goad him, telling him he had no bottle now that someone was standing up to him. I practically invited him to hit me.

By this time, the other detective was pissing himself laughing at him.

The little prick got up and left. I think that must have been the last throw of the dice for them. They didn't threaten me after that. I have to say that in all the times I was arrested, he was the only little shit to ever threaten me, or to mistreat me in any way.

The same insignificant little person, who doesn't even deserve a mention, went on to make a name for himself as a member of the so-called Heavy Gang, a squad of Gardaí sanctioned to beat confessions out of people, including three innocent men convicted for the Sallins train robbery a few years later.

I returned to my cell and was left in peace again until the following morning, but they were far from finished with me.

The key turned in the lock early enough. A Garda motioned me to gather my things and walk out with him. I stepped onto the landing but when I looked over the edge of the walkway, I couldn't believe my eyes. Dozens of Special Branch detectives were packed in below like sardines, all staring up at me.

My escort marched me down the stairs and the throng parted as I walked through them towards the Interview Room.

'Sit down,' a detective invited. 'Now, tell me your real name?'

As usual, I stayed silent and after asking a few more silly questions, and getting no answers, all pretext was abandoned. They called the Garda who had brought me down and told him to put me back in my cell. Out we marched from the room, to repeat the process I had just gone through, except in reverse. I expected each one of those cops would remember me in future. If I ever got out of here and returned to operations, these detectives would know what I looked like. I expect they were also hoping some of them might recognise me so they could charge me with something else. On that score, they were wasting their time.

A while later, a Garda turned the key, told me to get my belongings together again and follow him.

'What belongings?' I asked, but he didn't reply. 'Where am I going now?' I asked.

'I think they're letting you go,' he said.

I was delighted to hear this, but I had my doubts.

The detectives standing below were gone. The floor was empty. I was told to walk towards two large, barred gates leading to the street. My spirits soared as I shuffled towards them.

'Where do you think you're going?' came a voice from a little room to my left. 'Come in here for a minute, I have something for you.'

I turned to face the door and had barely taken a step when two detectives came out of the room.

'I am charging you with being a member of an illegal organisation, namely the IRA. Have you anything to say?' one of them intoned, before cautioning me formally and reading me my rights.

I didn't speak. When I returned to my cell, I sat down and read the charge sheet they had given me.

'So much for letting me go,' I thought.

Sometime later, I was taken downstairs again, handcuffed to a Garda and taken outside. I didn't see the open sky for long. We joined more of his colleagues in the back of a prison minibus. Sirens screamed from several unmarked patrol cars the entire short journey to Green Street Courthouse, home of the no-jury Special Criminal Court.

The 'Special Crim' was originally set up in 1939 to counter an IRA campaign during World War II, and was reconstituted in its current form in 1972 in response to the upsurge in modern IRA activity. Just in time for me to face it.

People stopped and stared as we sped past, probably wondering what kind of lunatic was inside. When we reached Green Street, the doors of the courthouse yard swung open, and we drove inside. My Garda companion took me to a holding cell, removed the handcuffs and the door clanked behind him as he walked out. When I looked around, there was another man in the corner, staring at me.

'How are you doing?' I asked him, glad to have someone to talk to other than cops.

'I'm doing okay, under the circumstances,' he said. 'What are you charged with?' I asked.

'It's to do with the helicopter escape,' he replied.

I eyed him with suspicion. I had never seen him before. And I wasn't aware of any arrests in connection with the job. I decided not to engage too much until I knew a bit more about him.

'What about you?' he asked. 'What are you charged with?' 'Membership,' I said.

I discouraged further conversation, passing the time reading the names written on the wall by prisoners who had passed this way before. Some had also written their charges, others their sentences, and the date when they had received them. A lot of less than complimentary descriptions – and suggestions of what they might do with them – were made in relation to the judges. When the wall was full up, the authorities would paint it. I would be seeing several fresh coats over the next few years.

Hours later, the door opened, and I was led up a narrow concrete staircase, into the body of the court. I was ushered into the dock where two rows of seats faced an empty judicial bench. As I entered and sat down, everyone seemed to be staring at me. Gardaí, secretaries, typists, and a few people in ridiculous wigs and gowns.

'You've got some cheek to be staring at *me*,' I thought.

After a while, three judges took their place on the bench. Some formalities were gone through with various people coming forward to whisper to one or other of them. Glances were thrown in my direction, a lot of nodding. A lot of bullshit – all part of the charade.

Everyone was called to order and we proceeded with the case of the State vs Francis Bernard Hughes. They had got my name wrong, but I wasn't about to correct them. In jail, everyone would call me Barney, which I didn't discourage either, believing it would only add to the confusion.

A Garda read out the charges: IRA membership; possession of a gun at Mountjoy Jail on October 31; and conspiracy to forcibly release Seamus Twomey from prison.

'How do you plead?' they asked. 'Not guilty.'

This triggered another flurry of whispers, and nods. Papers were shuffled and I was pretty much ignored, apart from a few gestures in my direction.

A judge remanded me in custody, and I was taken back downstairs to rejoin the other man. A tray of food arrived, which we ate in silence. When the door opened, we were both handcuffed to two Gardaí.

The irony wasn't lost on me. Two weeks ago, I had helped break three men out of Mountjoy Jail. Now, I was heading there myself.

We drove up the avenue to the front gates. Once inside, I was taken, still handcuffed, into a room laid out in cubicles. The handcuffs were removed, and I was told to wait. I sat on a narrow bench, waiting to see what would come next. A large screw made an appearance.

'Strip,' he ordered.

'Go fuck yourself,' I replied. 'Go and fucking strip yourself.'

'Look,' he said, 'There's no point being difficult. Everybody coming in here has to strip, bathe, and get clean prison-issue clothes. No exceptions.'

'Let's get this straight,' I told him. 'I am not stripping. I am not bathing, as you put it. And I am definitely not wearing your fucking prison-issue clothes. I'm happy with the clothes I'm presently wearing. Now, fuck off and annoy someone else.'

He stared at me, looking like he didn't know what to do next. 'I'll be back,' he said.

That was the last I saw of him. Another screw came and told me to follow him. He took me further into the prison, to the first-floor landing, known as 'The Twos'. I found myself in a cell with Dermot Teeling once more.

'I forgot to tell you about all that shit they go through on the way in,' he said, kindly. 'They try that on with everyone.' 'Don't worry about it, it's okay,' I replied.

I still didn't trust him, but he was one hell of an actor if he wasn't genuine. I just couldn't figure out what he had to do with the escape.

The door opened and a screw appeared with a tray of food. More rock-hard boiled eggs.

'More fucking eggs,' I muttered.

This being my first time in prison, the smell of the place did nothing for my appetite. All I did was drink the tea, which wasn't bad if you like tea, which I didn't. It was a case of take it or leave it.

It took them about an hour and a half to process a transfer warrant to the top-security Portlaoise Prison, where all republican prisoners had been sent shortly after the helicopter escape. They handcuffed us one more time and led us out to a waiting minibus. It was part of a large convoy that included a spare vehicle in case of a breakdown. It also contained two jeeps with 12 soldiers cradling high-velocity rifles, two unmarked cars with armed Special Branch detectives and a standard, marked patrol car. Four motorbike Gardaí rode point to make sure this convoy was stopping for nobody or anything, even red lights. They weren't taking any chance that other mad bastards like me might be around to engineer another escape.

I knew this road well. Seán Treacy's pub was only a few miles away from the jail – some of the screws even drank there.

Many people may find 'screws' a pejorative term but I bear no ill will against prison officers or individual Gardaí. A few gave me a hard time, but the vast majority were decent people doing a job. Like our side, there were mostly good, but some bad. And I'm sure there isn't a single soul embroiled in that conflict who might wish they had behaved differently on occasion.

Portlaoise Prison is a large rectangular, four-storey building, situated on the outskirts of the Midlands town from which it takes its name. It is a grim, foreboding and unwelcoming legacy of British rule in Ireland.

When we got out of the minibus outside the gates, armed soldiers were looking down at us from the several pillboxes that dotted its thick walls.

There are three sets of gates set into the main entrance to the prison. All of them are unlocked separately. The solid, outside gate opened to let us in. The second one, also solid, would swing inwards only after we heard the first one clank shut behind us. A screw looked out the peephole in the middle gate to make sure everything was in order before opening it. The final gate consisted of thick, metal bars. Two screws waited on either side of this gate until the middle gate was closed before turning separate keys to allow everyone inside.

Once there, we walked along what looked like a garden path. Even in November, flowers were growing on either side of it. A large clock tower was facing us: the time was frozen at twenty past four. I couldn't help but think there was a reason why nobody bothered to repair it. This was a place designed to make time stand still.

At the end of the path stood another, smaller gate, covered in sheet metal. On the far side of it, we were taken into a room to be searched. My few personal belongings were taken from me. I was patted down, and my shoes removed.

The screws escorted us the short distance to E Block, home to republican prisoners. On the way there, we had to negotiate several more gates. Each one of them was manned by an individual screw with a separate key.

I was shown to an unlocked cell and a screw told me I would have the place to myself. Lucky me! It was pretty miserable, even by my low expectations. Flaking paint with a single window high up on the cell wall. Just over the door, the only light was a dim, 40-watt bulb. A six-inch heating pipe ran the length of the back wall. A steel bed with a thin mattress, three grey blankets, two sheets and a pillow neatly folded at the bottom sat perpendicular. In the corner behind the door, the toilet consisted of a small plastic pisspot, with no lid. A battered table and chair occupied the wall facing me. The table displayed a saucer, cup, plate and fork.

My abiding memory of the place is the smell of stale urine and faeces. Prisoners were subjected to slopping out their bodily waste.

After each lock-up period, we had to walk along our landings with our pisspots in hand to empty the contents down a sluice. Looking back, at least it was winter when I first arrived. In summer, the smell could be unbearable.

After a few prisoners had used the sluice, the floor became saturated from spills and overflows. There was no way of avoiding walking in this mess. Returning to our cells, we would trail it back on our shoes. The smell would permeate our sheets, our clothes, and of course our shoes. We took it with us everywhere we went, including on visits with our loved ones. After a while, we no longer even smelt it. What a fucking kip.

I was sitting on the edge of my bed staring into space, feeling sorry for myself, when the landing's IRA Commanding Officer (OC) stuck his head around the door.

'I'm just here to welcome you – if that's what it can be called, given the circumstances,' he said.

He gave me a rundown on how things worked. Every prison has its own ways of operating. I would later learn that circumstances can dictate very different experiences of doing time, even in the same prison.

He also told me that my court companion was an unfortunate newspaper seller who had been charged with the weapons found inside the abandoned taxi and with harbouring a fugitive.

It took me a few days to get the hang of life inside. At the start, the boredom was the worst. I was used to constant movement. The more time I had to think, the more frustrated I became. Over and over, the same question haunted me: How had they got me after only 13 days?

The Rathmines flat hadn't been used before. I had a clean car. They had been chasing me for two years and had never come close. I knew the helicopter job had upped the ante but how did they know I was involved? And how did they get the address of the flat?

On December 10, Mallon was recaptured in a dance hall, of all places.

He had been free for all of six weeks. I remember hearing the news as I lay in my cell. It would be several years before they caught J.B. or Twomey.

It might seem incredible looking back on it but after several court appearances I was granted bail, set at a hefty £15,000 – enough to buy a very nice house in Dublin at the time.

And so, just before Christmas 1973, I walked out of Portlaoise Prison.

# 31

After I got bail, I weighed my options. On the face of it, the evidence against me seemed flimsy. They had found my fingerprints on that damned map but the dabs of 11 others were also on it.

There were several plausible reasons for my prints being on it; I may even have been browsing it in the shop before someone else subsequently bought it. They had also found a false licence in the name of J.P. Murtagh in the Rathmines flat, but that was hardly enough to hang a man. Two people had taken a good look at me in an identity parade, but they failed, or perhaps they were unwilling, to pick me out of the line-up. And, of course, I was nowhere near Mountjoy on that helicopter.

The only evidence against me was the word of a senior Garda officer who refused to give the source of his information that I was a member of the IRA.

I was free at the moment and had no intention of going back inside. My trial was due to begin on February 4, 1974, but I had already decided to go on the run. When I failed to show for the first day of my trial, the judge issued an arrest warrant.

My main defence lawyer, Tony Hederman, was rated among the best in the country. I met him that evening and he persuaded me to turn up the following day, confident that the prosecution didn't have a leg to stand on. He gave me a guarantee that I would walk, telling me I would beat all the charges. The evidence was circumstantial at best and there was no way they could convict.

I studied his face and attitude. I was convinced he could, and would, do what he said. After further assurances, I agreed to show.

So, on a beautiful, crisp, February day, accompanied by one of my bailsmen, Bill Fuller, who had put up £5,000 for me (veteran Clones Sinn Féin councillor Frank McCaughey also put up £5,000), I walked straight into the courtroom.

Bill was one of those larger than life characters. He owned a popular music haunt, The Old Shieling hotel in Raheny on Dublin's northside. Over the years, I had enjoyed many a great night there at the VIP table in the company of various politicians such as the future Fianna Fail Tánaiste (Deputy Prime Minister) and presidential candidate, Brian Lenihan Snr, and a coterie of well-known sports stars and celebrities, including the singer Dolly McMahon.

The future Taoiseach (Prime Minister) Charlie Haughey, who was sacked from the cabinet after being implicated in an alleged gun-running plot to help besieged Northern nationalists, was also a regular visitor, though I never had the pleasure of his company.

When I walked into the courthouse, I made it all the way to the bench before the President of the High Court, Justice O'Keeffe, spotted me. Instead of being grateful for my change of mind, he glared at me and demanded to know what a man with a warrant out for his arrest was doing standing in his court.

A Garda sergeant moved to put his hand on my shoulder, to arrest me but O'Keeffe roared at him, 'Don't arrest him, you fool, don't you know that you cannot arrest anyone within the confines of the court?'

He continued to glare at me, like he had just stood on dogshit.

Then he said that he 'could not understand how a man for whom a bench warrant had been issued could walk through a ring of Gardaí into the court without being arrested.'

All of the relevant parties were summoned to a huddle around the bench. Lots of glances were cast in my direction as they whispered among themselves.

They seemed to be at a complete loss as to how they would get me legally from the floor of the court to my seat in the dock. All they really had to do was ask. In the end, I got tired of waiting and I took my seat beside Dermot Teeling.

I told the judge I had missed the previous day's proceedings because I had been making arrangements for my three young children to attend school in the South.

When things got started, we were treated to a detailed rendition of the events leading up to the escape.

Irish Helicopters was represented by Capt John Hobday, fresh from being subjected to an IRA hijacking of his own in Co Donegal a few weeks earlier. He had been forced to fly over a police station in Strabane, Co Tyrone, where bombs packed in milk churns had been thrown into the barracks below.

Capt Hobday confirmed he had taken a booking in the name of a Mr Leonard. The pilot, Capt Boyes was unavailable to appear in court that day.

A few months later he was involved in a helicopter crash in Co Tipperary. According to his nephew, Stephen Boyes, although his uncle was badly injured and was not supposed to be moved, his wife and a daughter spirited him out of hospital 'and got him up the road' to his family home in Northern Ireland. He would never testify. The kidnapped taxi driver, Hugh Collins, and Martin Delaney, a Mountjoy screw, were also there to give evidence.

At the end of the day, the court adjourned, and the judge remanded me in custody. Teeling was remanded on continuing bail.

The court resumed at 10 the following morning. The first person called was the real John Patrick Murtagh, a farmer, who explained that the motor tax office had lost his licence when he posted it for renewal. That office had issued me with the same licence, but that's a story for another time.

A detective garda Flynn detailed my arrest. In the boot of the woman's car, they had found wigs, maps, and an envelope with Murtagh's name on it. He also reported that in the aftermath of the escape, Gardaí had found the abandoned taxi with the weapons concealed inside and poor Dermot's fingerprints on the boot.

The following day, Thursday, the defence opened its case.

My counsel demanded the immediate dismissal of all charges against me due to lack of evidence. He pointed out the flaws in the prosecution case, particularly the ambiguity over the fingerprints on the map and a failure to place me in the Leinster Road flat in Rathmines between October 7 and 31, during the alleged hatching of the hijacking.

Further, he said, there was no evidence to connect me with the helicopter, or the taxi. There was no evidence to connect me with any person identified as a conspirator. And there was nothing to put me in a helicopter at Mountjoy Jail on October 31, or any other date.

The State, he said, alleged that I had been seen in the company of one of the escapees, Kevin Mallon. There was no evidence before the court to say that the man who someone had seen with me was, in fact, the named escapee. Plus, two people had failed to pick me out in an ID parade.

O'Keeffe and his buddies went off into a back room to consider things, or maybe to drink tea or coffee or something. Before long they were back on the bench and he was telling us that, based on forensic evidence, we both had a case to answer.

My fate was sealed by the fingerprints on the map, Dermot's by his on the boot of the car.

On Friday, February 8, the court adjourned to let the three judges consider their verdict.

Hederman came down to see me in my cell below the court.

'Congratulations,' he said, sticking out his hand for me to shake. 'I told you I would win the case.'

'How do you know I'm getting off?' I asked.

'The prosecuting counsel has just shaken hands with me and complimented me on the result,' he replied. 'They have conceded.'

I was, of course, delighted to hear this, as was Dermot. But I still had my doubts and, when the court resumed, they were realised in full.

Back in the dock we listened to some preliminaries, and O'Keeffe proceeded to find us both guilty. The verdict was all the more crushing after Hederman's hollow promise. In fairness to him, he was fuming.

'I will take this case all the way to Europe, and at my own expense,' he told us. 'This is the worst travesty of justice I have ever experienced. I just can't believe it.'

This righteous indignation gave me little comfort. To him it was a game. Losing probably hurt his ego but he was no crusader.

We were both sentenced to three years. O'Keeffe attempted to soften the blow, telling us he had shown leniency because we had no previous convictions.

Even though I was guilty, and I had received a relatively light sentence, I was furious. I had been sacrificed at the altar of political expediency. The escape had embarrassed the Government and to hell with the law. Someone had to pay.

I should never even have been anywhere near a court. I had been betrayed by some low-life tout. Still, in hindsight, living the kind of life I did, I should have expected such treachery.

I never doubted Hederman's sincerity. He did his best. Everyone thought he had won, including himself, but the powers-that-be demanded a conviction and that's what they got. As usual, our first stop was Mountjoy. By now, the authorities had given up trying to strip republicans on their way into prison, so we sailed straight through to our cell and some more hard-boiled eggs.

Then it was off to serve out my sentence in Portlaoise.

I would be lying through my teeth if I said jail was ever anything but a hateful experience. I knew it had always been on the cards, so the thought of it didn't come as a shock, but the reality still took a lot of getting used to.

For now, at least, my high-octane life became one of caged subservience, where every decision would be made for me, even small ones like switching on and off a light or deciding to open a door. I would be spending years in a cell the size of an average bathroom. I would sleep, eat, socialise, piss and shit in that cubbyhole.

My cell was in E2, the republican block. I had to stand on the bed to see out the window. A screw is supposed to check every prisoner several times during the night to prevent suicides, or escapes. Like every other prisoner, I hung a coat over the peephole. No-one likes being spied upon when they're asleep.

In early November 1973, citing the helicopter escape, the Government had transferred every republican prisoner in the state, all 120 or so of us – to Portlaoise Prison, figuring it would be easier to manage us all in one place. Soldiers stood sentry with live ammunition. The gloves were well and truly off.

I asked Kevin Mallon if I could get on the escape committee. I knew it existed. Every republican prisoner of war has a duty to try to escape from jail, however short their sentence.

He refused, telling me an operation was already in train and my help wasn't required. I was pissed off with his attitude but I didn't have any choice but to accept this decision and get on with doing my time. Still, it didn't stop me from looking for weaknesses in the prison security.

I could have been paroled early had I been prepared to keep my nose clean but there was always the prospect of conflict with the authorities that would delay a man's release. I had no intention of staying in jail a minute longer than I had to.

# 32

To prisoners and screws alike, Portlaoise Prison was known as 'The Bog'. The name may derive from the surrounding landscape or the vernacular for a shithouse. Or maybe both.

The rebadged Maryborough Jail, built by the British in the 1830s, is set back just off the old Dublin Road on the outskirts of Portlaoise, some 50 miles from the capital. Nowadays, it is readily accessible by motorway, and this Midlands town has become part of the wider Dublin commuter belt. In the early 1970s, its remoteness made it a tough place for visitors to get to, particularly from the North, as there was no direct public transport.

It was also constantly overcrowded. By the mid-1970s, it had developed a notorious reputation for the ill-treatment of inmates, including forced strip searches. In 1977, prisoners were forced to go on hunger strike to demand a public inquiry into conditions.

I knew the drill from the time I spent there on remand before my trial, but this was different somehow. When you're sitting in your cell, you're already counting the days and they seem endless. Other men have told me of the relief they felt after sentencing. At least they knew what time they were facing.

I never felt that way.

The landing OC paid a visit to reiterate the rules – no talking to screws and all business was to be conducted through army command structures. He knew I had heard it all before.

In general, prisoners would spend as much time as possible outdoors. They would walk in small groups around in a circle, or up and down the middle of the yard. We talked about everything. Anything to pass the time, I suppose. Football, women, politics, and of course, escape. New arrivals would be grilled for all the latest news from the outside, particularly on how the war was going.

Some prisoners would also spend a lot of time making arts and crafts, mostly in the workshop situated on my landing. They would make replica wooden harps, Celtic crosses and other artefacts with intricate designs to present to friends and family or to be sold to raise money for prisoners' welfare, or their dependants. Some of these pieces would adorn many a cell and have since become valuable collectors' items.

Cards were also a popular pastime. Endless games of Don generated raised voices and bad-tempered arguments.

There were regular football matches, both Gaelic, and although frowned upon, soccer. Every summer, prisoners would organise an entire week of sports. Running, volleyball, handball and sprints were all taken very seriously. Medals were awarded. Nobody liked losing. Strangely, there was even a long-distance running event.

Mallon would sometimes run a book. Gamblers would stake bars of chocolate, or cigarettes.

But we all knew even then that passing the time was the real prize.

I had ample opportunity to study my new surroundings. A scattering of buildings framed by walls 25-feet high and very thick at the base.

Within the walls, 'ordinary prisoners' ran the prison, I observed. When I say 'ran', I mean that they did all the work. Without them the prison couldn't operate. Republicans didn't do jail work. We kept our cells clean and tidy. We even painted them in prison-issue pastel shades of green and yellow, probably designed to have a calming effect. We maintained our own landings, recreational areas and workshops but workwise, that was it.

Ordinary prisoners did the rest, including the kitchens, supervised by numerous screws. In return for all this effort and compliance, they would get 50% remission.

There were other buildings within the confines of the outer wall. There was a disused church, a former cellblock, and an administration block. The authorities had converted these buildings into offices and storage facilities. All the better to administer justice to the guests of the nation. The tower framing the frozen clock was attached to the administration block. Two exercise yards ran parallel along either side of our rectangular block. Adjacent to the front yard, was a medical building, used by shrinks, dentists, and regular doctors.

Heating was peat-driven from the plentiful supply beyond the walls. The flat-roofed, single-storey boilerhouse attached to the laundry on our first-floor landing would later become our springboard to freedom.

The governor's house was situated within the perimeter, but it was separated by an inner wall, just as high as the outer one, which formed a triangular oasis of sorts. A small, barred gate set into the wall afforded him access to the prison. A stout, wooden door was his exit to the outside world. Later, it would become our way out too.

I didn't have any direct dealings with the governor, but we would see him around the place and his sullen presence set a dour tone. I won't elaborate but suffice to say he blighted the lives of many men who were just trying to get their time in.

Everywhere you went, screws were watching, listening, and taking notes. They might have looked disinterested, but we knew they were on the ball.

When the jail was running smoothly, conditions were tolerable. But, when it wasn't, life inside could be hellish.

Among any large body of men, or women, you will always find a few petty-minded bastards. The Portlaoise screws were no exception. Most were fine but the bad ones I will always remember.

I chose to do my time in as light-hearted a way as possible. As I said before, I have always made a point of hanging around people with a sense of humour.

Like a lot of other prisoners, I had good days and very bad days. Depression took its toll but even now I somehow always manage to struggle out from underneath the black cloud when it hovers over me.

I spent a lot of time with a larger-than-life character called Liam Fagan from Ravensdale, near the Co Louth border with South Armagh. He had a terrific sense of humour. He built a loom, and along with a friend of his from Dundalk, known as 'The Minister', we would spend many an hour under his instruction weaving bookmarks, guitar straps and belts for Irish dancers.

Liam's mission in life at that time was to raise money to build a memorial to Michael McVerry, a South Armagh man, who had been killed while attacking an RUC station in Keady only a few months before. McVerry's exploits were legendary in IRA circles. He tunnelled his way out of the Curragh prison camp and later lost an arm in a premature explosion. Yet, he still went back on active service.

Liam had everyone doing work for him in their cells and in the workshop. We made Claddagh rings from two-shilling pieces and harps and crosses from wood and matchsticks.

Liam would spend his entire day ensuring our output was up to scratch. He would also suss out new arrivals to gauge their usefulness, and their willingness to join in.

He would fulfil his goal: the memorial was erected the following year near the place where Michael McVerry was killed.

I had always felt more comfortable working with country people, but Liam took it to extremes. He had no time at all for Belfast men, or 'Shafties' as he called them. Most of the Belfast men had cells on E3, the landing he was on. He used to torture them!

We all had large, aluminium beakers for carrying milk. They were around eight inches high by six inches in diameter. Liam would jam his mug onto his foot using tea towels. Pretending to be asleep, he would then stick his leg out from under the blankets on the blindside of the screw at the peephole and begin tapping the heating pipe that ran down the length of the block.

This would go on for hours, driving the Belfast men mad. Some of them would demand a move. Landing meetings would be held to get to the bottom of it but to no avail. He was never caught. He eventually stopped of his own accord. I think he took pity on them, but he would never admit this.

Next door to me on E2 was a man called Peadar Mohan from Clontibret, Co Monaghan. He was a lovely man and a solid republican. We had operated together on the outside and we would end up working together on the inside as well.

# 33

I was growing increasingly frustrated. The IRA command in the prison was continuing to ignore my incessant pleas to join the escape committee. In late June or early July, I found out why. The authorities had discovered a partially constructed tunnel outside the external wall, aimed towards the exercise yard at the back of our block. Several local men had been arrested.

I asked no questions. I didn't have to. I had a very good idea who was involved, and I was looking forward to a reunion with at least one of the unfortunate architects behind the attempt.

Sure enough, my old friend Ned Bailey was charged with having details of the tunnel. When he arrived in the prison, he looked worn out and slightly dishevelled after a few days in custody. He was taken for debriefing by republican staff, and I bided my time until the fuss died down before going to see him. I had questions of my own.

'What the fuck happened you, Ned?' I inquired. 'You look a bit rough. Never mind, a few days in this resort will soon straighten you out.'

'Brendan,' he said. 'Am I glad to see you. I'm fine. I've had no sleep for a couple of days, that's all.'

Tired as Ned was, I wanted the full story.

'It was that headcase, Seán Treacy,' Ned lamented. 'He was staying in my house and he had maps and plans of the tunnel. When he went to bed that night, he put them under the mattress. The Gardaí hit the place at dawn. Treacy was on his toes right away, out the window and gone before they could put a hand on him. He got clean away. Unfortunately, he didn't take the stuff from under the mattress and the cops found it. You can imagine the drop I got when they put it on the table.'

'What did you tell them?' I asked.

'Nothing, at that stage,' Ned replied. 'So, they arrested me and whipped me off to the Garda barracks. I accepted responsibility for anything found in my house. I had no choice, Brendan. They would have charged Beth if I hadn't, and I couldn't have that.'

Ned broke off the conversation when a couple of welfare officers arrived to organise his visits, but resumed his story shortly after completing the formalities.

'The Gardaí asked me what was I doing with all of the plans?' he said. 'I told them I was building a house.'

'What did they say to that?' I asked, smiling.

'When I told them it was a house I was building, I could see they were trying not to break out laughing,' he said. 'To tell you the truth Brendan, I was smiling myself. Both of them left the room and I could hear them talking and laughing outside the door.

'Eventually, one of them stuck his head in and with a big grin on his face, he asked me, "How many bedrooms Ned?" "What do you mean?" I asked him. "How many bedrooms in that house you're going to build?!" I told him to fuck off. They left me alone after that, the bastards! I mean, what else could I say? I stuck to my story and here I am.'

'Ned, my friend, you are a sight for sore eyes,' I said. 'Apart from the circumstances, it's great to see you again.'

'How are things with yourself ?' Ned asked. 'You were very unlucky.'

'Ned, I don't think bad luck had anything to do with it,' I replied. 'I wouldn't even put it down to loose talk, downright touting was to blame. They couldn't catch me for over two years and suddenly I get caught inside two weeks. Anyway, here I am. When you are in court again?'

'My trial is set for the 29th of this month,' Ned replied. 'I was only arrested at the end of June, and here I am up for trial at the end of July.'

'That's the Special Crim for you,' I said. 'They knew what they were doing when they set that up.'

We sat in silence for a moment. I had a question for Ned but after what he had just gone through and knowing what he was facing, I was nervous about asking it. I took a chance anyway.

'Ned, tell me this, do you think we can get some explosives smuggled in here?' He didn't bat an eyelid.

'To tell you the truth Brendan, I was considering that myself before I got caught,' he said. 'I had an idea how we might get it in. P.J. and I discussed it in detail. He's confident it can be done. Why do you ask?'

'Well,' I replied. 'I've not been allowed on the escape committee, but I have the bones of an idea. Don't tell anyone I asked you that question. I'll come back to you later if I ever get onto the committee.'

'No problem, I'm always at home these days,' Ned smiled. 'Same as that Ned, same as that,' I replied.

# 34

I had become despondent, but my conversation with Ned had lifted me no end. I would work on my own escape plan. I already had a way out in my head.

I had spent the months since I was sentenced looking into every aspect of how the prison operated. Experience had taught me that even the most secure places have basic flaws. I happened to be very good at finding them.

Trying to find that chink in the armour appeared daunting. The army sentries overlooked the walls from every angle and had even mounted a light machine gun on the roof of our block. The soldiers also had an observation post in the central administration block, a tall building with a parapet running all the way around the roof. They had an excellent view of the front and back gates and the 100 yards of open ground between the main cell block housing the IRA prisoners and the governor's house. They also conducted regular foot patrols in the narrow no-man's land between the coiled razor wire, marking the boundary of the back exercise yard, and the outer wall where the tunnel was detected.

Anywhere you went in the prison, you had to negotiate double, and sometimes, treble gates. Razor wire was also strung along the top of the chain-link fence that enclosed the two exercise yards that ran down either side of our block. On the far side of both, there were more rolls unfurled on the ground. Anti-helicopter wires strung from the roof to the top of the outside wall shrouded the back exercise yard. These had also been wrapped with razor wire to prevent anyone being able to climb up on them.

Underneath our cell block was a cellar, running the full length of the building. Access was possible but only by opening several doors. The screws checked it every day, sometimes several times. I could only imagine the thickness of the foundations.

At night, floodlights bathed the entire compound. The beams perched on the edge of the roof of every building augmented standalone lamp posts dotted at regular intervals throughout. These were designed to cast no shadow. There would be no hiding place within the walls of Portlaoise Prison.

During the night, the screws would check every cell on E Block regularly, starting at the bottom landing, E1, and working their way up to E4. They also patrolled outside the buildings day and night. There was a headcount several times a day to make sure we were all present. Prisoners used to make life hard for the screws by hiding during the counts. It was all about resistance. I think most of the screws just gave the correct number regardless.

Every time you left the cell block, you were counted off and an escort would accompany you. It didn't matter if you were going to the doctor or on a visit, you had an escort. Wearing his medical-officer hat, a screw would even stay in the doctor's room with you while you were discussing your symptoms. No privacy, even there.

This regime even extended to the mail, which was opened and read before they gave it to you. They could even see your feet while you were sitting in a toilet cubicle.

It was hard to find space. There were four landings in the block with an open area in the centre. Every landing had the same number of cells, running down each side. There was strong wire mesh between the floors to stop men falling, jumping or being thrown to the inner courtyard below.

The centre of the roof was one long skylight, running the entire length of the block. Soldiers had built two footbridges over it to allow them to cross quickly. On one end of E4 there was a set of unused stairs, which led to the roof. This door was locked on the inside and sandbagged on the outside.

This much I knew. But I could only surmise there were patrols outside the walls to contend with too.

While my mind was working overtime in a vain attempt to figure my way out, I happened to meet Martin McAllister from South Armagh. He was on the escape committee. One day, he showed me something that was gnawing at him.

'I've been watching this for some time, and I believe it has serious prospects,' he said, beckoning me from my cell one morning. 'It's easier to explain when you're looking at it. I've brought it to the committee, but they haven't shown any interest. I know it has potential.'

Martin brought me to his cell on the top landing. After checking there were no screws around, he stood on top of the bed, motioning me to join him.

'Do you see that wall at the end of the central administration block?' he gestured. 'That's not the outside wall – though it's hard to tell from here. It actually divides the main prison area from the governor's house and grounds.

If you look carefully, you'll see a small door. That door leads to the governor's grounds. It's a wooden door, but there's a barred, metal gate just behind it.

Now, look over the top of that wall, and you can see the outside wall. If you look very closely, you'll just be able to make out the top of another door. That one's in the outside wall. That door, my friend, leads to freedom.'

We climbed down and sat on the bed.

'I've been playing with this idea for a long time,' Martin said. 'But no-one gives it any value. I even requested a change of cell, knowing this one would give me a better view.'

He turned and looked at me.

'If we can get as far as that gate without being shot and we can get it open, we're out of here,' he said. That's how the governor and his family leave.

It stands to reason. If anyone in that house wants to go out at night, this is how they do it. After all, you couldn't have such respectable people, meeting riff-raff like us or expecting the screws to open the main gates for them every time.'

He was scanning my face for a reaction.

'My first impressions are good, Martin,' I said. 'But how do we get past the soldiers on the roof of the admin block? We'd have to run towards them, and below them. We'd be sitting ducks.'

'I have that covered,' he said. 'They come down off that roof when we come back in out of the exercise yard. They only stay there while we have outside access. If we choose the right time to move, there will be no-one between us and that inner gate.'

I agreed the plan was worthy of serious consideration and promised to give it more thought.

'Who else knows?' I asked.

'Only those on the committee,' he said. 'But they haven't even bothered to take a proper look. I suppose they couldn't see beyond the tunnel.'

'Well, if they're not impressed, I am,' I told him. 'It's different. It's definitely outside the box. It's obvious the screws haven't seen the possibility any more than the committee. If the screws have overlooked it, we're halfway there.'

I asked Martin whether he had been monitoring the governor's movements.

'I've often seen him use the inner gate to come into the prison, but to be honest I've never seen that door in the outside wall open,' he replied. 'His movements are unpredictable. We could never depend on getting hold of him and forcing him to open that outside door. Our best bet is to make plans of our own. We need a key.'

'Or explosives,' I ventured.

'Yes, if we had some,' Martin replied. 'I can assure you we don't have any.'

'Leave it with me,' I said. 'I'll work on it and in the meantime, you can keep a close eye on the governor. We don't even know if that outside gate's in use or whether it's sealed shut.'

When I got back to my cell, I mulled this gem of information again and again. I had been analysing the security measures for months, but this just might be the flaw I had been looking for.

I had approached Mallon several times, telling him I might have a plan to empty the jail. He hadn't even given me a hearing, saying they were working on something else. I was now sure that this 'something else' was the tunnel. Who knows would it ever have worked? Unlikely, given the foundations under that wall, but with those men from The Heath involved, it certainly stood a chance.

Anyway, that operation was over. Surely, I would now be given the hearing I craved?

Whatever the outcome, I knew I'd be working with Ned.

# 35

I was having breakfast when I heard Mallon waltzing along the corridor towards my cell. His fondness for singing the catchy rebel ballad, Óró Sé do Bheatha 'Bhaile, would often announce his arrival.

'I need to speak to you,' he said. 'You've been co-opted onto the escape committee. There's a meeting at half-ten, on the 3s, in Leo's cell.'

'That's no problem,' I told him. 'I'm not going anywhere today; my car is broken down.'

Mallon just shook his head.

'That's a shame,' he said. 'I'll get someone to look at it later. See you at the meeting.'

I could hardly wait. This was my chance to show my hand to the people that could give my plan the go-ahead.

That morning still stands out for me. It was the most excited I'd been since the helicopter job.

I had to squeeze into Leo Martin, the OC's cell. Mallon, Martin McAllister and two others were there ahead of me.

Mallon introduced me, telling the rest of them I had been very keen to join.

Bringing the meeting to order, we got straight down to business. First on the agenda was planning. Now that the tunnel attempt had failed, they were looking at smuggling in explosives to blow the back gate.

I could see the merit in this plan. It was the one nearest the back exercise yard and it was only a single, solid gate as opposed to the three at the front. But it was a plan I had already thought about and dismissed. I allowed them to elaborate further before being asked what I thought. I proceeded to dismantle the idea on the basis that it was under a pillbox that had been built specifically to thwart such an attempt.

The back gate was, in fact, to the right side of the main gate, rather than at the back of the prison. We would also be in full view of soldiers on the side of the roof where they had chosen to mount their machine gun. And if that wasn't discouragement enough, there was the further problem that we would have to use explosives just to get to the gate itself before blowing that too. The initial blast might give the soldiers justification to open fire on the basis that we were armed.

After agreeing to park that idea, the OC asked me if I had anything better. I began by ruling out both the front and back gates.

'The gate we need to use,' I said, 'Is the third gate.' 'What third gate?' someone asked.

'The gate Martin has been watching for some time,' I told them.

I laid out the opportunity in minute detail, beginning with the governor's residence and how he had his own private way in and out of the prison – a small gate in the outer wall.

'We would only need a tiny amount of explosives to blow our way through the inner gate into the governor's garden,' I said. 'Martin can confirm that it's made of wood and has a barred gate behind it. This is nothing special – it's like the regular barred gates you'll find all over this place. Blowing the lock won't be a problem.

We'll have to allow for the outside gate to be similar, so again that shouldn't be a problem.'

As I looked around the room, I could see they were interested. Even though Martin had told them about this, or tried, this time for whatever reason, they seemed to be all ears. Maybe it was because he was only 21 at the time and the rest of the men were older.

Nobody jumped in, so I continued.

'If you look at the security, and how it's structured, you'll see it is designed to cover the main and back gates. Maybe there were no decent explosives back in the day but for whatever reason, whoever built this place never considered the possibility that someone might use the governor's personal gate to escape.'

It also occurred to me that the escape committee hadn't considered it either. Then the questions began coming, thick and fast.

'That's all very well, but how do we get to the inner gate, without being shot?' Leo asked. 'What about the soldiers on the roofs?'

'The soldiers on the administration block leave their post after we're locked inside our cell block,' I said. 'God only knows what other posts are also stood down after they lock us up.'

I was confident the pitch was going well but I wanted to drive home the advantage.

'After studying this for several weeks, I suggest we make our move on a Sunday dinner time. Security is at its weakest then. There are no visits and we're locked inside the block. Have any of you noticed the rush of the screws to get out of the prison after mass on Sunday?'

'There is just one thing,' Mallon said. 'How do we get out of our block? If we blow our way out, the alarm will go off straight away and we would still have the open space to cross to get to the first gate.'

'No, we'll already have a key,' I countered. 'There are two screws on E2 on Sunday morning and another on the flat boiler house roof, accessible from the laundry.

Once we're locked inside for the day, one of the two screws on the landing opens the laundry door to let the other one in. He, in turn, opens the outside door to let the third one in from the roof.

Then the two screws inside the laundry knock on the landing door and the remaining screw lets them back into the block before locking the door again. All three are now on the landing. We'll use this flat roof like a stepping-stone – from there we can drop to the ground.'

I asked them if they were all still with me and continued when they nodded.

The screw who goes into the laundry has a key to the door that leads to the roof. He needs that to unlock that door from the inside, to let the third man in. That's the key we want. Once the two screws are in the laundry, one of them will knock on the landing door and the other screw will unlock it. That's our time to move. We overpower the three screws, and we have our key.'

'One more problem,' someone said. 'Leo asked you, how do we get to the gate without being shot? You said the soldiers on the administration block would no longer be there, but what about the ones on our roof?'

I had been turning this plan over in my head since the day Martin showed me a glimpse of that gate.

'Ah,' I said, confidently. 'That's simple enough. We'll dress some of our men as screws and they'll run along with us. We'll only need some blue shirts, black trousers, and a few hats. We can make the hats handy enough from cardboard and dye them black in the workshop. You're right. The closest soldiers will be on our roof, but they won't shoot us because they'll think there are screws trying to stop us. Even if they think we're only dressed as screws, they're not going to take the chance.'

I finished by assuring them that these were only the bare bones of the plan. I knew it would need more work, but I also needed their endorsement and their help to make it happen.

There was a brief discussion in front of me. I wasn't asked to leave. Everyone seemed to approve, and we agreed to meet the following day.

When I walked out, Mallon was right behind me.

'You haven't been wasting your time since you came in, have you?' he whispered.

'I had nothing else to do and it seemed like a good way to pass the time and keep the brain active,' I replied. 'I remember telling you before that my plan would empty this place. I still believe that. A few explosives and we'll be on our way.'

'Don't worry about that, I'm on top of it,' Mallon said. 'I'll be back to you about that later on.'

At the time, I trusted Mallon with my life, but I had moved out of his long shadow. I wasn't going to tell him that I would be working with Ned to solve this problem independently. He would make sure we had everything required in the line of explosives.

Now I could really start putting the plan together. The more I thought about it, the more I liked it. Like the helicopter job, when you broke the components down, it was a piece of piss. I would be leaving this shithouse very shortly.

To my mind, the only real difficulty would be in getting the explosives and I had no doubt Ned would manage that.

The other details, like making the hats and bringing in the clothes on visits, I would leave to the escape committee. Mallon would organise all the logistics on the outside, like making sure we had transport.

Apart from the committee, other prisoners would also have to know – but not until the last minute.

# 36

The committee met the following day to discuss the plan further and to dole out work. We discussed the urgent matter of how to smuggle in the explosives. Someone suggested that we approach Ned. He was local and had the ear of volunteers for miles around. I dared not tell anyone that I had already broached the subject with him. Even then, I knew solo runs weren't always appreciated.

I was asked again how I had come to settle on this plan ahead of other options. A tunnel for instance? I told them I had been reviewing the security with a fresh pair of eyes since I first came in and had concluded that whoever designed the jail was looking to protect the front and back gates. Gates are the main weakness in any jail – walls are harder to scale or burrow under.

I detailed how I viewed the security as crescent-shaped. It started at the main gate, covered the wall running between it and the back gate to the right of it and then along the back exercise yard to the inner wall that separated the main compound from the governor's grounds. The other side was a mirror image.

By abandoning the post on the administration block after we were locked in our block, they were compromising the entire security arrangements. Security was further fatally undermined by the way in which the screw on the boiler house roof regained access to the prison. Put together, these factors created the flaw I had been looking for.

By exiting the block from the boilerhouse roof, we would evade this security crescent. Nobody would expect an escape in that direction. We would be running into the heart of the prison – or at least, it would appear like it. The two small gates servicing the governor's house had been completely overlooked.

I already knew too that improvisation wasn't a strong point with soldiers of the calibre we were facing. They weren't trained to think and most of them were more like civil defence. If it wasn't standard procedure, they would be at a complete loss, waiting for orders. There is no way they would open fire on a mixture of screws and prisoners, especially if they saw them all running towards an inner wall.

Realisation wouldn't dawn until we blew a hole in that inner gate. Until then, they wouldn't have a clue why we were running, or to where. Even after the first explosion, they would still have the mixture of uniforms and prisoners to contend with.

And after we cleared the inner wall, it would give us cover. They would no longer have a clear view of us, even from the rooftops. This would make it all the more difficult for anyone, ordinary soldier or senior officer, to open fire.

Until now, I had also kept another nugget of information from the committee. While on the run, I had met a soldier stationed at the prison. This man told me there were express orders not to shoot unarmed prisoners. I very much doubted these orders had changed and told the committee about my encounter.

'But, of course, there are no guarantees in life,' I said. 'One of them might decide to open up anyway. Nothing is ever risk-free.'

I had by then also felt confident enough to tell them that I had approached Ned about getting explosives in.

By the time I had gone over everything, it was time to break up. We didn't want the screws to notice the same group of men meeting up regularly or for long periods. Meetings had to be short and low-key.

Afterwards, Mallon and I went to Ned's cell. He was lying back on the bed, reading a local paper. Sitting down, we began to tell him what we needed. If the explosives were concealed in mahogany donated by supporters for making our crafts, they would slip past security. This was long before the introduction of sniffer dogs.

Ned told us he could arrange this. He would get the ball rolling straight away. He was expecting a visit from P.J. that very afternoon.

'He'll know what to do,' he said. 'And Treacy will have the explosives.' 'That's great,' I said. 'Tell him we'll need black gelignite. It doesn't weep, and it's not as smelly as the ordinary stuff.'

Black gelignite, more commonly known as Semtex, is a powerful plastic explosive. It was used commercially – and by the IRA – to detonate a bigger charge of more readily available, often home-made, explosives. I was certainly no expert when it came to explosives, but I knew that if a small square of this stuff was placed on a lock, the blast and shock waves would destroy it.

I gave Ned the rest of the shopping list: detonators – both commercial and electric – and a length of black fuse wire. We would leave the dets till last because they were very volatile. They were prone to exploding if not handled and stored properly.

I could see Ned was under pressure. His hearing was scheduled for a few days' time and he was expecting to do a stretch – he just didn't know how long it might be. We understood that his mind would be focusing on his case rather than this new preoccupation of ours, so we didn't push him hard. We had other things to do in the meantime. Anyway, Ned Bailey wasn't a man you had to sit on. If he said he would take care of something, it would be taken care of.

The rest of the committee had been delegated to organise the makeshift uniforms and other aspects of the escape. Prisoners began asking their visitors for blue shirts, dark trousers or jeans and the odd dark tie. The inmates also began designing the hats. The component cardboard parts would be stored separately.

It fell to me to monitor everything that happened in the jail during the time we planned to escape. I discovered the same routine every day – the only difference on Sundays was the exodus after mass.

At 10 every morning, the main door to the block was unlocked, and prisoners were allowed out to the exercise yards. The boiler house roof overlooked the smaller of these two yards, facing inward.

Six days a week, prisoners could stay out until 12.30, but on Sundays we had to come in at 11 to facilitate those who wanted to go to mass. Regardless of the time, the routine was the same. After all the prisoners were locked up again inside, the screw stationed on the boiler house roof to survey the exercise yard, left his post via the laundry.

This simple oversight allowed us to drive a coach and four straight through their security system.

Meanwhile, Martin concentrated on trying to see if the governor's outside gate was ever opened. He had managed to acquire a door viewer peephole, standard issue on apartment doors, to check the identity of a caller. By manipulating it, he could use it as a telescope to get a better view.

He would also spend these hours standing on the end of his bed monitoring the inner wall. This enabled him to establish the likelihood of a clear run from the boiler house roof to that crucial door leading to the governor's garden.

His new toy also gave him a tantalising glimpse of the frame of the barred gate behind this wooden door. It was enough to confirm for him that there was nothing extraordinary about the gate itself, although he couldn't be sure. It was a risk we would have to take.

# 37

On July 29, 1974, Ned Bailey and Mallon appeared at the Special Criminal Court. Ned was sentenced to three years for his role in the attempted tunnel escape. Mallon was further remanded pending additional charges relating to his recapture at the dance hall.

Sometimes after the reality of prison dawns, people drift towards depression, or the 'Big D', but Ned came back full of beans.

'I thought they were going to throw the book at me,' he said. 'I can do three years standing on my head.'

I always regarded Ned as a tough old guy, but I know now that age is relative. He was nearly 50 at the time, ancient to most of us in our 20s, but a young man from where I'm standing now.

'Give me a little time,' he told me. 'I'll get on top of your little problem. I have it more or less sorted. Treacy is sourcing the black stuff and P.J. has worked out how to get it in. Fuck them. We'll beat them, one way or the other.'

Ned was a great man to work with, in jail or outside.

Mallon got hit with 10 additional charges, including encouraging a person to discharge a firearm to prevent his arrest. The remaining charges didn't really amount to much – he was already serving four years for the helicopter escape anyway. The rest of the sentences would most likely run concurrently. What did it matter? He didn't intend to see them out.

The thing is, I wondered, how long would he stay out this time? Not very long as it turned out – but that's life.

The committee was confident enough to set a launch date for a few weeks' time. Sunday, August 18. This would focus minds inside and kick-start the external logistics. A breakout on the scale envisaged would require a lot of transport and a network of safe houses.

People on the outside wouldn't have the same fixation as us. For them, life got in the way. We had to instil urgency. The longer we played around with this plan, the more chance there was of making a mistake. Or, of springing a leak. I was still smarting over getting caught so easily, and I didn't want to fall prey to another informer.

A few days later, Ned dropped into my cell. His wife, Beth, would be paying a visit that afternoon. She would be handing over a block of mahogany. Prisoners prized this dark hardwood. Its toughness lent itself to ornate carvings that often adorned the model harps and Celtic crosses that helped them pass the time.

This slab of dark wood was different. P.J. had drilled six, 15-inch-long holes about 1 inch in diameter into the end of it, then filled these with Semtex. After plugging the holes, he had cut an inch off the end of the slab, making his handiwork all but invisible.

'Jesus, Ned, I could kiss you man,' I exclaimed. 'You really are something else.'

'Fuck off, kiss somebody fucking else,' he laughed. We'll get another piece of timber on Beth's next visit,' he said. This will contain the rest of the jelly and some fuse wire. The wire will be cut into short lengths. They'll already have tested a piece of it from the same roll to check its burn time.

We'll leave the detonators 'til last. What do you think Brendan?'

'What do I think?' I replied. 'What else can I think? Without you and Beth, this entire escape would be going nowhere. By the way, Ned, will you be coming with us?'

'Ah now,' he said. 'What would I do on the run? And what use would I be? I'd only be a burden on people. No, I'll do the couple of years and when I get out, I'll just go back to doing what I've always done. But I definitely won't have that mad fucker Treacy staying with me again!'

After he smiled, and left, I could only admire this man who was so willing to help. His wife was also taking a great risk. The country was full of people like Ned, who gave their all, and asked for nothing in return.

I thought about the people of east Tyrone and north Monaghan, who had helped and cared for me, and people like me, down through the years. The old couples who made their homes available to the IRA. And who, when you were leaving, would try to give you money, as they splashed you with holy water. They laughed with you; and cried for you. And when you were gone, they would mourn your passing.

I remember one night. Four of us were planning to rob a post office in a town first thing the following morning. We were told to stay at a particular house. When we got to the cottage in the wee hours, a grumpy old man opened the door. He hadn't been expecting us and we'd got him out of bed.

He told us to sit down, threw some turf on the fire and a shot of diesel on top to set it alight. Then he turned to us and grunted, 'Pull the door behind you when you're going. I'm back off to bed. I'm not sitting up all night entertaining you boys!'

And off he went. We let ourselves out in the morning, did the job and drove off. I never saw him again and hadn't a clue who he was. People like him opened their doors to us and never spoke a word about it.

The committee held another meeting on August 1. We had less than three weeks to make our self-imposed deadline. The intelligence officers on the escape committee provided progress updates. Everything was moving along nicely.

We had enough clothing to dress six prisoners in passable warders' uniforms. There were enough components for 10 hats, and these had been stored, ready for assembly. The shirts and trousers were hidden among the prisoners' personal clothing. The first explosives were due in that day. I had ordered enough for three charges, one for each gate and a spare just in case one failed to do its job.

During the meeting, I suggested that on the morning of the escape, we get prisoners who weren't taking part to provide a diversion.

Beforehand, we would gather all of the crockery we could lay our hands into the cells on the opposite side of the block to the boiler house roof. When the signal went up to begin the escape, those prisoners who had opted not to go would start hurling it into the exercise yard below. I was hoping that the plates, cups, bowls and cutlery would create a serious racket on that side of the prison while we were escaping in the opposite direction.

If this went to plan, while we were taking the laundry, the soldiers on our roof would be distracted by the clatter on the opposite side of the block. By the time we were off the flat roof, I would expect they would have sounded the alarm, but its focus would have been on the smashing crockery, rather than on our sprint towards the inner gate.

By the time the soldiers crossed the walkways above the skylight running down the centre of the block, they would be looking down on dozens of prisoners and screws running towards the middle of the prison, rather than towards either the main or back gates.

I was hoping the confusion would give us a clear run to the crucial first gate and the cover beyond before the soldiers even realised what was happening. There would be so many men in screws' uniforms among the prisoners sprinting towards that gate that the soldiers couldn't possibly take a shot.

The radio traffic would be so congested as to be useless. Total chaos.

After I had painted this scenario, the meeting adjourned, satisfied that there had been enough progress to maintain the deadline.

Everyone was given more things to do or detailed to provide further surveillance.

I had been watching the movements of the screw on the boiler house roof. This was a handy number for me. I could monitor it from the 'comfort' of my cell, which was on the same level.

The hotplate where we collected our food on E2 was right beside the laundry door. We used to gather and chat there while we were waiting for it to arrive, so hanging around there didn't arouse any suspicion. This would play into our hands on the morning of the escape.

As far as I could see, the changeover routine had remained constant. You could set your watch by them. On weekdays, extra screws would sometimes be hanging around the landing, but never on Sundays. Because the laundry was closed to us on a Sunday, there was no reason for extra screws that day. The two screws running the landing were the only ones around during the changeover.

Mass started at 11 and was over around 45 minutes later. Then, all the screws who were going off duty would charge like cattle down the stairs and out the door of the block.

I found a window from where I could observe them. They all made a beeline for the front gate. Such was their rush to leave the prison that all the screws manning the gates, between the prison and the front gate, even ignored procedure and opened them all at once. This was enough to convince me this was when security was at its most lax. It was exactly what we needed. The more screws that went off duty the better.

I had figured out that they had all left the precincts of the prison by 12.30.

They were in their cars, speeding off home, miles away by then. Bear in mind, these were the days before mobile phones. There was no way even a prison alarm would turn most of them back – they would already be too far away to hear it.

The lack of order, or discipline, shown by jail staff at this time, reflected the confidence they felt in their security.

They thought that once we were locked into the block, we weren't going anywhere. As they were heading off for their Sunday roast, an escape was the last thing on their minds.

The soldiers' routine also displayed a confidence bordering on arrogance. After lockdown on a Sunday, there was no further sign of them at the central post on the roof of the administration building.

The more I studied our tactics, the more confident I became of success. Their security apparatus was asleep.

# 38

It turned out this top-security prison lacked the basics in many ways. Or at least in one aspect – and we aimed to exploit it. One flaw was all we needed.

This was helped by the ancillary procedures. It wasn't quite the case that someone would have been able to smuggle in a file hidden in a birthday cake, but visitors were allowed to hand in food, newspapers and other essentials.

These were the days before drugs were rife in prisons and in Irish society. It was still relatively easy to arrange a visit and pass messages and other contraband. When Beth presented the screw at the gate with a length of wood four feet long by nine-inches thick, it aroused no suspicion. The warders examined it before leaving it among a large pile of similarly cleared items on the floor of the first landing of our block.

Over the course of the day, prisoners would collect the items handed in for them. On that Thursday, Ned and I dropped down to collect the piece of timber only to find it was one of several. It so happened that a lot of wood had been dropped in that day but there was only one piece we were interested in.

After picking this out, I took it to my cell. I remember handling it very carefully. After closing the door over as far as I dared, I examined it in minute detail, but it appeared completely intact. I wondered for a moment if I had the right piece, but two tiny notches told me where to cut it. We had our treasure, alright. I decided it would be safest to leave it intact. The screws would pay it no heed during a cell search because it had passed security on the way in.

In the early evening, Ned dropped in for tea. 'Well,' he said. 'What do you think?'

'Ned, it couldn't be better,' I replied. 'Tell Beth I'm forever in her debt.'

'Do you remember what I told you about how P. J. had done it?' Ned said. 'Cut 15 inches off each end – or maybe 16 to be sure. You don't want to cut through the gelignite. After you've cut off both ends, you must split them with a chisel to get at the jelly. It's wrapped in plastic: it should just fall out.'

I assured him I hadn't forgotten a single word of his instructions but that I wouldn't be opening it until just before the escape.

'It's safer where it is,' I said. 'If we open it beforehand, we'll only have to find somewhere else to hide it.'

The talk turned to times past and absent friends before inevitably coming back to the impending escape attempt.

'Ned,' I said. 'We're making real progress and we'll shake these bastards to the core again if we succeed.'

'Don't I know it,' he answered. 'I expect things will get a bit rough after you leave.'

The escape had now consumed me, but I still had plenty of hours to kill. I continued to contribute to Liam Fagan's fundraising drive. I also spent many hours listening to the stories spun by Éamonn Mac Thomáis, a celebrated folklorist and veteran republican, who is buried next to the legendary republican leader Frank Ryan, in Glasnevin Cemetery.

Éamonn was an absolute gentleman. He would regale and entertain us endlessly with stories about the history of his beloved Dublin. There wasn't a street that he didn't have a story about. He also told us all about the history of Portlaoise Prison.

I loved nothing better than to sit in his company. I never ceased to be amazed at the extent and accuracy of his memory. Hours would pass unnoticed while he talked. He never used notes, it was all in his head.

Long after the escape, when Éamonn was nearing the end of his sentence, the screws subjected him to an inexcusable act of meanness.

He had spent most of his prison time researching and writing a history book, spending endless hours on it. Just days before he was due out, the screws raided his cell and took all his notes, writings and reference books. They didn't leave him so much as a scrap of paper. To the best of my knowledge, Éamonn never saw any of it ever again. It nearly broke his heart.

He loved his books, and he loved his history. He was a gentle, helpful man, who didn't have a bad bone in his body. The loss of these materials devastated him.

Éamonn had been the Editor of An Phoblacht, the republican newspaper that Dermot Teeling had been selling around the pubs on that fateful night when he had been asked to give the getaway taxi a push.

Éamonn would end up doing two separate stretches relating to his involvement with the newspaper – the only 'evidence' against him was the word of a senior police officer. And when they had him inside, they allowed him to write his book, only to destroy it.

After his release, the State set about trying to destroy him financially too. He got no work from any newspaper or the state broadcaster. He managed to keep himself going thanks to people buying his books or enjoying his popular walking tours around Dublin.

At the time, I didn't have many dealings with the man widely blamed for giving the order to destroy Éamonn's book, the then Chief Officer Ned Harkin, who would later become governor. Harkin was a man who seemed to enjoy mind games. His pet pastime was censoring prisoners' mail. A lot of the time, a letter might be the only contact that man had with his family. Prisoners would receive their letters, redacted to the extent they meant nothing. Letters from wives and girlfriends were his favourite targets.

I too would experience the full extent of his pettiness when I ended up in Portlaoise again later in life. My daughter was getting married and the law in the North at the time dictated that she needed her father's permission. My wife posted a letter to me with the required consent form.

When it arrived, Harkin summoned me to his office. He sat behind a desk piled high with mail. The neat piles of letters on the left lay unopened; those on the right, had been opened and read. The thick, black marker that he used for redacting purposes lay handy beside the official prison stamp.

'Hughes,' he said. 'I have a form here that you may have been expecting. I'm afraid I can't allow you to sign it. You see, when you are serving a sentence of penal servitude, you cease to become a legal entity. Therefore, I would be breaking the law if I allowed you to sign it. Do you understand what I'm saying?'

'Yes, I understand what you're saying,' I said. 'But I think you're mistaken. This was abolished under English law a long time ago. Therefore, the form is totally legal in the jurisdiction where it will be used. Isn't that the case?'

'No, Hughes,' he replied. 'I decide what is lawful and what isn't lawful in this prison. The situation is very clear, I am empowered to sign it on your behalf. That is the only option available to you. If you don't agree to this, I shall return the form unsigned.'

I really didn't have a choice. It was bad enough missing my daughter's wedding without adding injury to insult. Time was of the essence, and a challenge to his authority, might mean it would have to be postponed. Strictly speaking, he was correct. I couldn't legally sign the form, but I doubt the world would have stopped spinning if he had turned a blind eye.

The bottom line is that my daughter got married with the permission of a small-minded, vindictive, bully of a screw.

# 39

In August 1974, I was as happy as a man could be in this shithole. The prospect of getting out of this dump had cheered me up no end.

The 'uniforms' were ready to go, and I had enough gelignite to deal with the gates. Extracting it safely from its wooden coffin would present more challenges, but it wasn't anything we couldn't handle. Now we needed only detonators and fuse wire to finish the job.

Information was kept tight. The prisoners making the components for the caps, for instance, wouldn't have been told the purpose, even if some of them might have guessed. One crowd would be making the top of the cap, just a simple piece of cardboard, the size of a dinner plate. Others would be making strips of cardboard that would be glued into circles to form the base. The peak was just a crescent-shaped piece of cardboard. We would wait until the last minute to assemble and dye all the component parts, so as to conceal their intended use. It would also allow us to keep them in separate locations.

The jail could be stifling in summer, so the screws ditched their heavy tunics in favour of a more casual uniform of blue shirt and dark trousers. In the weeks before the escape, the prisoners' lockers had plenty of blue shirts and black trousers. When we did eventually spring into action, it appeared as if there were more men in uniform than not.

A week after the first batch of black, malleable Semtex arrived, a second followed.

On Sunday, August 11, 1974, with one week to go, the escape committee held its longest meeting.

We decided we would go the following Sunday at 12.30. The prison OC was charged with briefing the landing OCs on what was happening and what was expected of them. Each OC would in turn brief the volunteers under their command.

Most of the briefings would only take place the day before the escape. Jail is a strange place and if prisoners knew what was happening, they would begin to act differently. The screws would surely pick up on this. We were right to keep it on a need-to-know basis. A lot of dinners went uneaten the evening after the men were eventually told.

I would be pressing Ned into service again to arrange for two getaway vans outside. They would contain weapons, maps, and spare clothing. One would be on the Borris Road, which went in the general direction of The Heath and the other on the main Dublin Road.

Once we had blasted through the outside wall, the intention was to split into two groups. Mallon would lead the group that was heading towards the Borris Road. Another born leader, Brian Hearty from Co Armagh, would take charge of the group that would break towards the Dublin Road.

I always had good time for Brian. He wasn't a man to be messed with. One day, close to the day of the escape, he took me aside.

'Brendan,' he said 'I need to ask you something. You and I are friends, and I need your word. Can you assure me that our group is not being used as a diversion to take the heat off the people going in the other direction? I need your word. I'll accept that.'

I've never been a person who dealt in intrigue, so the question completely threw me.

'Brian,' I replied. 'I don't play games like that. I can guarantee you that's not the reason you're heading in that direction. I have no idea what awaits either group. As far as I'm concerned, we all have the same chance. I would never use you like that. You have my word.'

This seemed to square things with him. He nodded and walked away with a relieved smile on his face.

It only dawned on me years later why Brian had even asked the question. Intrigue was only an infant monster at the time but men like Brian were already well aware of it and knew the damage it could inflict.

We picked the team to take the laundry, all of them hardened volunteers, with experience in the North. Brian would lead them. Their job was to overcome the three screws by pushing them all into the laundry and to secure the key to the door leading to the flat roof. We assigned a large number of men to this task, to make sure the screws realised that resistance would be futile. We wanted to avoid excessive force and the heat it might bring.

Looking back on things, the hardest thing was organising the prisoners. Screws wander around a prison pretending not to notice things but, I can assure you, they miss very little. Unexplained meetings and huddles tend to raise antennae.

Luckily for us, the prison OC Leo Martin was a very canny, experienced man, and this gave us confidence that everyone would be where they should be when required.

At the meeting, I got the job of extracting the dynamite from the wood and finding a secure hiding place for it.

Peadar Mohan, my neighbour on E2, was a country man through and through. This quiet, reserved man minded his own business, and got on with doing his time. He also had other rural traits. He was very loyal and efficient

– and he could keep his mouth shut. He indulged his love of Irish country music by playing it incessantly and loudly, which annoyed the fuck out of people who couldn't stand it. Peadar didn't care. He always maintained that he had to put up with their shite music, so it was only fair they should have to listen to his!

On Monday, August 12, the day after the long meeting, I walked into Peadar's cell carrying two heavy lumps of timber. He looked at me suspiciously.

'What are they for?' he asked, thinking he was going to be recruited into Liam's memorial fund drive. 'I'm very busy at the minute. I have a visit this day week, and I have stuff to get ready for it.'

I could only smile. Peadar would be the first to put up his hand if Liam needed anything doing.

'No, Peadar, it's not like that,' I said, placing the pieces of timber gently on his bed. 'It's like this. There is enough jelly in these two pieces of timber to blow a hole in your wall.'

'Fuck off,' he exclaimed, staring hard at the wood. 'You're winding me up.'

'No, let me explain,' I said, shaking my head. 'On Sunday next, we're all going to escape from this shithouse. We're going to blow our way out with what's inside of these.'

He sat on the bed beside the wood, looking puzzled. 'And what exactly has this to do with me?' he asked.

'I want you to help me remove the jelly from the wood,' I said. 'The problem is we can't do it in the workshop. It has to be done in a cell – your cell – if you're up for it?'

'Up for it? Of course, I'm up for it,' he said. 'As long as you're not winding me up, I'm your man. I'll bite it off if I have to!'

'About your visit… I began.

'Visit? What visit?' he said. 'This is more important than any visit.'

'Well,' I said, 'I was going to say that I doubt if you'll be getting a visit.

And if this goes to plan, there may not be any visits for some time.'

Peadar told me he wouldn't be going on the escape because he only had a short time left behind bars, but promised any help he could. I closed over the cell door and started to explain what had to be done.

'Inside each of these is at least a pound of black jelly, maybe more.'

I picked one up and pointed to the tiny notches at either end that P.J. had left to indicate where it should be cut.

'Cut off the ends of both pieces and store them,' I said. 'After that, we need to get a chisel and split them in several places. It goes without saying this has to be done very carefully! Once the gelignite is exposed, it should slide out of the holes – it's covered in plastic.'

Peadar examined the wood carefully, turning it over. Then, after placing it under his bed he straightened up and asked, 'When do we start?'

'Now is as good a time as any,' I said. 'We'll have to smuggle a saw out of the workshop, so let's get over there.'

The workshop was on our landing. We sauntered along towards it, looking as nonchalant as we could. The screws would always pat down everyone on their way out to prevent the removal of tools but, as searches go, they didn't amount to much. And when two or more prisoners were leaving at the same time, there was little or no search at all.

We walked in and I indicated to a couple of men to block the view of the screws as I slid a saw down the back of my trousers, hiding the bulge under my untucked shirttail. Five of us left at the same time. A screw frisked us all quickly and we were away. It was only a few short yards to Peadar's cell, adjacent to mine.

I had already arranged for two volunteers to stand guard on the landing opposite. They could see directly into my cell, with its door wide open. Peadar's cell door would be closed over.

I borrowed an eight-track tape of his beloved country music, telling him I would be playing it loudly enough in my cell for him to hear it.

'If there's any problem,' I said. 'Those lads across the way will signal me and I'll turn off the music. Once that happens, stop what you're doing and put everything out of sight. When it's all clear, I'll put on your music again. If it's a bad problem, I'll be in to you. Okay?'

'Yeah, no problem,' he answered. 'I'll have the ends off in no time.'

The loud music would serve as a signal and it would also serve to muffle the noise of Peadar's sawing. Everything went well. Less than half an hour later, my comrade told me he was finished with the first piece.

'Let's get rid of the saw before tea break,' he said. 'They check the tools in the workshop around then.'

We used the same method in reverse to return the saw. This was much easier because they never searched you going in.

It was now getting near dinnertime, as the midday meal was called back then when nobody in Ireland knew what lunch was.

Peadar and I went to tidy up. We would have to wait again until two o'clock for the workshop to reopen. We needed a hammer and a chisel for the final part of the job.

Beforehand, I went to visit Oliver McKiernan up on the third landing, 'the 3s'. He was another member of the escape committee and he had volunteered to store the explosives.

Oliver was a large man with infinite patience. He spent his time hunched over a table making harps and crosses, some of them from matchsticks. Some of these would be two-feet high, requiring thousands of pieces. He applied each one individually; he even had to cut some of them to size.

He had one large Celtic cross made of mahogany nearly complete, and he had made a special base for it. Special in the sense that it was hollow. Oliver intended to store the jelly there.

'Are you ready to take the stuff, Oliver?' I asked, as I looked around his Aladdin's cave.

'Of course, I'm ready,' he said. 'When can I expect it?'

'Hopefully, this evening. Well, some of it anyway,' I said. 'It depends on how hard it is to remove it from the wood. I'll be back later to see you.'

'No problem,' he laughed. 'I had arranged to go out, but I'll wait in for you instead.'

We all used variations of this same joke, and it was already wearing thin.

Peadar had hidden the four timber ends among the other pieces of wood that were lying around his cell. Over dinner, we examined them closely, but no matter how hard we looked, we couldn't see any sign of the drill holes. P.J. certainly knew his job.

'How much gelignite do you think is in here?' Peadar asked me.

'I really have no idea,' I replied. 'I'm expecting at least two to three pounds' weight. That would be more than enough.'

After a long silence, I asked Peadar whether he might change his mind and come on the escape. I still had it in my head to empty the prison. I was also thinking 'the more the merrier' when it came to causing utter confusion on the day.

'No, Brendan,' he said. 'I've nearly finished my time and being on the run wouldn't suit me. I'm an old home bird. No, I'll finish my time, and when I get out, I'll still be of some use to the Movement. Don't worry, you know I'll help you all I can anyway.'

Two o'clock came and went. The prison hum returned as people began moving around again. Some men would be heading for the exercise yards, others to the workshops, and a fortunate few would be going on visits from loved ones.

Peadar and I knew exactly where we would be going. We waited 15 minutes before going back to the workshop in case someone noticed our sudden appetite for manual labour.

I taped a hammer and chisel together and concealed them down the back of my trousers. The risk was minimal because things were very quiet – there was no tension in the prison at the time. This was no accident. The prison

OC had his thumb firmly on the pulse. Anyone creating a problem was spoken to in very severe terms. We needed calm in which to operate.

Back in Peadar's cell I deposited the tools on his bed and told him the same drill would apply, 'I'll be playing the music. If it stops, you stop.'

My two sentries were outside my door. One of them called me over, saying, 'For fuck sake, can you not play something else. That music's terrible. I'm dreaming about Big fucking Tom!'

Big Tom McBride, a popular Irish country singer from Peadar's home county of Monaghan, was a particular favourite of his.

'I heard that, you pair of bollixes,' Peadar shouted from his cell. 'I'm not all that fond of the shite you play either.'

The pair grinned across at me.

'I'll play Philomena Begley for a change; if that's any better?' I suggested.

Both of them just shook their heads in mock horror. I was laughing at them; I didn't really mind country music. They went back to their post across the landing.

Peadar had been working for about 30 minutes when the sentries signalled to me. I switched off the music immediately, walked outside my cell door, and stretched my arms, feigning boredom. Looking down the landing, I saw two screws making their way in our direction. They were performing their daily routine of checking the doors to make sure they hadn't been tampered with.

I opened Peadar's door. He was sitting at his little table colouring a design on a linen handkerchief. These were very popular souvenirs, or they would be sold to raise funds. There was no sign of the wood or the tools.

'It's okay, Peadar,' I reassured him. 'Just screws doing their daily check on the doors. They'll be gone in a minute. That's if your door doesn't fall off when they kick it!'

He grinned at me. 'No, it's as tight as a duck's arse,' he assured me. I was leaning against his door when the screws arrived.

'Excuse me,' one of them said. 'We're just checking the door.'

'It's still there,' Peadar shouted. 'If you're worried about it, you can take it away with you. You could keep it in your office, and it'll save you the trouble of coming around here every day, checking if it's still here!'

'We like the exercise,' the screw replied, dryly. 'We'd have nothing to do at all then.'

As soon as they left, we got back to work. After another while, Peadar knocked the wall separating our cells, and I went in to see what he wanted.

'Brendan, this is a very slow business,' he said. 'The grain in this piece of wood doesn't lend itself to splitting easily. I've only got one piece done so far.'

'Well look, Peadar,' I said. 'Whatever you do, don't get caught with one only half done. You don't want that. In case you get searched in the morning, if you're not sure of finishing a piece before lock-up, don't start it.'

He took the lid off a tin box that was lying in the corner. Inside there was around half a pound of black gelignite. Or black gold, to us.

'How long did that one take?' I asked.

'About 45 minutes, allowing for the time when the screws interrupted us,' he said.

'We need to get the tools back to the workshop,' I told him. 'Our friends across the landing will help me bring them back if you deliver the stuff to Big Oliver. He's waiting for it. Give him a rough idea of when you'll have the next lot.'

Peadar closed the box, picked it up, stuck it under his jacket, which he had just put on specifically for that purpose, and left without another word.

I ran a piece of tape around the hammer and chisel, concealed them down the back of my jeans and returned them with the distraction of the sentries.

After tea at four o'clock, the workshop would close for an hour and a half before reopening until eight.

This would give Peadar another few hours to do the job, provided we could smuggle the tools out again.

I told my lookouts I didn't need them again until the next day. I wanted different lookouts in the evening, in case the screws noticed anything.

I recruited the guy in the cell opposite. He often stood outside his cell, reading a newspaper. I don't know why he had this habit, but it suited me, so now wasn't the time to ask.

Peadar started again at six. I played Philomena Begley. He tried one of the ends of the other slab to see if the grain was more compliant. He told me afterwards that compared to the first one, it was easy. It had a straight grain, running from one end to the other.

Around 7.15, I heard a knock on the wall.

'I've two more ends finished but I don't want to start the last one in case it turns out to be as difficult as the first. I'm going to leave it 'til the morning.'

That was good enough for me. I told him to take what he had to Oliver and set about cleaning up the wood shavings and fragments. I put them in a bag covered with a pile of handkerchiefs on top.

I examined the fragments carefully for any signs of gelignite. I should have known better. P.J.'s plastic wrapping had meant no trace was left on the wood. I always loved forward thinkers.

Nobody even looked at me as I walked into the workshop. I slipped the tools onto a table and separated them before tipping the fragments into a bin that already contained similar shavings and cut-offs.

I took the handkerchiefs with me. Colouring a few in might help me get some sleep, though I doubted it very much.

# 40

After breakfast the following morning, Peadar and I set about extracting the remainder of the gelignite. We wanted to start as early as possible in case the last piece would prove the most difficult.

I also told Peadar he should expect to find black fuse wire in one of the holes. I had been promised several short lengths, all cut from the same roll and tested to give us 20 seconds' burning time. We couldn't time the fuse wire inside the prison. Once lit, it would emit a plume of black smoke and if that didn't give the game away its strong, caustic smell certainly would. As it turned out, we would opt for only five seconds between ignition and detonation.

I decided to give Larry Cunningham a bit of a play today for a change. Hearing the Irish country crooner at full volume was enough to make the lookout on the landing opposite grimace and bury his head deep into his paper. Until then, I had never realised how much some people really hated Irish country music. Peadar knew though and used it with great effect to wind up the Belfast boys.

About an hour after I turned Larry on, Peadar knocked on my wall and I went to see what he wanted.

'I've finished it,' he said, a smile of satisfaction spread across his face. 'That was one difficult bastard, my hands are in bits.'

'Peadar,' I told him, 'It'll all be worth it when you see the faces of the screws on Sunday. They'll be in bits, just wait and see. There will be promotions and demotions, and discontent. Screws will be moved up and sent down. Some will be moved sideways, but things will never be the same again in this jail when we're through with them.'

'I don't give a fuck where they go,' he said. 'Another few months and I'll be gone out of here myself, and believe me, I'll never be back.'

I told him to deliver the latest package to Oliver and that I would clean up again.

'How's Oliver getting on by the way?' I asked.

'He's fine,' Peadar replied. 'You can't get into his place for the matches. If you stayed still for a minute, he'd have you covered with them! The place is coming down with cottages, round towers, harps and crosses, all in the course of construction. He'll never get to finish them now, but I doubt that'll bother him too much.'

'Tell him I'll call to see him later, probably this evening,' I said.

I picked up the tools and taped them. Then I cleaned up the chips from the cell floor, checking again that there were no black streaks on them. They were okay, so off I went to the workshop.

We had just completed a major part of the operation without any drama, and I allowed myself some satisfaction from knowing again that I had chosen my people wisely.

I didn't go to see Oliver straightaway in case anyone noticed me following Peadar and wondering what we were up to. As I said before, it would have been very foolish to take the screws for granted. If they got the slightest suspicion that something was up, they'd be all over you like a rash.

While the extraction had been going on, the rest of the escape committee had been busy too. Mallon was overseeing most of it and I knew better than most his ability to organise and manage people. We met up later that evening to discuss progress and we were both satisfied with each other's accounts.

'I got all the stuff out and it's stored,' I said. 'I'm hoping to have the detonators either tomorrow or Thursday.'

'Good, good,' Mallon said. 'We'll all be in Tullyhogue next week!'

Tullyhogue Fort was an ancient site in our native Co Tyrone where the High Kings of Ulster, the O'Neills, had been crowned until the Flight of the Earls in 1607, heralding the end of Gaelic Ireland. Maybe I knew more history than I gave myself credit for!

After the meeting, I made my way up to see Oliver. When I got there, he was his usual busy self. He was working on a large round tower and I couldn't hide my amusement.

'I can't stop working,' he said, almost apologetically. 'I'm trying to finish this before Monday. I'm due a visit then.'

'Oliver,' I said. 'There is absolutely no chance this will be going out on Monday. Whether we succeed or not, the screws are going to tear this place apart. There will be no visits for at least a week and Ned Harkin will smash your tower back to matchsticks.'

'Brendan,' he said. 'I know that but I'm a bag of nerves. I have to keep busy, otherwise I might throw a wobbler!'

The chances of this were slim to none. It would take a lot more than this to knock him off his stride. I knew he was just trying to get the last few days in as best he could. It didn't help when you couldn't discuss things with anyone. I was nearly as bad myself, but I had lots of work to do, and things to worry about, so I was more preoccupied.

'Give me a look at the dump,' I asked.

He nodded towards a very large Celtic cross on a table in the corner. 'It looks well, doesn't it?' Oliver said.

'How long have you been working on that?' I asked.

'I'd be scared to tell you,' he said. 'It's breaking my heart to leave it behind.' I tried to keep a straight face.

'Oliver,' I said. 'Do you want me to get permission to bring it with you?'

'Fuck off!' he replied.

'No, I'm serious, you could use it as a weapon,' I said, warming to my wind-up. 'We could put a fuse in the base of it and blow it up!'

'Listen you,' he said. 'I'm not all that put out about it. It took me two months to make but I can always make another one.'

'Oliver,' I said. 'On Sunday night that cross will be in hundreds of bits all over the landing. Ned Harkin might even take it home to light the fire.'

I examined the bottom of the cross and it was flawless. Without taking it apart, you wouldn't have been able to tell there was anything different about it.

'Seriously, Oliver,' I said. 'That's a really good job.'

'I know it,' he said. 'As long as it doesn't blow up before Sunday! I have the window open wide, but I can't get rid of this headache from the jelly. Sunday can't come quick enough as far as I'm concerned. Them screws can take over the headache.'

'If it does blow, I hope I'm not locked up because I'm out through the hole no matter what!' I replied.

'You have no sympathy for me at all,' he said, as I walked out the door.

I did have sympathy, but this wasn't the time to tell him about the headaches I had from moving gelignite we stole from a quarry one time. The car was so heavily laden with boxes that the exhaust kept bouncing along the unpaved access road. I watched sparks fly with every jolt. That jelly gave me one serious headache.

I left him to his work. He never minded a slagging – he was a nice man. I also knew he'd be one of the first through the wall if we made it that far.

I made my way back to Peadar's cell to inquire about the fuse wire.

'Everything is safe as houses,' he assured me. 'I took the rubber stoppers from two of the legs of the table and pushed the fuses up inside. They won't be seen in there. Just let me know when you need them, and I'll get them right away. No problem.'

The next few days passed in calm, measured activity. The committee members took the chances afforded by the exercise yard to update one another constantly.

On Friday, Mallon and I met senior members of the IRA staff in the prison to brief them for the final time. As the senior commander, Mallon did most of the talking. We also settled on the signal for the escape to begin.

One of the prisoners was nicknamed 'Mickey Do' and fellow inmates often used to shout out his name for no reason other than they liked the sound of it. So, when Mallon cried out 'Mickey Do' at the top of his voice on Sunday, everyone would spring into action, but the screws would pay no heed.

I wanted everyone to behave as normal on Sunday morning. Some men would go to mass, others would lie around on their beds, killing the time until dinner. The last thing I wanted was prisoners all standing around, waiting for something to happen.

On Saturday evening and Sunday morning we collected every bit of crockery and cutlery we could find. We gathered plates, cups, saucers, bowls, spoons and forks, and stored them on the third and fourth landings, the 3s and the 4s.

Those volunteers who didn't want to go on the escape would start throwing everything out the windows on the side of the block facing the outside wall. This would certainly trigger the very loud siren that served as the general alarm. At exactly the same time, we would be taking the laundry.

The penny would only likely drop after the first explosion. By then, we would be inside the walls of the governor's grounds and heading for that little outside gate.

I assumed once the first charge went off, the soldiers would feel free to open fire because they would think we were armed.

They still had to choose a target though and could they take the chance that genuine screws weren't among the prisoners?

I expected the alarm would wake the screws up but when they followed us outside to try to catch us, it would just bring more chaos for the soldiers stationed on the roof. So, I was still reasonably confident, the troops wouldn't fire.

The prisoners designated to wear the replica warders' uniforms had to stay out of sight until the cry of 'Mickey Do' went up. Other prisoners, who weren't causing a commotion, were ordered to distract the screws away from the laundry area.

The fuses and detonators still had to be introduced to the jelly. This was all taking a great deal of coordination but, as an organisation, the IRA had always been pretty good at maintaining discipline.

At Friday dinnertime, Ned came into my cell and presented me with a matchbox containing six commercial detonators.

'I just got them an hour ago,' he said. 'Beth left in a pair of shoes and these were in the heels.'

I shook his hand one last time.

# 41

Mallon and I spent the Saturday morning on the day before the escape conducting final briefings and making last-minute preparations. He designated me to look after every detail beyond the laundry door. He would handle everything up until this point. Brian Hearty would lead the team tasked with taking the laundry.

Martin McAllister and I were assigned to blow up the entrance to the governor's compound. Martin would carry the charges and I would have the detonators with the fuse wire attached.

We had a choice of engineers and the committee chose Jim Monaghan. He was probably the best engineer the IRA has ever had. He was inventive and efficient. When he came to a problem, he would always find a way around it. He was always on the lookout for new and innovative ideas. I met Martin later that morning and asked him to take care of the explosives. He was to deliver the dets, the fuses, and Oliver's cross over to Jim for assembly. I instructed him to deliver them in the evening and to collect the finished products the following morning. Lastly, I told Martin to meet me on Sunday morning at the hotplate on the E2 landing to collect the dets and fuses. He would be keeping the charges.

I wouldn't be wearing a replica uniform because I would be hanging around the hotplate for too long. I told him that after our rendezvous, he must stay with me no matter what until we were outside the main wall.

'Don't worry,' he said. 'I'll be sticking to you like glue. I'll be on your shoulder all the way.'

Then I went to brief the laundry team, consisting of Brian Hearty, Oliver McKiernan and Belfast man, Liam 'Farmer' Brown, who had already proved more than capable of taking care of screws when the helicopter landed in Mountjoy. I impressed on them again that success hinged on them getting the key from the screw, otherwise the entire operation would fail.

Farmer's job was to distract the screw outside the laundry door when he was on his own, asking to be allowed in to collect some wet clothes he had left by mistake the day before. This would ensure that he would be in the perfect place to push all three inside as soon as the isolated screw on the landing opened the door to let his two colleagues back in.

'When that laundry door opens, charge it,' I ordered.

'Carry all three screws with you, through the doorway and back inside the laundry. Grab the screw who has the key to the roof and restrain the others. Remember, your sole objective is to secure this key from his belt. We'll be right behind you. Once you get the key, give it to me and then watch my back while I open the door to the roof.'

Brian assured me that everything was in place.

'We've been going over this in our heads for ages now,' he said. 'Don't worry, nobody will interfere with you while you're opening that roof door.'

Brian was only around 5ft 7in, but he was solid muscle. Behind his long, black beard lay a cool, calculating mind. He had earned a ferocious reputation around his native South Armagh – not an easy thing to achieve in a place teeming with hard men.

Farmer was six feet tall and strong as an ox. Oliver too had a formidable physique. I was entirely confident these experienced volunteers would get the better of the three screws.

'When Mallon sees you move,' I continued, 'he'll give the general alert and all hell will break loose. I also want plenty of our people crowding around the laundry door to prevent any screws seeing what's actually happening inside. Mallon, Martin and I will be first onto the roof.'

I left Brian to make his final arrangements and went back to worry about things. What had I overlooked?

I had high expectations. I really did intend to empty the entire prison of everyone who wanted to leave and didn't see anything to prevent it happening. I wasn't giving anyone priority. Prisoners serving long sentences had plenty of motivation to escape. The first prisoners off the roof would set the pace over the open ground. As long as they kept running, we would get to that crucial inner gate. Most of the prisoners would only be told about the escape a few hours beforehand. It was a calculated risk but one we believed would give us the best chance of getting the maximum number of men out.

As I lay on my bed conducting these mental gymnastics, who should walk through the door but my old friend, Seán Treacy.

He was accompanied by Eddie Gallagher, a man I would get to know after the escape. Like Seán, he had only arrived the night before. They had been stopped at a checkpoint and charged with IRA membership.

'It doesn't matter,' Gallagher said. 'I'll be going with you tomorrow anyway.'

'We were arranging the transport for you when they stopped us,' Seán elaborated. 'We had a van with weapons in it arranged for the Borris Road and we were just sorting out the transport for the Dublin Road when they nabbed us. Beth and The German both know what we were doing, and they'll have taken over after hearing we were caught. I still expect the transport will be there, no matter what.'

I spent the next half-hour or so explaining the plan to Gallagher. Seán said he wouldn't be going.

'The OC will find work for you, Seán,' I said. 'We're staging lots of diversionary tactics, to give us the best chance possible.'

I then asked Eddie if he wanted to join the group heading for the Borris Road or the one turning left for the Dublin Road. He opted for the Borris Road, saying that he was familiar with that part of the country.

I couldn't settle at all. It was getting really close now. We had kept the lid on it so far, but my nerves were starting to talk to me. I knew Mallon and the others would be the same. We were spending all that last day quietly tweaking this and checking that. I was confident of success but there is nothing like adrenaline to make a man agitated.

I watched the laundry changeover at dinner hour one last time. Same old routine. They were still sleepwalking, and I was itching to wake them up.

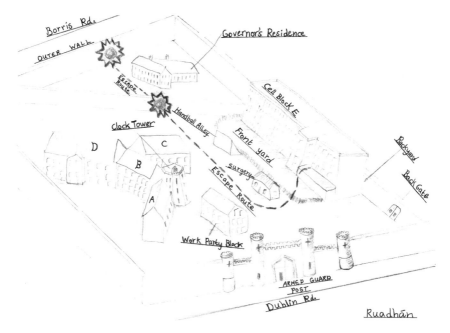

*Above: Sketch map showing the escape route from Portlaoise Prison.*

# 42

**Sunday, August 18, 1974**

I would have preferred to wake up to a dirty, wet day because people tend to keep their heads down when the weather is bad, but dawn heralded bright sunshine. I made the most of it, enjoying the heat from the window high above my bed. I had spent a sleepless night worrying about the little details and planning for things that might go wrong.

**10.30 am**

I took a walk up to Martin's cell to reassure myself that it hadn't been raided during the night. I found him out on the landing, smoking.

'I can't smoke in there,' he explained. 'It's like a fucking bomb factory! I have all the charges. They're made up. Jim did a good job on them. I only have to put them in a bag. They're literally ready to go.'

He handed me the six detonators, all of which had just over an inch of fuse wire crimped to them.

'According to my instructions,' Martin said. 'You'll have enough time to get clear but not enough time for anyone to interfere with the charge. There's a half a pound of black in each charge – enough to trash any gate in this prison.'

I conducted a cautious examination of the detonators, which were notoriously sensitive. I knew from bitter experience they had to be handled with the utmost care. I put them into a small cardboard box I had removed from the workshop and closed the lid.

'Be at the hotplate at 11.40,' I told him. 'I'll meet you there shortly after. Remember, you have to stay beside me all the way. Just hand me the charges when I ask for them, okay?'

Martin took a long drag on his cigarette before nodding and telling me that he'd be seeing me again very shortly.

As I was returning to my cell, I met Peadar on the landing. I gave him a final chance to change his mind about going.

'No,' he told me. 'I've not long to go, and I wouldn't miss the show after you leave for all of the world. Man, are those screws going to be pissed off.'

'Do you reckon they'll miss us, that they'll be sorry to see us go, and all that?' I joked.

'No,' he said. 'They'll only be sorry for themselves, and all the paperwork, and all the explanations and excuses.'

'Peadar, if I were you, I would keep my head down after we leave. Management won't be too happy with developments, and a measure of revenge will likely be on the cards. Just be careful, and good luck to you.'

'Good luck to you as well,' Peadar said. 'I'd shake your hand, but it might look suspicious, and we wouldn't want that now, would we?'

It would be the last words spoken between us. We would never meet again.

**11 am**

I checked the time, all the while monitoring the laundry door from my cell, looking for any sign of unusual activity.

**11.45 am**

Prisoners and screws began clattering down the stairs from the 3s above after mass. The prisoners would be going back to their cells, the screws out the gates. Give them 15 minutes and they would be well away.

After the rush had died down, I saw Brian and several of his team making their way towards the laundry. There were already a few men there, including Mallon.

A heated discussion ensued over sides at an imaginary football match scheduled for later that beautiful summer day.

**12.05 pm**

One of the two screws on the landing went into the laundry. This was my signal to move into place. Martin was already there with his shopping bag full of charges. I could see he was tense and ready.

'Where are you going?' I wise-cracked. 'Dunnes Stores isn't open on a Sunday!'

'Fuck off!' he muttered.

**12.30 pm**

Just then, we heard a knock from the other side of the laundry door. The remaining screw put the key into the lock, turned it, and swung the door open. As he did so, Farmer grabbed him and with the rest of Brian's team, they all tumbled inside.

'Mickey Do, Mickey Do, Mickey Do!'

When Mallon roared, the entire jail seemed to come alive. Prisoners began rushing from every landing towards the laundry. Plates, cups and saucers, rained down on the exercise yard opposite.

I too slipped inside, only seconds behind the men conducting the first onslaught. The quick-thinking screw who had come off the roof had managed to throw the crucial bunch of keys away. They rested beside a gaping hole in the floor. Another inch and we would never have been able to retrieve them. We would have had to blow the roof door, alerting the soldiers on the roof above the block.

Fortune had favoured us.

I grabbed the keys and barged my way towards the roof door. Glancing back, I saw a sea of anxious faces, all waiting to go. Mallon and Martin were on either side of me. Brian was watching my back.

I quickly isolated two possibilities and tried one. It didn't turn. I tried the other key, turned the lock and the door swung open. I stepped onto the flat roof only to encounter an obstacle I could never have planned for in a million years.

The army's commanding officer in the prison was standing in the open space between us and the first gate. Worse still, he was flanked by a corporal armed with a Gustav submachine gun. Apart from the explosives, which were no use defensively, we were completely unarmed.

I hesitated but Mallon shouted, 'Go on, go on,' and that was it. There was no turning back.

I draped down from the edge of the roof, dropping the final few feet to the ground. Others jumped, risking broken ankles from the fall. Mallon continued to shout orders as we sprinted in the direction of the soldiers.

'Don't go near them; don't touch them,' Mallon screamed.

Everyone obeyed. We swept past them on both sides, like water around rocks. They stood like statues, totally immobile. If we had attacked them, we would have lost momentum. We didn't have time. It would also have likely drawn fire from their comrades above.

We were near the first gate before I heard a burst of gunfire. From experience, I knew from the sound of the shots that they weren't firing in our direction. After the officer got over his shock, he had ordered the corporal to open fire over the heads of the men still spilling from the roof.

Unlike the first batch of battle-hardened Northern volunteers, most of the following waves weren't used to being under fire and they dropped to the ground. Their escape was over.

**12.35 pm**

I had reached the wooden door that had been my fixation for months. It wasn't even locked. I opened it to expose the barred gate behind.

Martin handed me a charge and I moulded it over the lock and pushed a detonator gently inside. I ran a piece of sandpaper over the matchheads taped to the fuse and they burst into flame. Black smoke appeared and everyone began taking cover.

By this stage, screws were running towards us but when they saw the smoke and the men dropping down, they turned on their heels and ran back towards the block. The crescendo from the explosion reverberating around the high walls seemed to add wings to their heels. We saw no more of them.

When I was placing the charge, I noticed a large greenhouse behind the barred gate. After it detonated, I was first through. All that remained of the glass structure was its concrete base and the buckled gate where it had stood only seconds before.

I began focusing on the outside door. It seemed to consist only of heavy wood, and we had planned for stronger.

**12.37 pm**

The door might even have been unlocked but I was on autopilot by then and took the charge that Martin handed me and hung it on the handle. I primed and lit it and sprinted to join the others in the shelter of the governor's house.

Seconds later, the explosion could be heard all over the town of Portlaoise. I put my head around the corner, the door had completely vanished, not even a splinter remained. We had cleared a path and the only thing between us and freedom was a rusty chain link fence. It took us only seconds to tear it down and we scampered across the gardens of the houses that backed up against the outside wall. A cacophony of barking dogs punctured the eerie silence.

Expecting to hear the sharp crack of machine-gun fire at any second, we found a laneway and charged out towards the Borris Road. We were so pumped up at this stage that we bolted past the waiting getaway vehicles.

Thankfully, the commotion had encouraged several people to stop their cars for a better look. Bad mistake!

**12.40 pm**

Brian Hearty's group hijacked a van and headed in the direction of the Dublin Road. Eleven of us piled into a green Triumph. With legs and torsos hanging out of every window, we drove in the direction of Borris, and the open countryside.

Eddie Gallagher, who told me he knew the road, had commandeered another car, a Morris Minor of all things, and had taken off in front of us with seven other men squeezed inside. You'd know we were on the skinny side back then!

After a few miles we turned off onto a quiet side road and who should we meet but Eddie, coming back towards us. He warned us the road was a dead end. So much for his local knowledge!

**1 pm**

Almost half an hour had now elapsed since we had taken the laundry. We knew it wouldn't be long until the Gardaí set up checkpoints on the main roads.

After continuing for a few minutes on the Borris Road, Mallon ordered us to turn off onto the first side road we came across. It was more of a rough track than a proper road, leading to a small farmhouse. Mallon and I went in, telling the rest of the lads to drive the car into an adjacent hayshed and hide it.

A farmer appeared at the door.

'Hello,' Kevin said, appearing as friendly as possible. 'I suppose you've heard all the racket?'

'Yes,' he said. 'I was wondering what was going on, alright. Who are you and what do you want here?'

'We are the Provisional IRA,' Mallon said. 'We've just escaped from the jail and need somewhere to take cover. Will you help us?'

Before he could reply, one of our comrades signalled to us. 'There are two men approaching with a gun,' he warned.

We squinted around the corner of the house and saw two men walking towards us. One had a rifle in the crook of his arm.

'Wait till they get close, and jump them,' Mallon ordered. 'Make sure you get control of the rifle before any shots are fired. They'll bring the whole thing down on top of us if that happens.'

I went back into the house and asked the farmer, 'Who's the man with the gun?'

'It's okay,' he replied nervously. 'It's only my son and his friend. They were out shooting rabbits. He won't give you any trouble. Just don't hurt him.'

We had no intention of hurting anyone. We quickly disarmed him and brought him and his companion inside. We asked the farmer again for help. He was very nervous, but I could understand this. I wasn't exactly calm myself.

The son offered to take us into the nearby forest where we could hide until dark. His father and his friend would stay in the house and put off any searchers.

Mallon ordered the son to guide us and asked the other young man if he knew where the Baileys lived. He also asked his name and where he worked. He left him in little doubt there would be repercussions if he refused his new commission. They knew the Baileys' house, and the young man agreed to deliver a message. We wanted a guide that would get us away from here.

'I'll do that for you, no problem,' the young man said. 'But I won't come back here in case I'm followed.'

'That's fine,' Mallon agreed. 'Just make sure to tell them where to find us and to wait until after dark.'

As soon as the messenger left, we went outside and briefed the rest of our comrades. We set off on foot, with the farmer's son leading the way. We reached the trees about a mile from the house and took cover. Mallon and I lay there all day, keeping watch with a pair of binoculars provided by our guide.

**2.30 pm**

Seeing a lone figure walking down the forest path in the direction of the house, we handed the glasses to the farmer's son.

'Who is it?' Mallon whispered to him. He didn't know.

After a few, tense minutes, the figure walked back along the path out of sight. We discovered afterwards that he was a Special Branch detective.

The farmer was a wily customer who feigned complete ignorance. He told the branch man he had no time at all for the IRA and would have nothing to do with them.

I was now thankful I hadn't got what I wished for weather-wise. It was relaxing lying there, basking in the sunlight, in the shade of the trees. We had time to consider our achievement. My only regret is that we failed to empty the place. We could never have anticipated the army personnel in the courtyard. Nobody had ever seen them there before at that time of the day.

I don't recall seeing or hearing a helicopter in the sky above as we spent the rest of the day hidden among the trees. This led us to believe that the Gardaí must be concentrating their efforts elsewhere. Time seemed to stand still. A church bell rang in the distance. I couldn't believe I was really free. Even lying here among the gorse and heather was freedom. The heat lasted well into the evening and we were so still that the songbirds congregated in the branches around us.

But we were keen to put more distance between ourselves and the prison. We knew it lay scarcely two miles away from our hiding place.

As dusk settled, we became more alert, waiting on someone to make contact. The enormity of what we had accomplished wasn't lost on us; we knew every effort was being made to recapture us.

Out of the twilight gloom, the ever-alert Mallon spotted someone walking in our direction. He suddenly sprung to his feet.

'I know him,' he told us. 'That's Eddie.'

He whistled softly, and the figure headed straight for us.

The two men shook hands and after a brief chat, Mallon told the farmer's son he could leave. We all expressed our gratitude to him. I'd say he was equally grateful to be rid of us.

# 43

We gathered around Eddie as he filled us in on the mayhem we had sparked. We would have to get out of the area as soon as possible. Gardaí and soldiers had saturated it for miles around. He told us that using the roads was completely out of the question, but Marion was organising transport and would meet us somewhere outside of the cordon.

We would have to walk. Beth was coordinating everything. We were all famished but Eddie had been afraid to bring us food in case he was stopped.

'I had no reason for being in possession of a picnic,' he told us.

We slipped quietly from field to field behind him, hugging the hedgerows and maintaining total silence. We avoided fields containing cattle because curiosity would get the better of them and we knew they would likely follow. After about two hours of hiking our way across country and burrowing through hedges, we reached a small hill, where we encountered a steel farm gate.

Mallon and a couple of others grabbed it to vault over but were thrown back. The farmer had electrified it.

Curses ruptured the silence as everyone else fell around laughing. Our leader wasn't amused.

'What the fuck are you are laughing at?' he fumed. Nobody answered him – we were too busy laughing.

We broke into the field through a hole in the hedge further along.

Mallon's mood was about to deteriorate further, and the rest of us wouldn't be laughing either. When we crested the hill, Portlaoise Prison lay below us, lit up like Disneyland. Mallon exploded.

'What the fuck are we doing here?' he asked Eddie. Our guide was devastated.

'I'm just not used to moving through the countryside in the darkness. I must have lost my bearings,' he said.

We all dropped down, acutely aware of how exposed we were on the brow of this hill. The moon was high in the sky and if we didn't find cover, we would be easily spotted from the air when dawn broke.

Just as we were debating what to do next, in the distance we heard the sound of a train.

Lying in my cell, late at night, I knew the sound of the freight wagons rattling up the line towards Dublin. How often had I wished to be on that train!

The sound gave Eddie his bearings.

'Follow me,' he said. 'I know where I am now. When we get to the train tracks, I can bring you to a safe area.'

Mallon glared at him, his confidence knocked. But with no better option, we all agreed this was our best bet.

I never blamed Eddie. Negotiating through unfamiliar terrain is difficult at the best of times and I knew he was doing his best. An hour later we were walking south along the tracks. This looks easy in the movies but negotiating railway sleepers is hard work. They don't match your stride, so you're always having to watch where you place your feet.

The rails stretched out in front of us in the moonlight but every time a bridge appeared up ahead, some of us would have to scout it. A dozen people walking along a railway line at night isn't exactly usual.

After a while, Eddie turned and said, 'I know exactly where I am now. If we turn off here it will bring us down to Emo graveyard.'

We trudged along a forest firebreak for an hour or more as daylight approached, tired, thirsty and hungry but thankful for the cover. Eddie stopped short of the road that ran to the cemetery. He pointed to a deep ditch and told us to hide there.

'The people in a nearby farmhouse are sympathetic and will help us if necessary,' he said. 'I'll report to Beth and try to arrange some food.'

After he slipped away, we burrowed our way deep into the undergrowth that covered what turned out to be a storm drain. Eddie had chosen well: it was so big it could have concealed the entire East Tyrone Brigade.

About three hours later, we heard the soft drone of a helicopter. The distinctive whirr of the propellers grew louder as it hovered nearby. Its downdraft ruffled the leaves on the bushes above our heads and it blew the grass around us flat. We didn't dare stir.

A fixed-wing aircraft also flew back and forth, and we heard our pursuers searching the forest nearby. They came within 100 yards or so of us. We could hear their radios and voices very clearly. This tested our nerves, but local knowledge had saved us. Eddie may have lost his bearings, but his choice of hiding place had more than made up for it.

Our pursuers scoured the forest for hours but gradually the search faded into the distance. We remained silent, motionless, and alert. We couldn't take the chance of spotters being left behind to watch for movement.

We only broke cover later that afternoon when Eddie returned with two large bags of food. He told us the search was now concentrating on another section of the woods, meaning we were safe for the time being.

We gorged ourselves. Never had lukewarm tea and sandwiches tasted so good. We were thankful for every sip and bite.

'I'm off now and I won't be back,' Eddie said. 'When it gets dark, Marion and her friend, Maggie, will be here with transport. You might have to walk a mile up the road to meet them. Try to be quick. Strange cars get noticed around here. Good luck to you all.'

We all took turns to shake his hand, showering him with thanks.

We kept watch in shifts. Then, when darkness fell, we crept into Emo graveyard. Not long afterwards, a car pulled up.

'Hello, Marion,' I said as she got out of the car. 'You must be my guardian angel.'

'Feck off you and your angel,' she replied. 'Every time I see you, you have a problem.'

I smiled at her, and she laughed.

'We have to cross the road and make our way along behind that wall for about half a mile,' she said. 'We have transport ready in a farmyard beyond. We don't have a lot of time. The roads are clear at the minute but that won't last.'

Mallon gave the order to go, and we crossed the road towards a high wall that marks the boundary of what is now Emo Park. We edged along, single file. In contrast to the previous night, there was no moon, and the shadow of the wall only compounded the darkness.

Curses would break the silence when someone fell into a drain, which were at least three feet deep and totally invisible. Briars scratched our faces and tore our clothes.

When we arrived at the farm, we were told we would be heading to Newbridge, the town where Tommy and I had gone after the helicopter hijack. We climbed into two cars. The two women drove ahead as scouts. If they encountered any problem, they would flash the brake lights to warn us. We criss-crossed back roads courtesy of local knowledge. Every section along the way had been cleared by local volunteers. It took about 30 nerve-wracking minutes to reach our safe house.

We spent much of Tuesday morning listening to the news reports about the escape. Later in the day, five of our number boarded a Dublin-bound lorry. I shook hands with Oliver. It would turn out to be the last time I would shake his hand for almost 40 years. It would take the authorities eight years to catch him. Not bad for a man afraid he might throw a wobbler!

After the last of them climbed into the back, the driver stacked building materials behind them. They reached Dublin without incident, dispersed and re-joined their units.

The rest of us were expecting our own transport later that evening. We were told we would be going to a place on the Wexford-Wicklow border, north of Gorey.

Marion and Maggie remained our main contacts with the outside world. They seemed to know every side road and boreen within 50 miles of Dublin. And if they weren't sure, they could always rely on local IRA intelligence.

The longer we remained free, the more embarrassed the State would become. Our escape had undermined constant assurances to the Brits that the government had the IRA on the run. Two high-profile prison breaks in a year didn't make them look good.

Late on Tuesday night, two cars arrived, and we piled in. The plan was to reach the next safe house unseen. This would leave us outside the dragnet. We would then stay put until things cooled down a bit.

A bridge in the scenic village of Tinahely was to prove our undoing. Crossing a bridge is never a good idea. There is a reason tolls were placed on them in the days of yore: they are choke points that are tough for fugitives to cross.

All the gold in the world wouldn't have got us through the checkpoint set up at Tinahely Bridge unnoticed. Fortunately, the Gardaí didn't have a car, but we had no choice but to smash through their blockade. We were never in any danger of being stopped, but we had just given away our position. They would also know the likely direction we were going, scuppering our plan to lay low for a while nearby.

We continued to our intended destination. The safe house was set well back from the road. The cars dropped us off at the bottom of the long, straight driveway that led to the front door. The house was empty, forcing us to break in. The owner was lucky. Later when questioned, he could deny all knowledge.

Mallon and I agreed we had come far enough from the checkpoint to be safe for the night. We also took note of the forest that bordered the bottom of the garden, which would give us cover in case of emergency.

We slept soundly enough considering, taking turns to keep watch. The following morning news bulletins reported that two cars had crashed through a roadblock in Co Wicklow. In solemn tones, the newsreader announced that the nationwide search would now concentrate on our area. He also said the search was costing £20,000 a day and there was an interview with a very displeased British government official questioning the inability of the Irish state to control a small group of desperadoes.

There were complaints from gardaí about having to sleep in ditches. And about the lack of food for days on end.

The Irish army was also concentrating on our area after the previous night's incident. The announcer said every outbound ferry was being searched, houses were being raided and security beefed up on both sides of the border. Yet not one of the 19 escapees had been recaptured so far. The obvious frustration in every Government interview buoyed our spirits.

Around midday, a car collected Marion and Maggie, who set off to arrange our next move. An hour or so later, a newsflash announced the arrest of two women in Co Wicklow, in connection with the escape. We knew immediately our guardian angels had been snared. But where? We had to assume it was nearby. We knew they would never betray us, but Mallon ordered an immediate evacuation.

The Gardaí would start raiding houses within a certain radius. Known or suspect safe houses would be first on the list. We gathered our meagre belongings and wiped down all traces of our presence. We all worked feverishly. After taking a good look around outside, we left by the back door and made for the forest.

Mallon and I lingered at its fringes, keeping an eye on the main road from the cover of a small hedge.

We had hardly settled into position when the first of a long line of Garda cars careered into the driveway. A helicopter also appeared overhead, followed by a spotter plane. The chopper then landed on the lawn. We beat a hasty retreat into the trees, regrouped and took refuge. The forest was so dense that we had to negotiate it on our hands and knees.

As we crawled away, we heard the door of the house being smashed in. Radios were crackling garbled messages. The helicopter took off and joined the fixed-wing plane scanning the carpet of trees.

We crawled deeper and deeper into the undergrowth until we reached a logging road. We continued to take cover in the trees, camouflaging ourselves as much as possible. We sat tight, praying they wouldn't sweep the forest on foot.

I have to admit, the strain on me was beginning to tell. Maybe it was a culmination of years on the run, coupled with the stress of the last few days. It wasn't the best place to have a meltdown, but my muttered words of desperation received short shrift.

'Pull yourself together,' Mallon ordered. 'What the fuck is wrong with you? Get a grip.'

My own wobbler had been short-lived! We lay there all day, listening to the aircraft inching its way back and forth across the sky above. Sometimes it was directly overhead, sometimes off in the distance. Occasionally, we would hear voices close by, but they would always fade away.

When darkness fell, we moved cautiously towards the rutted road, thinking to cross over. Garda cars were crawling past at regular intervals, forcing us to stay put.

When we eventually decided to go, we were just about to step onto the road when two Gardaí on foot appeared out of the darkness. I don't know who was more startled. They didn't have radios and it turned out they were raw recruits who hadn't even finished basic training.

'Don't be shouting now and you'll come to no harm,' Mallon said, in a voice full of authority. 'We only need you to be quiet for 10 minutes while we cross this road and get into the woods on the other side.'

The young recruits nodded agreement, standing transfixed while we went on our way again. We crossed the road and entered another thicket so dense in places that the lead person had to throw himself forward to bring the bushes and young trees down with him. The next in line would step over him and repeat the process. The foliage sprung back again after we passed, covering our tracks.

I have no idea how long it took to negotiate this formidable barrier, but it seemed like hours. We heard no sound of pursuit, even though we expected the young Gardaí would surely have reported their encounter.

When we came to the open country again, we headed north. Or so we thought. The night was pitch black. We had no moon or stars to navigate by, so we kept going in what we thought was a straight line. It didn't take us long to realise it was far from straight.

# 44

Around midnight, we emerged onto a single-track road. Stopping to catch our breath and get our bearings, I looked around, filled with a creeping realisation of déjà vu. I wandered off on my own for about 50 yards and came to an opening leading up to a house. This wasn't just any house, it was the one we had left this morning.

I signalled Mallon over. 'What's up?' he asked.

'I'll tell you, what's up,' I said. 'That's the house we stayed in last night.'

Mallon couldn't believe it, but I had stayed there previously so I was certain, even in the dark of night. It was all lit up, but it appeared deserted. We didn't dare approach, just in case. We thought we had been putting miles between us and this place but here we were again, right back to where we started. We had walked in a complete circle. We were all shattered. For all our efforts, we hadn't even gained a few yards.

'What the fuck are we going to do now?' Mallon asked.

'We could always send for Eddie!' I joked.

Mallon fixed me with a withering stare.

I could hear waves breaking not far away, so I suggested we follow the coast north towards Dublin until daybreak, or until we came across an opportunity to take cover. We had good contacts in the city; we had no connections further south.

And that's what we did. We stopped for a minute to rest, savouring the tangy sea air before ploughing on. We struggled along the spongy sand, walking just below the waterline to cover our tracks. Sometimes, we had to wade thigh-deep when we were negotiating a rocky outcrop.

We trudged north for about four hours before taking cover as dawn approached. We followed a small track leading away from the beach, towards some bushes. After reaching them, we followed a path until we came to a clearing. There we found a caravan with a small car parked outside.

One of our number still had what looked like a garda uniform, including the peaked cap stuffed in a pocket, so we sent him to knock on the door. A lady answered and nearly keeled over in shock. Media reports had been depicting us as a gang of gun-toting thugs to be avoided at all costs. Instead, we surely presented a pitiful sight.

Mallon and I began trying to instil some calm. We confirmed who we were, assuring her that the last thing we wanted was to harm or scare her in any way. We just wanted shelter for a few hours, until we figured out what to do next.

It took a while, but she accepted our assurances and began to relax. She had begun making us tea before telling us that her sister was in the other room asleep. She would wake her, so as not to alarm her. Opening the door to her sister's room, the lady turned around ashen faced.

'She's gone,' she gasped. 'She must have jumped out the window. She'll have gone for help.'

We grasped the situation straight away. We had to get out of there – and fast. We took a look around outside but there was no sign of her. We asked for the keys to the dinky Renault 4 car and the lady handed them over without complaint. We squeezed inside. I had never driven a car with a gear stick protruding from the dash before, but I soon got the hang of it.

We drove along some narrow, winding roads until we reached a junction with a signpost for Dublin. Negotiating the next bend, we ran into a checkpoint manned by two Gardaí on the main Dublin to Wexford road.

We spotted each other almost simultaneously. Both Gardaí scattered as we revved past and swung left, south away from Dublin. Their patrol car was sitting to the north of the junction and we didn't fancy our chances against it in our little French tin box!

We barrelled down the road in that ridiculously small car. Even with my foot flat to the metal, we were barely managing 50 miles an hour. After swerving around the first bend and out of sight of the checkpoint, we turned right for the Wicklow mountains.

The car found the going even tougher as the road began to climb. The labouring engine whined in protest. Our only chance lay in hijacking a bigger, more powerful car. Salvation came in the form of a Volkswagen Passat, being driven by a couple heading for the Rosslare ferry. We stopped them, politely handed them out their luggage and switched cars.

We knew that if we didn't go to ground before sunrise, the game would be up.

As I continued driving across the hills in the grey light of dawn, I saw a plane off in the distance to my left. It dropped behind a copse of trees, and it never reappeared. None of the others had seen it and try as I might, I couldn't convince them of its existence.

A short time later, we came to a large, gloomy presbytery. Given its connections to Christian charity, Mallon thought someone there might be sympathetic to our plight, but we were told in no uncertain terms to go away and not to come back. As we drove off, it occurred to us that such hostility indicated they would most likely call the Gardaí and we had better get off the road as soon as possible. So Mallon told us to turn into the next house we saw.

By now, we were several miles further on. I turned onto the drive of a farmhouse. Mallon and I alighted from the car and knocked on the front door. A slight, elderly gentleman answered. We exchanged greetings before Mallon told him we were the IRA escapees and we needed somewhere to hide for a while.

He looked us up and down, without saying anything at first. Then he asked how many of us there were. Our presence didn't appear to have ruffled him at all – he was calm and calculating.

'There are six of us,' Mallon said. 'You had better come in then,' he said.

He turned around to his son, who was standing at his shoulder, and ordered him to take the car to a shed and cover it with hay.

We couldn't believe our luck as we fell onto the sofas in the living room. When we were settled, he stood to address us, drawing himself up in a formal manner.

'Let me put my cards on the table,' he said. 'I am a Blueshirt, a real Blueshirt. Not one of those arseholes you see on television and read about in the papers. I fought in Spain with O'Duffy and I'm proud of it. I have no time for your politics but as a military man myself, I have to respect what you people have achieved in getting out of prison. On that account, my son and I will give you whatever assistance we can. Now that's as fair as I can be. Relax, you're safe here. We'll all have a cup of tea, while we figure out what we are going to do with you.'

We were amazed at the honesty and integrity of the man. He was willing to risk his freedom, and that of his son. He just wasn't helping us in some passive way, he was prepared to get his hands dirty. We tried to thank him, but he only brushed it away with a wave of his hand.

'It's nothing,' he said. 'You men have earned some help.'

Who knows, maybe he had other reasons. Like many people in the South, the recent loyalist bomb attacks in Dublin and Monaghan, which killed 34 innocent civilians and maimed hundreds more, had appalled the entire country. There were already whispers of British military collusion in those murders that persist to this day. One thing was certain – there was no containing the conflict within the artificial British border in Ireland.

His son returned from covering the car and a short time later we found ourselves sitting at a table in front of one of the most memorable breakfasts of my life. We gave them a rundown of the last five days and details of how we had managed to escape. They sat wordless throughout.

Conversation eventually turned to what we might do next. His son agreed to take a message to an address in Dublin where he would ask for Brian Keenan, the IRA's Dublin Quartermaster, who was waiting to hear from us.

All day long, a helicopter and a plane buzzed the surrounding countryside in a vain effort to flush us out. Our host never once glanced skywards. Gardaí and military vehicles passed constantly but his countenance never changed. He was a solid man, confident in his actions and at peace with his commitments. I liked him, regardless of his politics.

In the early evening, his son returned to tell us he had met Keenan and appraised him of our situation. The message he brought back was simple. He told us to be ready the following morning, and transport would be there for us. We were not to worry, he had everything in hand.

We cleaned ourselves up as best we could and spent a pleasant evening in the company of these two men. We also enjoyed our first untroubled rest since leaving Portlaoise Prison.

The following morning, around 10.30, two long black limousines decked out with red and pink ribbons pulled into the front yard. We had already washed and shaved in preparation. Three young ladies sat inside each, all dressed in wedding attire. We were all given black suits, white shirts, and bowties, complemented with shiny black shoes.

We bade our hosts farewell and took our place beside our new partners; carnations in buttonholes and stinking of aftershave. We drove straight up the main road to Dublin. Along the way, we were waved through several checkpoints. Our odyssey was over.

We had endured a gruelling ordeal for the past six days. Along the way, I had often thought of the Irish patriots hunted and sheltered in these same mountains over the centuries.

After we left, the son dumped our car in a forest several miles away. Its discovery provoked another spate of fruitless searches.

In later years, I tried to find this house again, to no avail. I would have liked to express my thanks. Their actions only served to underline the complexity of politics in Ireland.

Some 44 years later, on a cold, blustery New Year's Day, I reunited with Oliver at his home. A Celtic cross has pride of place in his living room. Somehow it had survived the aftermath of the escape and a fellow inmate had sent it out for him. The same man had the foresight to change the original base, which was contaminated with explosive residue.

Several years after the escape, I found myself back in Portlaoise Prison for other offences. A screw approached me one day.

'Can I ask you something?' he started. 'I've been meaning to ask you this for a long time, but I wasn't sure if you'd speak to me.'

'It depends on what you have to say,' I replied.

'I served in the Irish army and I was wondering, were you in the house we raided in Co Wicklow after the Portlaoise escape? I know it's a long time ago, but I can give you an interesting perspective on it.'

'Yes,' I said. 'I was in that house. Why do you ask?'

'On the day we raided,' he said. 'We were given orders from the top that we weren't to confront you under any circumstances.'

'Well, you could have fooled me,' I laughed.

'No, seriously,' he said. 'We were told you were all heavily armed and we were not to engage you in a firefight. We weren't entirely sure that you had even been in the house, but we were instructed not to search the forest.'

I didn't press him for any more information. I thought it strange, but I had no reason to disbelieve him. It did jolt me back to the time when I saw the plane disappear after it surely spotted us on the exposed road. Apparently, it ran out of fuel, but this is hard to believe given that it was early morning and it was likely to have just taken off.

Like many things that strike a man as odd in hindsight, I'll probably never know.

Looking back to that time, I should have called it quits when I was ahead, but it wasn't that easy. My options were limited. I returned to active service, but I would soon find myself on the run from the very organisation for which I had been prepared to give my life.

Following this escape, another banned song soared to the top of the Irish charts.

'There's nineteen men a-missing and they didn't use the door, Just blew a little hole where there wasn't one before,

Now the army and the Gardaí are searching high and low,

For the men from Portlaoise Prison who have vanished like the snow.'
– Dermot Hegarty

Perhaps one day I'll get decorated for services to Irish ballads!

# 45

After a few weeks of laying low, during which I took the opportunity to reunite with my wife and kids, I went straight back on active service. I knew that operating would no longer be as easy for me. My face had been on the front page of every newspaper and on TV. And after that episode in the Dublin Bridewell, every Special Branch detective now knew what I looked like.

So, I was given elements of my old job back. I would operate behind the scenes, running a secret unit with much the same personnel, reporting directly to GHQ.

I told GHQ at the time, 'You give me information on any building or job in this country and I'll take it.'

Once I got the information, it was simple. There is always a weakness, always a flaw, always a lazy fucker. If the ins and outs of your security are known, then it's no longer secure. I was confident of getting around anything.

In December 1974, the secret unit took £147,000 from Chase Bank of Ireland International at Shannon Airport – the biggest bank robbery in the history of the State.

I wasn't involved on the day, but I certainly had first-hand accounts from some of those who were, including Mark, who led the operation.

It all began with a meeting in a quiet corner of a pub near the border. After Mark sat down, his contact pressed a large key into his hand.

'This is the back door key to a bank at Shannon Airport,' the contact said, matter of factly. 'I want you to rob it.'

'Where did you get it?' Mark asked. 'And how do you know it'll work?'

'I got it from a building worker who was doing some repairs,' the contact said. 'He got the original and cut a duplicate.'

Mark agreed to scope out the job and travelled to Shannon to meet the supplier of the key. The Co Clare town was full of northern refugees who had resettled here, taking work in the industries spawned by the nearby international airport.

The airport bank was considered among the most secure in the country. Aside from its sophisticated internal systems, a Garda station was situated right beside it.

Mark met the building worker and asked him whether he could still move around the vicinity of the bank without attracting too much notice.

'Yes,' I believe so,' the man said. 'We're still on site there.'

'Right,' Mark said. 'Can you go down there on Monday, then again on Wednesday and then again at the weekend? I want you to unlock the door, trigger the alarm, close it again quickly, turn the key again and walk away every time. I need to gauge the reaction after the alarm goes off.'

He agreed and Mark began to conduct some detailed surveillance.

At first, as soon as the alarm went off, a Garda would emerge from the station to check things over.

After the man had done this three times as requested, Mark asked him to repeat it the following week. He could already see that complacency was setting in. Every time the Gardaí checked the back door, they found it locked.

## Chapter 45

Eventually, instead of arriving quickly, one of them would dawdle out and give the door a perfunctory kick.

The alarm had cried wolf.

After Mark had established that the security could be breached, he assembled a small group of experienced Co Tyrone volunteers, including a woman from Dungannon, at a nearby Co Limerick motel. Everyone stayed in the same room the night before the robbery.

They put gloves on, cleaned their weapons, oiled the magazines and reassembled them. Then they set them on a bed. Mark ordered everyone not to touch them again until they were ready to go and sat them down for a final briefing. There were also some locals present and he knew they would be feeling the heat afterwards.

'Tomorrow, you're going into a very tight spot,' he said. 'They're going to lift you afterwards. Now, listen very carefully to what I have to tell you. They're going to threaten you with jail but that's nothing to what I'll do to you if I catch you. If you mention anyone's name, I will come back and I will kill you. If you get picked up, all you have to do is say nothing.'

The three men from the unit designated to carry out the job waited until dark before using the key to let themselves in. As anticipated, the alarm went off and rang for a short time. A few minutes later, they were cowering inside when they heard the clang from the garda boot giving it the usual cursory kick.

The following morning, a security guard walked in to open up. He was a former soldier and the IRA had information that he might be armed. They weren't taking the chance. Mark jumped him and stuck a revolver in his mouth.

'If you give me any trouble, a bullet will be going into the back of your head,' he said.

Then he frisked him. He was unarmed.

By this time, the others had rounded up the rest of the staff who had walked in behind. They tied all of them up, apart from the manager. They forced him to open the huge vault. The door was so heavy it took two men to push it ajar. There were safe deposit boxes all around the wall. Bags of cash awaiting collection lay in the middle of the floor.

Just as they began breaking into the boxes, more security guards entered the building. The unit hadn't bargained for this but managed to overpower them. However, it cost the volunteers valuable time.

They were on a tight schedule. The plan called for speed and surprise. It had to be completed before the branch was scheduled to open for the day.

They grabbed the sacks but decided that smashing the boxes open would take too long. They later discovered that these contained at least £1m worth of gold bars and diamonds.

When they walked out, Mark flashed a light to alert the getaway driver that it was time to pick them up. The car didn't move. They found out later that he had fallen asleep!

A van belonging to a cleaner was sitting outside the bank with the keys inside. They loaded the bags into it and drove away to meet the 40-foot trailer truck that was waiting for them a few miles away.

There was a false compartment built into the front of the trailer. The men transferred the money and sat inside along with it. The driver then closed it in. By the time the Gardaí had set up roadblocks all over the Midwest region the men and the cash were already in Dublin.

Several of those involved were questioned afterwards but no prosecutions followed. During the interviews, Gardaí attributed the operation to me, but that job was solely down to Mark.

# 46

The unit's final operation would end in both failure and death. Just before 8 pm on Monday, March 17, 1975, an armour-plated truck trundled towards the boundary of Portlaoise Prison. Henzy, an IRA inmate from South Derry, had spotted a security flaw and Mallon, who had been recaptured again in January, sent out word to mount yet another escape.

We aimed to drive a heavy vehicle through the lightly fortified prison farm adjacent to the outer walls and smash the back gate of the main compound. At a pre-arranged time, IRA prisoners who had gathered in a recreation room to watch a movie would blow open a door and rush towards this gate.

The unit had stolen a quarry truck the previous Friday night, and a team of mechanics and engineers, led by local men, Liam O'Mahoney and Brian Fenlon, spent every waking minute that weekend welding steel to the body plating and modifying the cab to provide access underneath, giving prisoners cover as they crawled inside. They were expecting heavy fire from the machine-gun mounted above the gate.

But minutes before the truck was due to start its four-mile journey, the engineers discovered a serious flaw.

A damaged water pipe would cause the engine to overheat – the chances of making it were slim. The armour plating designed to protect those inside also prevented vital running repairs.

Taking the decision to abort the mission, the Co Tyrone man in charge drew the two drivers aside to inform them. But Eamonn O'Sullivan and Gerry Quinn refused to stand down. 'If there's any chance at all, no matter how slim, we have to go,' Eamonn said.

When the vehicle began lumbering towards the prison, the unit cut the electricity to the town, including to the jail itself. Although the prison had back-up generators, these couldn't power every light. Cars were torched at junctions off the main roads, both as a distraction and to ensure a clear run for the vehicles waiting to transport the escapees.

Later, the commander regretted a failure to install extra headlights on the truck to compensate for the poor visibility the unit had created, but this didn't prevent it getting to the farm, breaching its perimeter, and lurching towards the back gate.

Inside, the waiting prisoners who had blasted their way out of a recreation room, knew the game was up when they heard the engine stall only a few yards away without penetrating the gate. Worse was to come. Soldiers had opened fire, killing Dublin volunteer Tom Smith and wounding six others.

If the engine had held out for another few yards, the unit's final operation would have been a success. Instead, it ended in failure. Eamon and Gerry were arrested.

March 17 is celebrated as St Patrick's Day around the world, but this is a day I always remember Tom Smith and what might have been. I also recall the bravery of Eamonn and Gerry and salute the expertise of all those people who worked so hard to ensure a successful conclusion. We had so nearly made it.

# 47

Around Christmas 1974, J.B. O'Hagan, one of the senior men I had helped spring from Mountjoy, had approached me to join the IRA Army Council, a near-mythical group that decided strategy.

J.B. always had high regard for me, but I declined his offer of promotion to the top table, telling him that I preferred to be out in the field. I also pointed out that, contrary to orders, I had recognised the court during my trial in connection with the helicopter job.

IRA policy at that time dictated that volunteers should refuse to recognise the authority of the court to judge them because they didn't accept the legitimacy of either state on the island of Ireland. I never saw the point of this. I always felt it was better to go down fighting. In later years, this order was dropped, and guerrilla tactics extended to the legal system, resulting in many volunteers literally able to fight another day.

I told him that, given my actions, I would have felt very uncomfortable ordering other men not to recognise the court. I didn't tell him that I was never very good at obeying orders.

I have always felt that turning down the offer of a position on the Army Council was the beginning of the end for me as far as the IRA was concerned. It also coincided with a time when I needed a break.

In the early days, I would see my wife every few weeks, but I never went home. She would cross the border to see me. She didn't care what I was doing. She was a very independent woman.

We never thought I'd have been gone for so long – maybe a couple of years and I'd be home again. I could have caught up with the kids then. But over the years, I became hardened into it – it took on a life of its own and I kept at it.

Around the same time as I declined J.B.'s offer, the IRA agreed a ceasefire with the British Army. It ended the following month but was renewed again in early February, 1975, and held until the following year.

For the record, I was opposed to it, believing that the Brits weren't interested in ending the war but were using the truce to gather intelligence and give themselves some breathing space. History will judge me correct on that score.

One night, a house I was staying in near Dungannon was surrounded by British troops. Although there was no attempt to arrest me, they were letting me know that they were fully aware of my presence and were marking my movements. As far as I was concerned, the fact that they were gathering intelligence on me contravened the ceasefire.

I went to GHQ, pleading to be allowed to mount a couple of operations to put manners on them. My unit could have inflicted serious damage. It was so secret that we could even have denied involvement publicly, but it would certainly have sent them a message. I was explicitly ordered not to do anything unless the Army Council agreed to it. I was also told to write down the names of all the members of the unit.

I refused point blank to give up any names, saying that if they wanted to replace me as head of the unit, I would give the names to my successor.

I also told them in no uncertain terms what they could do with their order.

After that, they banned me from providing finance to the volunteers under my command. This meant I had responsibility for the safety and security of several men and women, but I was to leave them hanging.

I asked Marion to check three arms dumps under my control. She found them empty. I asked my superiors where the arms had gone and was told they had been moved because they expected another pogrom in Belfast. More bullshit!

That was when the penny finally dropped: I had fallen out of favour, and so, I resigned.

I asked for some money to relocate to the United States for a while with my wife and family. I always had full intention of returning to the IRA, but I badly needed a long break. I was given the okay but when they offered me only £300, I went berserk. I felt it was disrespectful after all the years of work and the money I had brought in. I suppose that, stupidly, I had developed a sense of entitlement.

I decided I would bankroll myself. I would go freelance, in other words, instead of robbing for the Movement, I would rob for myself.

I wasn't looking to raise much – maybe a few grand to set things up and have a good time. So, I tapped up another few men of similar mindset and set about looking for suitable targets.

I was driving through a large town when I noticed someone carrying what looked like a large sack of cash into an imposing bank branch on the main square. There didn't appear to be much security, so I decided to take another look at the same time the following week.

In the meantime, I booked a room in the hotel opposite, to keep the place under surveillance. When we discovered a repeat of the previous week's routine, we couldn't believe our luck.

The following week, three of us parked up on the square. I decided against a mask, opting instead for a shower cap. I was working on the assumption that if you wear something unusual, that's all people will notice.

I jumped out of the car and pointed my gun into the open door of the security van.

I told the guard to throw out a few bags and I heard the rattle of coins at my feet. I cocked my pistol.

'The next bag that makes any noise when it hits that floor – I'll shoot you dead'.

He began throwing bags of cash towards me. £135,000 - the second-biggest heist in state history after Shannon. A complete fluke and an amount that would cause us no end of trouble. We couldn't believe it but we could hardly leave it behind either!

We stashed most of it in a friend's house, taking just a few grand each to keep us going.

I travelled on my own passport but when I landed in New York, someone met me and took me through a side door to avoid Immigration officials. My wife followed me over.

Someone told me later that the IRA knew I was going but decided it was easier to let me leave because trying to stop me would have caused them more trouble than it was worth.

'The only problem is that you came back,' he added.

I had a job arranged in New York working in a couple of Irish bars owned by Alan Clancy, a well-known republican who used to own The Four Seasons hotel in Monaghan town. He used to deliver food and drink to Mallon and me in the Garda station after we had been arrested. Thanks to him and to the hospitality of the local Gardaí, it usually turned into a very pleasant few days' rest before they released us.

After a few months around New York, my wife and I were both ready to go back when I got word that the IRA had sent a hit squad after me. When I had carried out that last robbery, I didn't know that GHQ was holding a meeting nearby. The police follow-up around the bank had kept senior officers pinned down for nearly two days. They weren't happy.

I was working in two bars but had to quit. We also moved elsewhere, and I armed myself but nobody ever knocked on my door.

Years later, at a funeral, I met one of the men who had been sent to execute me.

'You were lucky that you never found me,' I told him. 'You would have been staring down the barrel of a .44 Magnum and gone home in a box.'

He agreed that he had been extremely fortunate. I often wonder how hard he actually looked.

By the time I went home shortly afterwards, the IRA had found the rest of the money from the robbery. I had been intending to use it to 'buy' my way back in or at least be left in peace.

I was now in a worse situation than when I left. It's hard to negotiate from the bottom of a trench. Not only was I penniless, the IRA was also out to kill me, believing that I might join a newly-formed organisation that opposed the ceasefire, the Irish National Liberation Army (INLA).

This grouping, comprising an assortment of former IRA members disenchanted with the ceasefire and the general direction of the Provo leadership, was carrying out bank raids across the Republic to arm itself. I knew many of them, of course, but I had no hand, act or part in the INLA. Nor did I support it. The Provos were the only game in town as far as I was concerned.

I had only wanted a holiday but in the febrile atmosphere of the time and given my reputation as a maverick, the leadership wasn't prepared to give me the benefit of any doubt.

I returned to robbing banks for personal gain. In February 1976, three of us got away with almost £11,000 from the Allied Irish Bank branch in Balbriggan, a town north of Dublin. We followed this up in March, taking around £28,000 from the Bank of Ireland in Navan. I fired warning shots high above the head of a Garda sergeant who was trying to stop us getting away after the building was surrounded. I believe the bullet holes are still plain to be seen.

I was willing to face an IRA court-martial for my freelance operations but was told by former comrades, who remained friendly with me, that I could look forward to a kangaroo court. I was a very hard man to find in those days, but Pete Ryan went out of his way to warn me.

'If you hand yourself in, you're for the mulberry patch,' he assured me.

The mulberry patch could have been any one of a number of lonely boglands where the IRA buried informers in unmarked graves. I was no tout, but the message was clear: I wouldn't be seen again if I surrendered myself. I would be joining 'The Disappeared'.

In desperation, I sought a meeting with Phil Flynn, the vice-president of Sinn Féin at the time. Although Sinn Féin was meant to be the purely political wing of the Republican Movement, he reputedly had enormous influence with the Army Council, and I believed that he might be able to call off the dogs. I assured him I was ready to rejoin the Movement – all I wanted was a fair hearing.

I drove from the meeting in Bettystown to Canning's Bar, an isolated pub in the village of Galtrim, about six miles from Trim, Co Meath, where the Special Branch arrested me, along with Eugene O'Hanlon, on that afternoon in March, 1976.

In follow-up raids, the Gardaí found around £30,000 and a cache of weapons in a safe house we had been using. This was negligence on my part: I had the address in my pocket when I was caught. It caused the family unnecessary harassment, and I can only apologise for the trouble I brought to their door.

I was never captured on any job, but I was certainly betrayed. When I was bundled into the back of the patrol car, I saw the false number plate of the vehicle I was driving written on the dashboard. Very few people knew what I was driving and fewer still knew the registration of the car.

The media at the time reported that my arrest had been coincidental but I never bought this line. All the evidence I needed was on that dashboard in front of me. I had been betrayed yet again. And this time, I had run out of chances.

They threw the book at me. Eugene and I were sentenced to 20 years for the Navan robbery and shooting at a Garda. It was small consolation that we beat an attempted murder charge.

The judge handed us another 15 years concurrent for Balbriggan – another man, Frankie Taggart, got 15 years for this one too. Eugene and I got another 12 years concurrent for our part in a robbery of a hotel and the three of us were given another concurrent 10 years for possession of gelignite and a detonator at Balbriggan and a final 10 years concurrent for possession of weapons at that bank. There was no leave to appeal.

The three of us sat the whole time in the dock of the courtroom with only socks on our feet after Portlaoise Prison authorities refused to allow us to wear our own shoes.

When I arrived back inside to start my sentence, one of the screws joked to me, 'Welcome back, Brendan – you wouldn't have a milk churn buried somewhere that I could look after for you until you get out?!'

I didn't. I had as much money then as I did when I walked out again all those years later – none.

I was only 29 years old.

This time, I was housed among a mishmash of outcasts – mainly former IRA volunteers who had fallen out with the leadership because of disagreements over direction. The Provos initially labelled us 'The Mavericks' but when we wore that as a badge of honour, they began referring to us as 'The Bits and Pieces'. Many of the men on my landing were members of republican splinter groups, mainly the INLA.

The future IRA Chief of Staff, Kevin McKenna, a fellow Tyrone man who already held senior rank, issued a standing order banning everyone from speaking to me. We knew each other well but we never did get along – you could say there was mutual disrespect. Apart from a few noble exceptions who ignored this, such as Pete Ryan and Jim Lynagh, the order to shun me was obeyed.

Mallon, who was very much his own man and could have ignored the diktat, even made sure that nobody even passed on the local Tyrone newspaper for me to read.

I don't know to this day why he took such a set against me. I can only surmise that he felt that my actions had reflected badly upon him.

It is a grudge that has lasted almost five decades now and given his response to a request for input into this book, will likely continue.

McKenna's boycott extended to my wife and kids. They would never receive any help. They would never even be offered a lift to the prison to see me. It is a tribute to them that they struggled down so often to visit me despite the odds stacked against them.

Sometimes neighbours from Coalisland on their way to visit other prisoners would literally drive past them as they stood on the side of the road, soaked to the skin, looking to hitch a lift. These people knew my wife and kids were trying to get to Portlaoise.

My time in prison began courtesy of the helicopter escape but those who benefited most ensured that I became an outcast – and this extended to my family. Those who don't understand loyalty will never understand the hurt of betrayal.

Even former friends and comrades were forbidden from visiting on pain of expulsion from Sinn Féin. But people like Maureen Shiels and her sister Eileen defied these bullies. We remain friends to this day, and I will value their loyalty forever.

I did time hard. My family did time hard.

I was eventually released in 1991 after almost 16 years. My marriage broke down shortly afterwards, and by this time my kids had grown up without me.

I rustled up some seed money and set up a small, open-air market in Dublin. It wasn't long before the Special Branch came around and leaned heavily on the stallholders not to become involved with the likes of me. I had to shut down.

In 1993, Dominic McGlinchey, another former IRA volunteer who fell foul of the leadership and went on to become leader of the breakaway INLA, approached me to get involved in robbing a busy Dublin pub. We knew each other from time spent together in Portlaoise. After he split from the IRA while in prison in the early 1980s, he too was exiled among 'The Bits and Pieces'

He said he was stuck for a driver. I reluctantly agreed, out of loyalty to a man I had got on well with in jail. It was a fiasco and I ended up being sentenced to another eight years in Portlaoise. For the record, we were armed solely with a .22 rifle, which was more usually a weapon for hunting rabbits.

I was released for the final time in 1999, as the jails were emptied after the Good Friday Agreement. Since then, I have ducked and dived, doing casual jobs and keeping my nose clean. Neither my record nor my age lent themselves to gainful employment.

Still, from my perspective, even having little in your pocket is always better than doing time. I literally couldn't do one more minute in jail. I've had more than enough.

# Epilogue

So, what prompted me to write this book? About 10 years ago, Tony McNally approached me concerning a graphic account written by the high-profile informer Sean O'Callaghan, of how he had fired bullets over my head to save the life of an innocent young Protestant man I was allegedly beating in a field.

This couldn't have been further from the truth. I remember the incident well at the 1975 Easter Commemoration at Carrickmore, Co Tyrone.

Someone told me that this young fella was being held by two volunteers, who were awaiting an order to execute him. I went there and immediately realised he was being held in the wrong. I ordered his release. I wasn't wearing a mask and I told him, 'My name is Brendan Hughes. If anyone ever causes you any difficulties, mention my name and I will sort it out.

At that commemoration, I shared the platform with Kevin McKenna and Sinn Féin leader, Dáithi Ó Conaill, and I read out the Roll of Honour of the local republican dead. At the time, the newspapers described Ó Conaill and I as two of the most wanted men in Ireland. Thousands of people attended and the security forces stayed well clear. This was our heartland and, besides, the ceasefire was still holding at this point.

O'Callaghan's twisted fiction was a pack of lies but it prompted me to set the record straight. I intended to confront him through this book but he died before I could do so.

I pressed on. I had been written out of history but I was determined this would no longer be my fate.

Even though I was young and resilient when I started out, the entire experience was very trying. Going to sleep in a different place every night and forever being in dread of the early morning knock on the door aren't things I would recommend.

I didn't leave the Provos in 1975, they left me. I had always meant to return. I just needed a long break. I became embittered.

This was a dark period in my life, a period of madness and bad decision making.

I had let myself, and most of all my family, and close friends down. I make no excuses for my behaviour, but it seemed like the best option at the time. I can only apologise to all those people who believed in me. I lost the plot. Instead of helping my family, I destroyed their future and mine.

I take this opportunity to thank those people of East Tyrone and North Monaghan who opened their doors and their hearts to me and others like me who dared to take up arms for their rights and freedom.

I also think of those many people like the wee man in the hills of Pomeroy, those who reared me, and those who stood by me even in the darkest of times. I would like to pay particular tribute to my good friend, Eugene O'Hanlon, without whose enduring loyalty I would probably never have lived to tell this tale.

I also must mention Micksy Martin for all his help and welcome advice and my son, Craig, who bought me a laptop to help put this story down. Leo Magee in the National Archives also went out of his way for me.

I served my time in the best way I could, but it took a heavy toll on me and on my family. The events recounted here happened decades ago, but some people still believe they have the right to indulge in snide innuendo.

While attending Tony McNally's funeral in 2017, a man called Tommy Cassidy whispered in my ear.

'You know, Hughes,' he hissed. 'All I ever done during the war was fight. I never had any interest in money.'

I suppose some of my former comrades feel they have the right to judge me but ignorant individuals like Tommy Cassidy are all too common. He has more than earned the nickname 'Foggy' based on a ridiculous character in the classic BBC comedy, Last of the Summer Wine, who bored his friends to tears, boasting of his unlikely exploits. This was a barbed provocation too far. So, in his cack-handed way, he did me a favour.

During my time in the IRA, I did my best to behave with integrity and fairness. All a man can do is his best, and that's what I tried to do. I wish I could have done more, and done it better, but there it is, and there it remains.

My good friends have often asked, 'Was it all worth it?' This is a question every activist must answer for themselves.

I don't regret what happened to me. I would do the same again. I was defending my community. I regret the innocent lives lost but there is nothing I can say to lessen the pain of those left behind. I have also lost many comrades over the years. Some were killed in combat, more by loyalist murder gangs and undercover Brits. It was a dirty war. When we set out, we thought we could finish it, but we were only skirmishing around the abyss before we fell in.

After half a century, we emerged but the old distrusts continue.

I am certain of one thing: the current situation beats sending our children out to die, or ending up in prison for long, soul-destroying years. The Peace Process may not be everyone's cup of tea but I sincerely hope that we never again have to resort to armed conflict.

I would not advise any young person today to become involved in a campaign of violence. Education and politics are where it's at now.

When we started out, life for Northern nationalists differed little from 1921, when the sectarian statelet was born. Now, our people are much better off. Housing, education, and jobs are more fairly distributed, but the spectre of sectarianism still haunts the place.

If our children were educated together, I believe it would lift this curse. I also believe a united Ireland would hasten this process, north and south, and that we are closer to it than ever.

I never felt more alive than I did back then. But don't listen to any of that shit about living fast and dying young. I may have treated it like a game at times, but it wasn't like that.

Dark thoughts plague me, too. Of a screw switching cell lights on and off as he checks on the ghosts of the men inside. Then it's my turn and it wakes me with a start. I console myself that I'm now safe in my own bed. Somehow, I survived.

Some night soon, I hope his footsteps will cease and I will finally be finished with this thing.

# Hunger

'Twas not the food that they hungered for

Brave Irish comrades, men at war

From Mac Swiney in a British cell

to Bobby's men in that squalid hell.

Don't dare to call them terrorists

'Twas ye who brought the guns

To shoot them down in Derry

Brothers, fathers, sons.

Never let their names leave your lips

Go tell the young and the younger

No lack of food did take their lifes

'Twas for freedom they did hunger.

*Leo Magee*

**Kevin Mallon** received a 10-year-sentence in 1975 for ordering his female companion to open fire on Gardaí during his arrest in a dance hall the previous year. She was acquitted. He was released in 1982. He turned down a request for his input into this book in emphatic fashion. Referring to Brendan Hughes, he texted: 'You travel in much hated company you shave (sic) sense and run away do not contact me again.'

**Tony McNally** emigrated to the U.S. and died suddenly in 2017. He was buried in his native Co Tyrone.

**Tommy McKearney** continued to play a leading role in the republican movement and remains politically active.

**Maurice Conway** died in 1999, aged 62. The congregation at his well-attended funeral in his native Coalisland heard Tommy McKearney describe him as 'an elegant enigma'.

**Seamus 'Sig' Dillon** was murdered by loyalist gunmen in 1997 while working as a hotel doorman. It is believed he was targeted in direct retaliation for the prison assassination of the notorious loyalist leader, Billy Wright, only hours before. He was 45 years old.

**'Mark'** enjoys early morning walks in the Dublin mountains and says that his greatest achievement is 'being above ground'.

**Marion** later served many years in jail for her republican activities.

**Michael 'Pete' Ryan** became an IRA legend and was among eight prisoners who shot their way out of Belfast's Crumlin Road jail in 1981. He always featured at the top of 'Most Wanted' lists, until British special forces eventually shot him dead – along with two comrades, Lawrence McNally and Tony Doris – in his native Tyrone in 1991. Reports of wild celebrations after the shootings reflected the damage he had inflicted upon his enemies over the years.

**Joe 'J.B.' O'Hagan**, one of the three helicopter escapees, was recaptured in Dublin in 1975. He died in 2001, aged 78. The Catholic Church forced his family to remove the Irish Tricolour from his coffin before requiem mass, but in a final act of protest, his family replaced it before carrying his body to its final resting place in his native Lurgan.

**Seamus 'Thumper' Twomey** became IRA chief of staff for a second time following his escape from Mountjoy. He was recaptured in Dublin in 1977, after a high-speed chase through the city. An uncompromising militarist, he remained true to the Provos until his death in 1989, aged 69.

**Seán Tracey** and his workmate **Robert Dunne** died in a building site accident in 1998. At his funeral he was described as a 'brave republican soldier'. He was 57 years old. Brendan Hughes says that his inability to attend the funeral due to incarceration in Portlaoise remains one of his biggest regrets.

**Ned Bailey** died in 1997, aged 73. His massive funeral featured a republican guard of honour. Special Branch detectives were present to take video and photographs of the mourners.

**Beth Bailey** died in 2008, aged 83. She is buried along with Ned in the new cemetery at Emo. Brendan Hughes still visits their grave.

**Jim 'The German' Hyland** died in 2007. Describing him as 'no ordinary man', in a glowing eulogy to his life-long friend, former Sinn Féin vice-president Phil Flynn wrote about The Heath: 'Through the most difficult stages of the struggle this was a hive of activity, a centre of action: of training, technical and general logistical support, supply lines, prison escapes, shelter, sustenance and active service volunteers. Central to all this was Jim Hyland.'

**Liam 'Mr Leonard' Quinn** became a key member of a highly effective IRA unit, known as the Balcombe Street gang, that wreaked havoc across London in the mid-1970s. He shot a policeman dead while trying to evade arrest and fled to the U.S. He was extradited to England in 1986 and given a life sentence. He was repatriated to Ireland in 1988 and released in 1999 under the terms of the 1998 Good Friday Agreement. He lives in San Francisco.

**Thompson Boyes,** the Mountjoy helicopter pilot, was involved in a serious crash when his chopper hit electricity wires only months after the escape. He recovered and continued to fly. According to his nephew, Stephen, he rarely talked about his career. He died aged 63 in 1989, a few months after his wife Mary.

**Dermot Teeling**, the unfortunate newspaper seller, remained active in republican politics. In 2007, the New York Times described him as a senior member of Sinn Féin President Mary Lou McDonald's election campaign team.

**Liam Fagan**, the master craftsman in Portlaoise Prison, sided with Republican Sinn Féin in the 1986 split, becoming that organisation's Vice-President for Life. The IRA veteran died after a long illness in 1989, aged 61.

**Martin McAllister** used a smuggled compass to navigate his way towards safety after the Portlaoise escape. He was badly wounded in a firefight with the British army only weeks after the escape and was incarcerated in Crumlin Road jail, Belfast. He remains a political activist.

**Oliver McKiernan** is living a quiet life, enjoying the peace in his beloved, native Co Fermanagh.

**Brian Hearty** is retired and living abroad.

**Liam 'Farmer' Brown** is retired. He walks every day and reminisces with friends in The Rock Bar on The Falls at weekends. They call him 'Bomb Scare' because of his ability to clear a place with his singing. He claims that management pays him handsomely to do so!

**Peadar Mohan** made good on his promise never to return to jail, although he remained active in the republican movement. He died in a car accident in 1981.

**Leo Martin**, the Portlaoise OC, a founding member of the Provisional IRA in Belfast, had been arrested in Co Sligo in 1973 after Gardaí stopped a car containing guns and ammunition. Like Liam Fagan, Martin sided with Republican Sinn Féin after the 1986 split. He remained a priority target for loyalist assassination. He died in 2011.

**Bill Fuller**, the legendary hotel and dance club owner who stood bail for Brendan Hughes, probably merits a book of his own. In later years, this colourful north-Kerry native would relocate to Las Vegas, where he paved the way for the success of many Irish showbands. He would go on to own a chain of music halls and hotels, as well as a construction company. He died in 2008, aged 91.

**Brian Keenan**, the senior IRA commander who organised the wedding cars for the Portlaoise escapees, was sentenced to 18 years in jail in 1980 for conspiracy to cause explosions in England. After his release in 1993, he played a key role in the peace process. He died in 2008, aged 66.